"Bill Hull provides a comprehensive guide to the central issue of contemporary Christianity: discipleship of Jesus Christ. Those already aware of Bill's continuing leadership in this arena will not be disappointed. Essential reading for anyone concerned about being truly Christian in the twenty-first century!"

—LARRY HART, PhD professor of Systematic Theology,
Oral Roberts School of Theology

"Bill Hull is the modern voice on disciple-making for the church. His writings never fail to convict me, provoke me, and move me to action. This latest work has what I have been hungry for: a historical perspective on disciple-making with a helpful bibliography and introduction to little-known masters. I will use this book with my leadership as we seek to be faithful to Jesus' Great Commission. May it find a broad readership in the church!"

—SANDY MASON church planter and senior pastor,
Desert View Bible Church, Phoenix, Arizona

"In the last fifty years, the U.S. Church has been duped into substituting quality of church programs for quality of individual *Christlikeness*, and the result is too many churches with too few disciples! *The Complete Book of Discipleship* is a real treasure of motivation, ideas, and applications to help counter-balance this problem. No other book provides so much practical help in making disciples in the local church."

—BOB GILLIAM President, T-NET International

THE NAVIGATORS REFERENCE LIBRARY

THE COMPLETE BOOK OF
DISCIPLESHIP

ON BEING AND MAKING FOLLOWERS OF CHRIST

BILL HULL

NAVPRESS®

BRINGING TRUTH TO LIFE

OUR GUARANTEE TO YOU

We believe so strongly in the message of our books that we are making this quality guarantee to you. If for any reason you are disappointed with the content of this book, return the title page to us with your name and address and we will refund to you the list price of the book. To help us serve you better, please briefly describe why you were disappointed. Mail your refund request to: NavPress, P.O. Box 35002, Colorado Springs, CO 80935.

The Navigators is an international Christian organization. Our mission is to reach, disciple, and equip people to know Christ and to make Him known through successive generations. We envision multitudes of diverse people in the United States and every other nation who have a passionate love for Christ, live a lifestyle of sharing Christ's love, and multiply spiritual laborers among those without Christ.

NavPress is the publishing ministry of The Navigators. NavPress publications help believers learn biblical truth and apply what they learn to their lives and ministries. Our mission is to stimulate spiritual formation among our readers.

ISBN 1-57683-897-8

Cover design by Wes Youssi / www.thedesignworksgroup.com
Cover image by Martin Barraud
Creative Team: Kent Wilson, Brad Lewis, Amy Spencer, Darla Hightower, Arvid Wallen, Pat Reinheimer, Brooke Graves

Some of the anecdotal illustrations in this book are true to life and are included with the permission of the persons involved. All other illustrations are composites of real situations, and any resemblance to people living or dead is coincidental.

Unless otherwise identified, all Scripture quotations in this publication are taken from the HOLY BIBLE: NEW INTERNATIONAL VERSION® (NIV®). Copyright © 1973, 1978, 1984 by International Bible Society. Used by permission of Zondervan Publishing House. All rights reserved. Other versions used include: the *Revised Standard Version Bible* (RSV), copyright 1946, 1952, 1971, by the Division of Christian Education of the National Council of the Churches of Christ in the USA, used by permission, all rights reserved; *The New English Bible* (NEB), © 1961, 1970, The Delegates of the Oxford University Press and The Syndics of the Cambridge University Press; *New King James Version* (NKJV). Copyright © 1982 by Thomas Nelson, Inc. Used by permission. All rights reserved; and the *King James Version* (KJV).

Hull, Bill, 1946-
The complete book of discipleship / Bill Hull.
     p. cm.
Includes bibliographical references and index.
ISBN 1-57683-897-8
1. Discipling (Christianity) 2. Spiritual formation. 3. Christian life. 4. Church history. I. Title.
BV4520.H7795 2006
253--dc22

                                   2006016252

Printed in the United States of America

3 4 5 6 7 / 11 10 09 08

FOR A FREE CATALOG OF NAVPRESS BOOKS & BIBLE STUDIES,
CALL 1-800-366-7788 (USA) OR 1-800-839-4769.

CONTENTS

985

11 9240

CHAPTER 2:
ORIGINS OF DISCIPLESHIP

CHAPTER 5:
THE DISCIPLE-MAKING ENVIRONMENT:
WHAT MAKES THINGS GROW

CHAPTER 6:
THE STAGES OF DISCIPLESHIP

CHAPTER 7:
CHRISTIAN SPIRITUAL TRANSFORMATION

CHAPTER 8:
PERSONAL APPROACHES TO DISCIPLE-MAKING

CHAPTER 9:
THE ROLE OF SMALL GROUPS IN DISCIPLESHIP

CHAPTER 10:
CONGREGATIONS, PASTORS, AND DISCIPLESHIP

CHAPTER 11:
SPIRITUAL GENERATIONS

CHAPTER 12:
THE FUTURE OF DISCIPLESHIP:
LIVING THE JESUS WAY

INTRODUCTION

" Christianity without discipleship is always Christianity without Christ."[1]

The reasoning behind this dramatic statement by Dietrich Bonhoeffer provides the rationale for this book. Without discipleship, Christianity doesn't exist, because following Jesus activates the Christian faith.

Bonhoeffer expanded his thought:

Discipleship means adherence to Christ, and, because Christ is the object of that adherence, it must take the form of discipleship. An abstract Christology, a doctrinal system, a general religious knowledge on the subject of grace or on the forgiveness of sins, render discipleship superfluous, and in fact they positively exclude any idea of discipleship whatever, and are essentially inimical [detached] to the whole conception of following Christ. With an abstract idea it is possible to enter into a relation of formal knowledge, to become enthusiastic about it, and perhaps even to put it into practice; but it can never be followed in personal obedience. Christianity without the living Christ is inevitably Christianity without discipleship, and Christianity without discipleship is always Christianity without Christ.

It remains an abstract idea, a myth that has a place for the Fatherhood of God, but omits Christ as the living Son. A Christianity of that kind is nothing more or less than the end of discipleship.[2]

Unfortunately non-discipleship "Christianity" dominates much of the thinking of the contemporary church. In addition to sucking the strength from the church, Christianity without discipleship causes the church to assimilate itself into the culture. And sadly, whenever the difference between the church's and culture's definition of morality ceases to exist, the church loses its power and authority.

Many mainline churches depart from orthodoxy because they reject the absolute authority of Scripture. However, many evangelical churches pose an even more subtle danger by departing from the gospel that calls on all believers to be disciples and follow Christ in obedience. As a result, we evangelicals accept and even encourage a two-level Christian experience in which only serious Christians pursue and practice discipleship, while grace and forgiveness is enough for everyone else. Dallas Willard notes, "We have not only been saved by grace, we have been paralyzed by it." Willard adds that the church stresses who is saved and who isn't. However, when we see faith as agreement with a doctrinal test and understand grace as forgiveness of sin alone, we lose the idea that discipleship is normal. And when we lose discipleship, we also lose vibrant Christianity.

Willard both defines and describes discipleship: "Discipleship is the relationship I stand into Jesus Christ in order that I might take on his character. As his disciple, I am learning from him how to live my life in the Kingdom as he would if he were I. The natural outcome is that my behavior is transformed. Increasingly, I routinely and easily do the things he said and did."[3] In other words, we can't truly follow Christ without desiring to become like him. Following him requires regeneration or new birth. If we're reborn, we'll follow him — unless we're taught that we don't need to.

I'm going to reveal my heart early in this book with the following statement: I find it both sad and appalling that we've used the great doctrine of justification by faith and God's grace to teach that people don't really need to follow Jesus to be Christians.

My heart tells me that it's time to speak up! The goal of this book is to address the mistakes we've made with discipleship, including making it a limited training period for spiritual newbies, and allowing the consumer culture of the contemporary church to diminish the radical nature of following Jesus.

Further, this book will encourage those with an intense hunger to follow Jesus and who desire to help others do the same. I'm referring to the kind of person the great scholar Augustine described:

> Give me a man in love; he knows what I mean. Give me one who yearns; give me one who is hungry; give me one far away in this desert, who is thirsty and sighs for the spring of the Eternal Country. Give me that sort of man; he knows what I mean. But if I speak to a cold man, he just doesn't know what I am talking about. . . . You are surprised that the world is losing its grip? That the world is grown old? Don't hold onto the old man, the world; don't refuse to regain your youth in Christ, who says to you: "The world is passing away; the world is losing its grip, the world is short of breath." Don't fear, for thy youth shall be renewed as an eagle.

If you feel a fire burning in your soul when it comes to discipleship, you know what I mean — and this book is for you.

THE MERGER

Although many mergers don't work, some do. Fortunately, a merger of three streams of thought regarding discipleship now taking place seems to be born of God's Spirit, bringing new and vibrant life to the people of God. Let's take a brief look at those streams.

Classic Discipleship

The first stream, classic discipleship, gained momentum in the mid-twentieth century with the rise of organizations such as The Navigators and Campus Crusade for Christ.

The characteristics of classic discipleship included one-on-one mentoring, a disciplined program of Bible study, Scripture memorization, and training in witnessing and speaking. Classic discipleship made significant inroads into the church as the baby boomers it reached became pastors and leaders of the church. In addition, the movement produced its own literature, music, and curriculum.

The strengths of the classic discipleship movement include focus, method, and the ability to process large numbers of people through a curriculum. However, classic discipleship didn't address the disciple's inner life as much as it measured performance. As a result, people grew weary of a spirituality that required completing programs but often didn't offer lasting change. For many people, as soon as the program ended, so did their growth.

The essential and lasting strength of classic discipleship is its commitment to Scripture and the importance of sequence and segmentation in training people well.

Spiritual Formation

The spiritual formation movement recaptured ancient exercises practiced by Jesus, his disciples, and the monastics. Following the Reformation, Protestants had stripped the gospel of its imagination by throwing out many ancient practices: the Eucharist, holy days to remember saints, church calendars, sacraments, icons, and art. However, Anglicans, desiring to benefit from their own reformation yet maintain the positives of their Catholic heritage, continued many of these practices.

By definition, spiritual formation is a process through which individuals who have received new life take on the character of Jesus Christ by a combination of effort and grace. The disciple positions himself to follow Jesus. The actual process of reforming, or spiritual formation, involves both God's grace and the individual's effort.

The weakness of the spiritual formation movement — at least from an evangelical viewpoint — includes its associations with theological liberalism. These connections sometimes made the movement susceptible to infiltration from secular worldviews, other religions, and Eastern philosophy. Thus it became important to distinguish the movement as "Christian spiritual formation."

Fortunately, the richness of the ancient traditions emerged from behind monastery walls and outside the ivy-covered halls of academia, finding its way into the mainstream of evangelical interaction. As a result, the spiritual formation movement introduced practices such as silence, solitude, frugality, meditation on Scripture, and filling instead of emptying the mind. This movement also espoused more ancient ways of reflecting on Scripture for life application rather than simply accumulating more biblical data.

One of spiritual formation's greatest strengths is that it causes us to slow down twenty-first-century life long enough to ponder what's going on in us and around us. Recently the spiritual formation movement has also incorporated the focused and "let's get things done" nature of the classic discipleship movement, creating a richer and more thoughtful approach to transformation.

Environmental Discipleship

Some might call this third-stream psychological discipleship or relational discipleship. Other associated words include *community* and *congregation*. In essence, this movement encompasses the ways people get along.

One of the least-developed concepts in discipleship has been how the environment of a group determines what grows or dies within that environment. The most important issues in spiritual transformation are the presence of acceptance, integrity of relationships, and trust. The classic discipleship movement mandated trust: "You must be accountable to me." The spiritual formation movement required submission: "If you want to be a part of our society, you must subject yourself fully to it. No negotiations."

The therapeutic society we live in has developed its own environment, which accepts nearly anything, no matter how damaging it might be. The culture has determined that intolerance is the only real sin; it labels conviction as hate speech. Fortunately, some thoughtful Christians have "spoiled" the therapeutic world, introducing some very important insights that create trust and allow disciples to flourish.

A NEW MONASTICISM: NOTHING LIKE THE OLD

These three movements—classic discipleship, spiritual formation, and environmental discipleship—are now converging to create a new, full-bodied discipleship, with the potential to transform the church in the next twenty-five years. Of course, this merged form of discipleship will be of little or no significance if it doesn't lead to the transformation of millions now outside of Christ and change the cultures we all live in.

My goal in this book is not just to recap some current methods and explore a few of the latest ideas concerning discipleship. Rather it is to delve into some very old but proven ideas that have changed the world. As you read, I hope these ideas will revolutionize both you and those you touch.

CHAPTER 1

BIBLICAL FOUNDATIONS OF DISCIPLESHIP

IN THIS CHAPTER
- DISCIPLESHIP: GOD'S VERY BEST FOR HIS PEOPLE
- DISCIPLESHIP: GOD'S PRIMARY WORK
- DEFINING TERMS:
  DISCIPLE
  DISCIPLE-MAKING
  DISCIPLESHIP
  SPIRITUAL FORMATION
- NON-DISCIPLESHIP CHRISTIANITY
- EXPLORING A FAITH THAT EMBRACES DISCIPLESHIP
- THE KIND OF PERSON THE GOSPEL CAN CREATE

For two years, one of my friends followed the rock group The Grateful Dead. He was known as a Deadhead. He didn't follow The Dead casually like a fan who follows baseball. He traveled from city to city, living out of his car. He wanted to live the same life the band lived.

My friend might have been misguided, but he was totally committed. He was a true disciple in much the same way the New Testament describes discipleship.

DISCIPLESHIP:
GOD'S VERY BEST FOR HIS PEOPLE

Jesus taught that faith means to follow. That was his first test of a person's faith (see Luke 9:23-25). Following, however, isn't short term. Discipleship isn't a program or an event; it's a way of life. It's not for a limited time, but for our whole life. Discipleship isn't for beginners alone; it's for all believers for every day of their life. Discipleship isn't just *one* of the things the church does; it *is* what the church does. It's not just part of the advancement of God's kingdom; the existence of serious disciples is the most important evidence of God's work on earth. Without enough of these workers, the task languishes and the work remains incomplete (see Matthew 9:35-38).

Simply, discipleship means learning from and following a teacher. However, while we can define discipleship in these simple terms, something about the discipleship movement has never quite made it into the heart of the church. I find it particularly puzzling that we struggle to put disciple-making at the center of ministry even though Jesus left us with the clear imperative to "make disciples" (see Matthew 28:18-20).

So why don't we automatically place discipleship at the center of every ministry? Perhaps certain words put people off: influence, vision, submission, accountability, vulnerability, confession, study, sacrifice, and discipline. With just a few powerful words, the apostle Paul touched on another reason people tend to avoid discipleship: "Train yourself to be godly" (1 Timothy 4:7). Let's face it—discipline isn't something most of us like. We avoid discipline if we can, because it disrupts the normal and comfortable pattern of our life.

The great Christian apologist C. S. Lewis wrote that the word he detested most was "interference."[1] Interference occurs when someone sticks his nose in your business. However, that's precisely what discipleship is all about. If you want to grow in a meaningful way, you not only must tolerate another person's intimate knowledge of you, you must also willingly invite that person into your life. Even more startling, you'll grow to love and depend on the "interference."

Most of us want to reap the harvest of a discipline while living a life of relative sloth. We want all the benefits of humility and growth without being humble or working to grow. Yet Scripture states clearly that we require a great deal of interference to stem the tide of our self-indulgence. This positive interference lies at the very heart of making disciples — a process Jesus described as teaching others "to obey everything I have commanded you" (Matthew 28:20).

DISCIPLESHIP: GOD'S PRIMARY WORK

Why is the call to make disciples the very heart of God's work? Why is God pleased when we make a total commitment to discipleship? What does discipleship do that nothing else can?

Let's start with the obvious. Discipleship ranks as God's top priority because Jesus practiced it and commanded us to do it, and his followers continued it.

Jesus Said So

Jesus told us to be disciples and to make disciples. When he issued the Great Commission, he could have spoken about contemplation, study, worship services, or gathering people together for revival meetings in the temple. He could have restated the Great Commandment.[2] But he didn't. Instead Jesus got straight to the point with simple words: "All authority in heaven and on earth has been given to me. Therefore go and make disciples of all nations, baptizing them in the name of the Father and of the Son and of the Holy Spirit, and teaching them to obey everything I have commanded you. And surely I am with you always, to the very end of the age" (Matthew 28:18-20). With the Great Commission, transformation became mission.

Jesus' words reveal his heart and priority. They also indicate a method that will fulfill God's plan to rescue the world. A commitment to be and make disciples must be the central act of every disciple and every church.

God Gave His All to This Mission

Jesus came "to seek and to save what was lost" (Luke 19:10). He came not "to be served, but to serve, and to give his life as a ransom for many" (Mark 10:45). He held back nothing to reach those he loved. When he claimed, "All authority in heaven and on earth has been given to me," in effect he was saying that all the authority of all realms and all time was being marshaled so that, through him, imperfect disciples could go and make other imperfect disciples. The words of William Law come to mind:

> Christianity is not a school for the teaching of moral virtue, the polishing of our manners, or forming us to live a life of this world with decency and gentility. It is deeper and more divine in its designs, and much nobler ends. It implies an entire change of life, a dedication of ourselves, our souls, our bodies unto God in the strictest and highest sense of the words.[3]

Making disciples has nothing to do with winning others over to a philosophy or turning them into nice people who smile a lot. Rather the Great Commission launches a rescue mission; all followers receive orders with full authority to take action wherever they happen to be. Discipleship involves saving people from themselves and eternal oblivion, permitting the transforming power of God to change them from the inside out. *All* is the Great Commission's key word—*all* authority, *all* sacrifice, *all*-out effort, *all* the time, for *all* people. How could anything else the church thinks up be nearly as important?

A Transformed Person Can Change the World

Jesus addressed this imperative command to his eleven remaining disciples, the first examples of his disciple-making. Many English translations use the word *nations* to describe the target of discipleship. However, the Greek New Testament uses *ethne*, which means "various people groups."

The focus of reaching others has been universally accepted among orthodox Christians since the beginning. But the ambitious impulse to fulfill the Great Commission sometimes gives it a mechanical or programmatic feel. In particular, the church in America has superseded the theoretical for pragmatism, creating a marketplace model of church and society. This isn't a new phenomenon. Alexis de Tocqueville, a Frenchman who toured America in the 1800s and recorded his impressions, said, "Where you expected to find a priest, you found a politician—or a salesperson."[4]

This marketplace emphasis became deeply rooted in American church culture. Eventually the idea of disciples making other disciples became a church-growth method, a way to increase numbers and satisfy the American thirst for progress. After all, it's a great plan to train eleven people who will go out and reach others. In turn, the reached will reach still others.

As many writers and teachers have proclaimed, when all who become disciples make disciples through several spiritual generations, the result should not be reproduction (adding disciples one at a time) but multiplication (one disciple makes two, who make four, who make sixteen, and so on). I've heard sermons (in fact, I've preached a few) theorizing that if we just follow this multiplication plan, the entire world will be converted to Christianity in thirty years. That was more than thirty years ago.

In spite of how logical it sounds, this plan runs aground repeatedly on the rocks of human frailty and ignorance of how people really change. We must admit that this mathematical formula has never worked in any broad way. It might have limited success in controlled environments, but it would be wrong to claim that multiplication has worked to the extent of reaching whole cities, countries, or generations.

The principle behind discipleship does involve one person influencing another, which does result in a change in heart and mind. The success of discipleship doesn't depend on soldiering forward in a mechanical strategy of reproduction and multiplication. And discipleship doesn't involve developing a well-trained, elite sales force. Rather discipleship occurs when a transformed person radiates Christ to those around her. It happens when people so deeply experience God's love that they can do nothing other than affect those around them.

The heart of being a disciple involves living in intimate union and daily contact with Christ. Discipleship—the effort both to be a disciple and to make other disciples—is about the immense value of God at work in one individual's life and the resulting impact on other lives.

A Company of the Committed

When someone claims to have faith in Christ, he must also commit to follow Christ. Remember, Jesus taught that faith meant to follow him (see Luke 9:23-25). Anything less is something else—a wish, a desire, or a good intention. But it's not faith, because faith means to follow.

Participation in the Great Commission doesn't require great

learning or ability, but it does require regeneration—being a transformed person. Only the habitation of God in a disciple enables her to answer the call to follow Christ. Two acts of submission flow out of this regeneration:

1. To be baptized—to go public: Although baptism remains significant in the present, it lacks the risk and courage it required in the first century. Then the act of baptism proclaimed that someone had indeed decided to follow Jesus. Being baptized in the name of the Trinity—Father, Son, and Holy Spirit—meant the follower entered into the reality of experiencing God in his fullness. This separated the believer from all other gods and philosophies.

In the twenty-first-century Global North,[5] where Christianity is established but shrinking, we don't face the risks that followers of Christ had to take in the first century. In much of the Global South, however, baptism remains a courageous act. Being baptized can put a person on a government watch list, make him an enemy of his people, and even make him a hated member of his own family.

Baptism means going public as a disciple. It was never meant to be a private ritual that takes place inside church walls. For Christianity to flourish, disciples must start out public and remain public. A single disciple creates a light, and the community of disciples shines like a city on a hill. Keeping your light under a cover isn't an option (see Matthew 5:14-16).

2. To be taught to obey everything Christ commanded—to submit to transformation: Catholics speak of tradition and Scripture. Anglicans speak of Scripture, tradition, and reason. Protestants speak of *sola scriptura* (Scripture alone). With these differences clouding church history, can we hope to extract what's most important?

Before Catholics, Anglicans, or Protestants existed, Jesus provided the process to follow: All disciples were to be taught to obey everything he commanded. He commanded 212 things, summed up in three statements:

1. Love God with all your heart, mind, soul, and strength.
2. Love your neighbor as yourself.
3. Love your enemies.

Learning to Obey

Although Jesus provided these summaries, when we look at all he commanded we see that the "curriculum" for being and making disciples is extensive, covering all of life. But before we get concerned with *what* we need to obey, we first need to understand *how* to obey. Four ingredients are necessary.

1. As disciples, we need a vision to inspire us. Vision provides hope, and hope fuels our efforts as we walk into the future. Just as a great athlete fulfills a childhood dream to win an Olympic medal or play in a professional league, disciples should dream to be like Christ. The apostle Paul had this goal for himself and for all those he loved and trained (see 1 Corinthians 9:24-27; Galatians 4:19; Colossians 1:28).

Our goal should be to absorb the example of Christ into our lives by studying and meditating on the characteristics of his life. Because the core character trait of Jesus is humility, that's the place to begin. This vision can pull us into the future, inspiring us for all of life.

2. As disciples, we need accountability to receive training. Because training involves constant repetition, it requires discipline. But because consistent self-discipline is rare, we need others to hold us accountable.

Unfortunately, accountability is often couched in the negative, such as when a disappointed person comments, "He failed because he didn't have anyone to hold him accountable." However, accountability is a biblical concept—a contemporary term for the ancient principle of helping fellow disciples keep their commitments to God.

Accountability can serve as our best friend, even when we don't want that friend around. It's like a chaperone for life—always in the room with us, but tucked discreetly in the corner. We submit to accountability when we have a passion to please God, to avoid moral failure, or to avoid wasting away the years through neglect and sloth. Accountability means submitting ourselves to at least one other person. That individual has permission to ask any question and keep us honest about life.

3. As disciples, we need structure to empower us. One of the least appreciated necessities in life is structure. Everything from speed limits to the rails on a baby's crib protect us and make life work better.

Just as accountability involves submitting ourselves to other people, structure is about designing life for success. If you want to lose weight, you first need to ask a friend to help you keep your commitment. Then you create a structure that will help you lose weight successfully. This structure might include purging your home of foods that will sabotage your goal, coming up with ways to prepare food at home, and learning how to eat meals in uncontrolled environments. The structure empowers you and makes your goal attainable.

When it comes to developing spiritual habits, a good devotional guide provides structure for me. I meet twice a month with a friend who works and journals his way through the same guide. Our relationship provides accountability and the guide provides the structure. This is just one example of a structure that works. In fact, it doesn't even need to be a great structure. A structure should simply compel us to take action, setting into motion the Holy Spirit's action to reshape us.

4. As disciples, we need relationships where we experience love. Most of us have never experienced the true power of community. The social-oriented programming that many churches call small groups or *koinonia* groups have little affect on character.[6] True community means living in submission to each another. It requires the work of the Holy Spirit to submit to others and to allow others to play a meaningful part in our growth.[7]

Submission involves trust. Most of us take in only the truth that we trust. If someone you don't trust tries to convince you to believe something or change your mind, she almost always fails. However, when someone you admire and trust does the same, you'll almost always believe that individual. As disciples, our character develops in a faith community where we feel loved, affirmed, and safe enough to trust other members of the community.

DEFINING TERMS

In trying to understand that discipleship offers God's very best to us, and that he sees it as the primary undertaking of the church, we've already used all of the following words. But let's pause briefly to make sure we have a clear understanding of what each one means.

Disciple

A disciple, *mathetes*, is a learner or follower—usually someone committed to a significant master.[8] Michael Wilkins, New Testament professor of language and literature at Talbot School of Theology, further describes the term this way:

> Disciple is the primary term used in the Gospels to refer to Jesus' followers and is a common referent for those known in the early church as believers, Christians, brothers/sisters, those of the way, or saints, although each term focuses upon different aspects of the individual's relationships with Jesus and others of the faith. The term was used most frequently in this specific sense; at least 230 times in the Gospels and 28 times in Acts.[9]

A disciple, then, is a reborn follower of Jesus. I've already mentioned my distaste for the teaching that a difference exists between being a Christian and being a disciple. The common teaching is that a Christian is someone who by faith accepts Jesus as Savior, receives eternal life, and is safe and secure in the family of God; a disciple is a more serious Christian active in the practice of the spiritual disciplines and engaged in evangelizing and training others. But I must be blunt: I find no biblical evidence for a separation of Christian from disciple.[10] In answer to the age-old question, "Are disciples born or made?" I contend they are born to be made. The vision Jesus set into motion meant finding and training more people like the Eleven, a lifelong experience where imperfect people would be shaped into his likeness — marked by progress, not perfection.

At the moment of salvation, when someone decides to follow Christ, he shouldn't experience any interruption on his journey from that point forward. As a new Christian, an individual doesn't take a "second step" toward becoming a disciple. Instead he embarks on a seamless journey of growth that passes through spiritual childhood, adolescence, and adulthood to maturity. Of course, all disciples experience good seasons and bad ones. All enjoy victories and suffer defeats. All experience stagnant times, and even times when they seem to travel in the wrong direction. But a disciple's heart consistently yearns for and desires to please God.

When the distinction between disciple and Christian disappears, so does the damaging belief in a two-tiered church. A disciple, then, is the normal Christian who follows Christ. Of course, the way individuals follow Christ will be different. Some followers will be highly educated or literate people who love reading, philosophy, and the ascetic life. Others will be more activist by nature and less contemplative and will find more meaning in serving than in reading or in long seasons of prayer. While people will follow Christ in different ways, no one should think that only the elite practice serious faith and no one should hold the even more destructive idea that being a casual Christian — who decides to believe in Jesus but not to follow him — is somehow normal.

Discipleship is what a disciple does. If she's not following Christ, then Christ gets left out of the process. This individual has only "signed off" on Jesus and doctrine, but doesn't enjoy a real relationship with Christ. Signing off isn't enough — it's not faith, but merely agreement.

Disciple-Making

The term *disciple-making* comes from the verb *matheteusate*, which means to "make disciples" (Matthew 28:19).

Three dimensions distinguish disciple-making from discipleship:

1. Deliverance: The first step in making disciples is evangelism, the part of the Great Commission that tells us to "baptize them." One reason contemporary disciple-making doesn't produce new disciples is because churches limit disciple-making to training people who are already Christians.[11] Instead, all disciples should be actively involved in finding others who need Christ and then — through the disciples' gifts, opportunities, and faith community — introducing these individuals to the life of following Jesus.

2. Development: Once a disciple makes a commitment to Christ, the next step is developing character and capacity. This comes from the "teaching them to obey" component of the Great Commission (verse 20). Many Christians traditionally refer to this single step as discipleship (or, in more recent times, as spiritual formation).

3. Deployment: Once a disciple is trained, the final step is sending. This comes from the "go" (verse 19) aspect of the Great Commission and means deploying the disciple in mission where he lives, works, and plays. The disciple gains an awareness that he lives among lost and broken people and that God's kingdom grows best organically through relationships. Deployment also includes certain "called" individuals who cross cultural and geographic barriers to reach others.

Discipleship

Discipleship, the widely accepted term that describes the ongoing life of the disciple, also describes the broader Christian experience. This word isn't a pure biblical expression, but a derivative. Yet most Christians generally accept discipleship as the process of following Jesus.

Ship added to the end of *disciple* means "the state of" or "contained in." So discipleship means the state of being a disciple. In fact, the term *discipleship* has a nice ongoing feel—a sense of journey, the idea of *becoming* a disciple rather than having been *made* a disciple.

Spiritual Formation

The term *spiritual formation* is derived from Galatians 4:19: "My dear children, for whom I am again in the pains of childbirth until Christ is formed in you." The word *formed* comes from *morphe*, which means "to shape." When combined with Greek prepositions, it is rendered as "conformed" in Romans 8:29 and "transformed" in 12:2.

Most accurately, *spiritual formation* describes the sanctification or transformation of disciples. The term has become popular for those who want to avoid the baggage that *discipleship* has carried in recent years. *Disciple* does seem to dominate the Gospels, while *spiritual formation* describes spirituality in the Epistles.

However, because *discipleship* has stood the test of time and links believers directly to Jesus, I've chosen it to describe the contents of this book.

WHAT DISCIPLESHIP IS NOT

That's a quick look at terms describing discipleship. Yet sometimes people try to make discipleship into other things that end up diminishing it. Unfortunately, that causes leaders to make the wrong choice their main focus. So it's important to knock down these diluted forms of discipleship before we continue.

Not a Program

The most common mistake made by well-intentioned leaders, particularly acute in the Global North, is turning discipleship into a curriculum that a serious disciple completes and then graduates from. Instead of supporting an ongoing process, a program focuses on finishing the material, learning the information, and developing certain skills such as giving a testimony or using different methods of Bible study.

But because discipleship is fundamentally about the choice to follow Jesus, it needs to be a way of life for all of life. Yes, many good programs provide information and skills, but they're just tools of the growth process, not discipleship itself. When someone says, "I finished the two-year study; I've been discipled," she implies that she doesn't need to continue in the process of discipleship.

Further, program-based discipleship can divide a community of people into those who have been through "the program" and those who haven't. The most damaging result is that churches categorize discipleship as just one of the ministries of the church, rather than the core of the ministry. When discipleship takes a place alongside leadership, evangelism, preaching, worship, counseling, support groups, and other programs, it ceases to be what it was meant to be: the heart of what it means to be a Christian.

Not a Production Line

Earlier I mentioned that some people try to turn discipleship into a production plan based on multiplication for reaching the world. Again, this concept is certainly attractive. It's like the challenge most kids have heard from their grandparents: "Would you rather have a million dollars right now or a penny today, two pennies tomorrow, four the next day, and doubled every day for a month?" Almost every kid answers, "I want the million dollars." I know I did. But the right answer is to take the penny; in thirty-one days, you'll have more than ten million dollars![12]

Of course, no one ever thinks about the practical problems of who'll deliver the pennies or how many trucks it will take to transport them — not to mention who'll provide all that money. It's always the practical problems of real life that ruin the most attractive scenarios.

The truth is that only disciples who are passionate for Christ will be able to sustain any effort to reach others around them. In real life, God doesn't have a production plan; he uses us to reach others in a wide variety of ways. His glorious method is unpredictable, not smooth or symmetrical. It bursts forward with spasms of energy. It zigzags across the planet in disorganized patterns, propelled by the passion of faithful disciples.

The Great Commission happens as it did with John Wesley, who preached to thousands and placed them in societies and classes for nurture and training. Or in the present day, with Billy Graham as a crusade-preacher, Rick Warren as a pastor-writer, and Michael W. Smith as a singer. God uses some disciples to open entirely new vistas that other faithful disciples, with their own gifts and opportunities, can enter.

In other words, only God orchestrates the call to be and make disciples, and disciple-making can be accomplished only through the events and conditions that make up life. Of course, disciples should certainly be encouraged to train others and to reproduce in others, but discipleship is much more about the depth of character and spiritual passion of each disciple than it is a plan for church growth.

Not Just for Beginners

When I hear people say that discipleship is only for new Christians, I want to pull out the short white hairs left on my head! Yes, new disciples need basic training, but it's a huge mistake to think that we can simply learn the basics, flow into the general population, and live off that training.

Churches around the world are filled with people who've learned basic information about being a follower of Jesus, but who no longer study the Bible, memorize Scripture, or pray as daily disciplines. This would be like a basketball player who learned the basics of dribbling, passing, shooting, and rebounding, yet no longer practices the basics. You don't know any really good basketball players like that, do you? That's because it's impossible to continue to play at a competent level without continually remastering the basics and staying in good playing condition.

Far too many Christians no longer practice the basics and are out of shape spiritually. The cause of Christ has paid a terrible price because of the mistaken concept that discipleship is only for beginners.

Not Just for Leaders

For much of the history of Christianity, only church leaders — bishops, elders, pastors, priests, monks — received spiritual training. Of course, this changed as a result of the Reformation, as lay people gradually worked their way into training environments. Yet a residual bit of disparity still exists between clergy and laity when it comes to the amount and level of training available.

Some pastors still maintain a spiritual aura that makes average nonprofessionals feel left out. Usually this elitism is unintentional. Many lay people simply feel inferior spiritually to the "real" disciples — those who have chosen full-time church service as a vocation or profession. Sure, pastors know more about religious matters than most lay people, but this doesn't mean they're more spiritual.

Any residual spiritual elitism can be trumped by some basic tenets regarding discipleship:

- *All* Christians are disciples who are born anew to spiritual life when they choose to follow Jesus.
- Both the starting point and the goal of spiritual formation and discipleship is transformation to the image of Christ.
- Together discipleship and spiritual formation provide a full New Testament perspective of the process of the growth of Christians.
- Spiritual formation and discipleship must be biblically and theologically grounded.[13]

Not Just for the Highly Literate

One of the dangers of some discipleship training ministries is that they reward only those who love to read and think bigger and higher thoughts. With the recent blending of ancient mystics and scholars into mainstream evangelical popular literature, everyday people have been introduced to Francois Fenelon, St. Augustine, Lancelot Andrews, Gregory of Nyassa, Benedict of Nursia, and others. These scholars and mystics wrote about topics such as ladders of humility, spiritual labyrinths, and Stations of the Cross. Their literature contains riches, and those who spend hours contemplating it receive great reward. In fact, all Christians can benefit from such experiences, even if only periodically in a retreat format.

However, God also rewards those who read less and instead find most of their spiritual pleasure in service. Certainly the majority of people who served Christ well during much of church history could not read or write. Their spiritual formation occurred by attending daily church services, hearing the words of the liturgy, and taking in the stories of faith depicted in the décor of their churches. In the Middle Ages, for example, spirituality was more communal than individual: people experienced Christ as the community gathered around the reading of the Scripture and the Lord's Table.

God meets people where they are, based on who they are, and using the tools they have available. I'm not encouraging anyone to read less or to spend less time in spiritual contemplation. However, I do want to encourage those who feel less spiritual or less useful because they don't approach their spiritual life from an academic angle.

You should read, but you might grow more through active service. You must pray, but you might pray as you serve on the frontlines. Use the mini-retreats that life offers when others run late or you're stuck in a traffic jam or a backed-up airport. You can be just as intimate with God as someone who studies great spiritual literature. God can use you just as powerfully without spectacular experiences in your private moments.

Not Just for People Who Like Structure

Remember, discipleship isn't a program, although many of us have been taught that it is. Certainly, in an attempt to help groups of people follow Jesus, organizations and publishers have developed various plans or programs. Most of these are good and needed. However, when we strip down discipleship to just completing a curriculum, it becomes much less than God intended.

The apostle Paul wrote to Timothy, one of his disciples, "Train yourself to be godly" (1 Timothy 4:7). Paul wrote this because he knew that people can't be godly—conformed to the image of Christ—without discipline.

Discipline is tough to learn on your own. You're much more likely to learn it with the support of a group and a clear, measurable plan. Eventually you can remove some of the program scaffolding as you internalize the disciplines. Yet the brutal truth is that around 90 percent of people who leave behavioral change programs revert to their former behavior. So we shouldn't be surprised if a similar percentage of people who desire to grow spiritually need the structure and support of that nasty thing called a program. The truth does sting, doesn't it?

Perhaps broadening your understanding of discipleship can help you see that programs serve as an explosive trigger. A program sets you in motion with energy. Even if you're not drawn to structure, it will enrich your life in Christ. You might never feel at home in structure, but when you make peace with it, you'll learn to embrace its value.

THE CREATION OF A NON-DISCIPLESHIP CHRISTIANITY

The church culture in the Global North—along with Australia, New Zealand, and South Africa—has largely accepted the idea of non-discipleship Christianity: People can be Christians without making any effort to submit to and follow Christ. The fact that we've developed this two-tier form of Christianity forces us to retrace our theological footsteps back to the actual message we proclaim. We need to ask ourselves, "What kind of person does non-discipleship Christianity produce?"

Does Non-Discipleship Christianity Make Disciples?

What kind of people does this altered gospel message naturally create? Does it create spiritually reborn disciples of Jesus committed to the Great Commission, or does it create consumers of religious goods and services? Unfortunately, the gospel we teach has become drenched in American culture.

This isn't a surprise, and it's not all bad. As Lesslie Newbigin, pastor and former missionary to India, wrote, "No gospel is pure, it is always embodied in a culture."[14] However, church historian Philip Schaff called America a motley sampler of all church history.[15] The American gospel is predominantly activist rather than contemplative and usually moves toward individualism rather than community.

And our altered gospel message contains several negative characteristics. Let's look at the three most harmful.

The American gospel limits grace to forgiveness of sin. In America in particular, we've crafted the gospel message to produce results. We place the focus of grace on conversion instead of on the whole journey. We measure God's blessing by how many people decide for Christ by coming forward or raising their hand. This emphasis on conversion exerts a tremendous influence on our understanding of grace. While we dole out grace in major doses at conversion, we then watch it trickle for the remainder of a disciple's journey.

Perhaps this is why the words of Ephesians 2:8-9 are quoted regarding God's grace without 2:10. "For it is by grace you have been saved, through faith—and this not from yourselves, it is the gift of God—not by works, so that no one can boast." Verse 10 continues, "For we are God's workmanship, created in Christ Jesus to do good works, which God prepared in advance for us to do." By limiting this awesome passage—even unintentionally—to a lifeboat that rescues us from our plight, we limit the extent of God's grace. Grace, then, is God's continued gift of enabling us to do good works and to give great effort. These are as much a part of his grace as the act of salvation or conversion.

So we must work to restore the grace of God that is active, powerful, and transforming to the way we proclaim the gospel. Grace provides divine enablement for all of life, for the entire journey. We should expect it to flow freely all of our days.

The American gospel separates justification from sanctification. Of course, justification and sanctification do have different meanings: the reality of the new birth and the process of becoming like Jesus, respectively. However, we've incorrectly made the line of demarcation meant to distinguish them into a wall that divides them.

Most of the damage we've done to the gospel with this separation is subtle and without malice. The problem is that separating these two theological terms gives the impression that being a Christian means obtaining a protected status before God. We've taught that this act of justification settles the issue — "Come in where it's safe and secure" — rather than teaching that a call to believe in Christ should also compel following him. In other words, the point of salvation (justification) isn't the finish line; instead it's the starting line for a lifelong journey (sanctification).

Discipleship flourishes when we present the gospel as a seamless journey of transformation that begins with new life given by God and moves right along with the joy of following Christ every day.

The American gospel teaches that faith equals agreement with a set of religious facts. Believing in Jesus has no meaning if we don't follow him in discipleship. Believing without discipleship isn't believing, it's agreeing to a set of facts about a religious figure.

The problem we face is that we have created and taught a faith that doesn't transform people. Survey the members of your church. Ask if they think discipleship is optional for believers. I bet they'll say yes. However, in Scripture, that kind of Christianity doesn't exist.

Both Jesus and Paul taught that following Jesus is proof of being a Christian.[16] The gospel of the kingdom Jesus delivered in the Sermon on the Mount is the same gospel preached in Acts and the same gospel Paul presented in Romans, Ephesians, Philippians, and Colossians. When Jesus commanded, "Make disciples," he wasn't simply referring to converts. He wants followers who follow — people who submit to his teachings and his ways.

But because we've preached a different gospel, a vast throng of people think they are Christian/saved/born again when they really aren't! We've made the test for salvation doctrinal rather than behavioral, ritualizing it with walking the aisle, praying to receive Christ, or signing a doctrinal statement.

Perhaps we've made it so easy to get into "the life" that we've made it nearly impossible for people to live the life. The life that

Jesus calls us to—a life of following Him—a life of humility, sacrifice, submission, and obedience.

This has led to what some call bar-code Christians—people who believe the right things but who don't follow Jesus. The real gospel requires us to repent of our sin. To believe means to follow Jesus daily. The gospel requires us to make disciples who learn to obey everything Christ taught. The evidence of salvation is living a life of transformation. I'm not speaking of earning salvation; I'm talking about proof of salvation. Perhaps the question we need to ask ourselves is, "Does the gospel we preach produce disciples or does it produce consumers of religious goods and services?"

The most basic issue confronting us is restoring the gospel message of Scripture that will create healthy followers of Jesus. For many, this will require the redefining of the very nature of faith as a faith that follows, a faith that forms the inner person, a faith consistent with the call of Christ to "follow me, . . . and I will make you fishers of men" (Matthew 4:19).

EXPLORING A FAITH THAT EMBRACES DISCIPLESHIP

The statement "exploring a faith that embraces discipleship"[17] implies that a faith exists that doesn't embrace discipleship. We've been talking about that kind of faith, one that results in non-discipleship Christianity. It requires agreement with religious ideas or facts, but doesn't require the development of character to take action. Because that's what much of faith has become, let's briefly explore the faith that requires disciples "to follow" Jesus. In fact, this kind of faith started thousands of years before Jesus ministered and taught on earth.

The Great Cloud of Witnesses

The writer of Hebrews wrote about the active pursuit of a faith that embraces discipleship:

> Therefore, since we are surrounded by such a great cloud of witnesses, let us throw off everything that hinders and the sin that so easily entangles, and let us run with perseverance the race marked out for us. Let us fix our eyes on Jesus, the author and perfecter of our faith, who for the joy set before him endured the cross, scorning its shame, and sat down at the right hand of the throne of God. Consider him who endured such opposition from sinful men, so that you will not grow weary and lose heart. (Hebrews 12:1-3)

The writer earlier created a list of heroes of the faith from the Old Testament era (see Hebrews 11:4-38): By faith Abel offered a proper sacrifice. By faith Noah built an ark. By faith Abraham packed up his family and moved. By faith Joseph ran from evil. By faith Moses chose a life of self-denial, confronted Pharaoh, and led the people through the Red Sea. By faith Joshua led the people around Jericho's walls. By faith Gideon showed courage in his obedience even though he was afraid. Samson, David, and Samuel — the world wasn't worthy of them.

These are our great cloud of witnesses; they taught us faith. Notice that with their actions, they showed us what it means to believe. What kind of disciples is the gospel meant to create naturally? The answer is people like these, whose faith embraced following their Lord. Without this kind of faith demonstrated by obedience, can a person really please God (see Hebrews 11:6)?

The lesson here is clear: Faith that doesn't result in action isn't faith, but something less. The apostle James, the half-brother of Jesus, wrote, "What good is it, my brothers, if a man claims to have faith but has no deeds? . . . In the same way, faith by itself, if it is not accompanied by action, is dead" (James 2:14,17).

Jesus, "the author and perfecter of our faith" (Hebrews 12:2), taught James about faith. He demonstrated it by obeying in spite of the shame and suffering he faced and endured on the cross.

In fact, Jesus' own words about faith couldn't be clearer:

> "Why do you call me, 'Lord, Lord,' and do not do what I say? I will show you what he is like who comes to me and hears my words and puts them into practice. He is like a man building a house, who dug down deep and laid the foundation on rock. When a flood came, the torrent struck that house but could not shake it, because it was well built. But the one who hears my words and does not put them into practice is like a man who built a house on the ground without a foundation. The moment the torrent struck that house, it collapsed and its destruction was complete." (Luke 6:46-49)

Characteristics of a Faith That Embraces Discipleship

The qualities of the discipleship-based faith taught in Scripture are both basic and important to understanding how to both be and make disciples. Here's a recap:

- A faith that embraces discipleship is only real when we actively obey it.
- A faith that embraces discipleship is defined historically by people who took action.
- A faith that embraces discipleship distinguishes itself from mere agreement or intellectual assent with demonstrated proof.
- Jesus distinguished a faith that embraces discipleship as thoughtful obedience instead of religious words.

The Kind of Person the Gospel Can Create

So far, I've declared that you can't be a Christian without being a disciple and that faith as modeled and taught by Jesus requires more than just agreeing to religious truth. It means a commitment to follow Christ daily. Discipleship describes the process of following Jesus; it's the centerpiece of the Christian experience, because as Dietrich Bonhoeffer said, "Christianity without discipleship is always Christianity without Christ."[18] The Christian faith and following Jesus are irrevocably linked. You can't have one without the other.

Before we close this section, let's briefly list the characteristics and the competencies that will be found in the kind of person the gospel produces.

Personal Characteristics of Disciples
- A disciple abides in Christ through the Word and prayer (John 15:7).
- A disciple bears much fruit (verse 8).
- A disciple responds to God's love with obedience (verses 9-10).
- A disciple possesses joy (verse 11).
- A disciple loves as Christ loved (verses 12-13).[19]

Personal Competencies of Disciples
- A disciple submits to a teacher who teaches him or her how to follow Jesus.
- A disciple learns Jesus' words.
- A disciple learns Jesus' way of ministry.
- A disciple imitates Jesus' life and character.
- A disciple finds and teaches other disciples for Jesus.[20]

SUGGESTED RESOURCES

ON DEFINITIONS OF DISCIPLE

Following the Master: Discipleship in the Steps of Jesus by Michael J. Wilkins (Zondervan, 1992). The best work theologically, done by an outstanding scholar.

The Divine Conspiracy: Rediscovering Our Hidden Life in God by Dallas Willard (HarperSanFrancisco, 1998). Particularly, check out chapter 8, "On Being a Disciple, or Student of Jesus."

A New Kind of Christian: A Tale of Two Friends on Spiritual Journey by Brian McLaren (Jossey-Bass, 2001). Defines what it could mean to be a disciple in the present culture. Challenges many of our traditional notions of discipleship, providing in the relationship of the two main characters a beautiful depiction of how one person can affect another.

ON THE PRIORITY OF DISCIPLESHIP

The Master Plan of Evangelism by Robert Coleman (Revell, 2006). The classic of classics on making disciples. Short and accessible, very nicely outlined with good footnotes. Makes the case for discipleship as the first priority for all serious Christians.

The Cost of Discipleship by Dietrich Bonhoeffer (Touchstone, 1995). A not-so-accessible classic in discipleship literature. The first half of the book on "cheap grace" and the Sermon on the Mount is worth the effort. It was written by a very brave and brilliant theologian who lived under the tyranny of the Nazi regime and was executed for his participation in a plot to assassinate Adolf Hitler.

Jesus Christ, Disciplemaker by Bill Hull (20th anniv. ed., Baker, 2004). Develops the case from the life of Jesus that he practiced the principles of discipleship that he later called his followers to practice. Also shows how his life makes the case for disciple-making and discipleship as the core of God's work.

CHAPTER 2

ORIGINS OF DISCIPLESHIP

Haldis Gundersen of Kristiandsund, Norway, wondered if she experienced a miracle one weekend when she turned on her kitchen faucet and discovered that the water had turned to beer. Two flights below her apartment, horrified customers at a local bar wondered what went wrong when water came out of the beer taps.

Apparently a very clumsy plumber had hooked the beer pipes to the water pipes for Gundersen's apartment. A local beer distributor, who came to the rescue and helped bartenders properly connect the pipes, said, "The water and beer pipes do touch each other, but you have to be really creative to connect them together."[1] This story certainly makes you question the competence of the plumber, and it makes you realize that life doesn't work too well without competence.

But even competence isn't enough. We also need character.

From the earliest days of life on earth, the mature have taught the young. They've passed on both character and competence to their children, friends, and associates. We find this concept in Scripture. The apostle Paul told Timothy, "What you heard from me, keep as the pattern of sound teaching, with faith and love in Christ Jesus. Guard the good deposit that was entrusted to you—guard it with the help of the Holy Spirit who lives in us" (2 Timothy 1:13-14).

We've already noted that many people try to reduce the call to follow Jesus to a study course, a limited program only for new believers, or a rigorous life only for monks, missionaries, and ministers. Worse, many think that discipleship involves the completion of tasks, the acquisition of skills, and the accumulation of knowledge. We need to clear these half-truths from our minds.

Losing the context of Jesus' command to make disciples leads to this kind of misunderstanding and misapplication. So, in order to understand what "make disciples" should mean in the twenty-first century, we need to explore what it meant in the first century and throughout church history.

PRE-CHRISTIAN EXAMPLES
OF DISCIPLESHIP

Passing on wisdom to the young for the purpose of character formation has always been around. It meets the human need for friendship, guidance, and intimacy. It's also crucial for accomplishing a task, achieving a long-term goal, and—for spiritual people—doing the will of God.

Throughout history, mentors or spiritual guides have helped temper people's tendency to be lazy, lose focus, or give into temptation. What we now call discipleship provided the following human needs:

1. relationships to nurture
2. apprenticeship for competence
3. accountability for tasks
4. submission for shaping
5. wisdom for decision making

The Greco-Roman World

Historians agree that Greece was the birthplace of Western civilization. Plato's *Republic* described the foundations of democracy, and when we think of philosophy, we immediately recall Socrates' teaching techniques and Aristotle's articulation of theories.

Alexander the Great led the Grecian empire to world domination. When he died at age thirty-three, his kingdom was divided into four parts, and one of those parts became the Roman Empire. That's where the name Greco-Roman comes from — a word that describes a thousand years of seminal culture. In the world of togas, sandals, the Parthenon, temples, and little white homes perched on hillsides overlooking the sea, discipleship permeated Greek life — from aristocrats to peasants, from philosophers to tradesmen.

In the first century, the apostle Paul stood on Mars Hill and said, "Men of Athens! I see that in every way you are very religious. . . . I even found an altar with this inscription: TO AN UNKNOWN GOD. Now what you worship as something unknown I am going to proclaim to you" (Acts 17:22-23). Paul's speech demonstrates that the Greek philosophers were confused about God. But they were also astute in passing on their confusion as they lived out discipleship and even created some of its language and technique.

The Greek masters' use of mathetes, *or disciple:* As explored in chapter 1, *mathetes* is translated "disciple." We can find the concept of disciple — a person following a master — among the great masters of Greece. Plato, Socrates, and Herodotus all used *disciple* to mean "learner" or "one who is a diligent student." These and other Greek philosophers generally understood that the disciple's life involved apprenticeship, a relationship of submission, and a life of demanding training.[2]

Michael Wilkins summarizes discipleship during the Greco-Roman period:

> In the earliest written use of *mathetes,* the term was used in three ways: it was used with a general sense, in morphological relation to *manthanein,*[3] to refer to a "learner"; it was also used quite early with a technical sense to refer to an "adherent" of a great teacher, teaching, or master; and it was also used somewhat more restrictedly by the Sophists to refer to the "institutional pupil" of the Sophists. Socrates/ Plato (and those opposed to Sophists)[4] tended to avoid using the term to designate his followers in order to avoid Sophistic misassociations, but used the term freely to refer to "learners" and "adherents" where there was no danger of misunderstanding.[5]

The inclusion of the meaning "adherent" at the time of Christ and the early church made *mathetes* a convenient term to designate the followers of Jesus, because it didn't emphasize learning or being a pupil but *adherence* to a great master. So a "disciple" of Jesus, designated by the Greek term *mathetes,* was a person who adhered to his master, and the master himself determined how the disciple followed.[6] Of course, that leads us to Jesus' call to all who were interested: "If anyone would come after me, he must deny himself and take up his cross daily and follow me" (Luke 9:23).

Five hundred years before Jesus was born, a disciple was one who committed his all to follow a master teacher. The meaning remained the same until the time of Jesus, providing our first major clue about what Jesus meant when he told his disciples to "make disciples."

The Semitic World of the Hebrews

While Plato, Aristotle, Socrates, and other Greek philosophers were making their own kind of disciples, religious leaders were using the same kinds of activities in the Semitic world. This culture actually pre-dated the Greco-Roman world. While the philosophies in Athens pointed in many directions regarding truth, the dominant beliefs in Jerusalem pointed to Yahweh and the coming of the Messiah. We need to examine both the words and the concept of *mathetes* in the Hebrew culture.

The words: mathetes *as* talmidh: The Hebrew equivalent to *mathetes* is *talmidh*, which literally means "taught one."[7] The prophet Ezra used this word to describe a community of musicians in the temple (see 1 Chronicles 25:8). Isaiah used a closely related word, *limmudh*, several times to speak of disciples (see Isaiah 8:16; 50:4; 54:13). "Bind up the testimony and seal up the law among my disciples" seems to indicate that Isaiah had some disciples (8:16). In Jeremiah, *limmudh* is translated "accustomed to" in the familiar saying, "Can the Ethiopian change his skin or the leopard its spots? Neither can you do good who are accustomed to doing evil" (Jeremiah 13:23). Here it means that someone has been discipled or taught to do evil. These uses make it clear that all of us are someone's disciple. Who we follow makes the difference.

The use of *talmidh* and *limmudh* also indicates a personal relationship as the master teaches and trains a pupil/disciple. Ancient Hebrew culture didn't naturally lead to the kinds of formal discipleship relationships we have now. Yet the words do indicate a teacher-student relationship. This was true in families, among elders at town gates, and among the wise men who served as keepers of Israel's wisdom and traditions.

Still, words have limitations. They find their meaning in the context of life. For example, a store can more specifically be a grocery store, a department store, a sporting goods store, or a storehouse. So looking at the words for discipleship in the Old Testament is just a beginning. We also need to look at the context of discipleship relationships in the Hebrew culture. As Wilkins notes, "Even though the terms for disciple are not found in abundance in the Old Testament, various relationships in Israel were true 'discipleship' relations since they share universal characteristics of discipleship relations."[8]

The concept: Moses and Joshua: The premier mentoring relationship in the history of Israel was that of Moses and Joshua. Their relationship lasted the longest, and its context is rich with applications. Notice how their relationship manifests itself in the five characteristics of what humans need to grow and develop.

1. Relationships to nurture: Moses needed a lot of encouragement because he faced great and demanding tasks. With help from his imperfect brother, Aaron, and his very capable father-in-law, Jethro, Moses obeyed God and rescued God's people from Egyptian tyranny.[9] Then, when Moses went up the mountain to meet with God, he took Joshua as his aide (see Exodus 24:13). From that time forward, Joshua served by Moses' side.

2. Apprenticeship for competence: From the time of the visit with God and through many personal and organizational crises, Joshua observed and learned how to lead difficult people in challenging circumstances—even when the leader is filled with self-doubt. He saw Moses slam the tablets to the ground. He saw Moses make mistakes, such as striking the rock for water rather than speaking to it in a trusting way. At the same time, he listened outside Moses' tent and heard the cries of his mentor pleading with God to show mercy on the people.

3. Accountability for tasks: Moses' task seemed so simple: Take the people into the land. Yet it was a daunting one. By administrating much of the work, Joshua learned the daily grind of managing two million people.

4. Submission for shaping: Joshua remained faithful to God and

to Moses, even when he faced pressure from others close to him to go along with various disagreements: when Moses' sister and brother, Miriam and Aaron, rebelled; when the people demanded meat rather than manna; when conflict arose over Moses' new wife; and when all but one of the spies reported that entering the land of promise would be too dangerous. Joshua's submission to the Father and to his servant Moses shaped him into a man of strong faith and character.

5. Wisdom for decision making: God selected Joshua to replace Moses because Joshua was ready. God chose him, Moses trained him, and then God anointed him (see Deuteronomy 1:38; 31:1-30). Moses told Joshua to "be strong and courageous, for you will bring the Israelites into the land I promised them on oath, and I myself will be with you" (Deuteronomy 31:23). Joshua then crossed the Jordan River, took the city of Ai, conquered the five kings of the region, went on to capture the entire land of Canaan, renewed the covenant, divided the land among the twelve tribes, and faithfully served until the Lord gave Israel rest from her enemies. Still faithfully serving at the end of his life, Joshua charged Israel's leaders with the wisdom he'd learned from Moses and from God: "You yourselves have seen everything the LORD your God has done to all these nations for your sake; it was the LORD your God who fought for you" (Joshua 23:3).

We can see the influence Moses had on Joshua and the influence Joshua had on others in the epilogue to the book that bears Joshua's name: "Israel served the LORD throughout the lifetime of Joshua and of the elders who outlived him and who had experienced everything the LORD had done for Israel" (24:31).

The Prophets

Some of Israel's prophets also had followers or disciples. Again, Isaiah spoke of "my disciples" (Isaiah 8:16).[10] The prophet Samuel apparently had a large following. He ordered Saul to meet with "a procession of prophets" in preparation for Saul's ascension to king (1 Samuel 10:5). These prophets seemed to be under Samuel's control; he knew in advance what they would say and do. Prophets also seemed to have a special relationship with kings: Isaiah with Hezekiah, Nathan with David, and Samuel with Saul. While not always pleasant for the kings, these odd relationships were often necessary for the spiritual direction of the kings.

Elijah mentored Elisha, and Elisha later commanded a "company of the prophets" (2 Kings 4:38). Through the years from Samuel to Elijah and Elisha, a primitive guild of prophets existed, perhaps formed to resist the policies of Jezebel.[11] These men, known as the "sons of prophets," met with and learned from Elisha.

Wise Men and Scribes

Israel had three primary sources of spiritual wisdom and authority: (1) the high priest and the priestly clan known as Levites represented the people to God; (2) the prophet represented God to the people; and (3) the wise man or sage explained and protected the accumulation of wisdom. These men worked to pass on the wisdom literature, orally from fathers to sons and eventually in writing. When the wisdom began to be written down, a new class of scholar—the scribe—came into being. One of the best known was Ezra, the primary teacher during the return to the land under the leadership of Nehemiah.

The Bible's wisdom literature exists because of the work of these professional wisemen, the scribes. Their work required formal training, including a master-disciple relationship. Scribes first existed in the royal court with elders and court advisers. Their training also called for apprenticeship in reading, writing, transcribing, and expounding on wisdom and scripture. For example, Baruch was a trained scribe who helped Jeremiah put together his work, and trained wise men helped Solomon compose Proverbs.

Wilkins summarizes for us: "Individual master-disciple relationships within the leadership of the nation enabled the leadership function to be passed from one leader to the next until God has accomplished his purpose through them to meet the need of his people."[12]

DISCIPLESHIP DURING THE TIME OF CHRIST

The Middle Eastern world that Jesus was born into was steeped in the tradition of apprenticeship. Various schools of religious thought all claimed their ground with great passion, and each required a great deal of their disciples. Let's look briefly at four groups. The way they made disciples is helpful to us today, because when we understand the requirements of the first century, the fog lifts from how we should be and should make disciples now.

The Pharisees

The Pharisees, passionate nonpriestly members of a renewal movement, saw it as their calling to protect the law by retaining written and oral traditions. They believed in resurrection and the importance of daily rules. They were highly committed, but their zeal often caused them to go too far. They were tragically misguided and missed the entire point of Jesus (see John 5:39-40). However, these well-intentioned men were very curious, and they took Jesus seriously. Some people might snore through the Sermon on the Mount, but not the Pharisees. They scrutinized every word, remembered it, discussed it, and then became enraged because they understood Jesus' words. They knew he was taking them apart point by point when he declared, "Unless your righteousness surpasses that of the Pharisees and the teachers of the law, you will certainly not enter the kingdom of heaven" (Matthew 5:20). On a number of occasions, they tore their robes, threw dust in the air, and attempted to kill Jesus (see, for example, John 8:59).

The Pharisees also sponsored a formal rabbinical school, and a number of their rabbis became very popular. The reliable Jewish historian Josephus noted that so many young men gathered around rabbis in Herod's day that they were like an army.[13] Gamaliel II reportedly had a thousand disciples who worked on mastering the complex and extensive Torah. The Pharisees' demanding discipleship system rewarded only the best and brightest and was the doorway to a wonderful religious career.

Disciples of John the Baptist

John the Baptist proclaimed a purist form of Judaism focused on repentance, seeking God, and serving God—a manifestation very close to the kind of discipleship Jesus espoused. John had many disciples, and only two left him to follow Jesus in the early stages (see John 1:35-50). Many of John's disciples, twelve in one recorded case (see Acts 19:1-7), believed on Jesus at a later date. John's semi-monastic disciples were sacrificial; for instance, they were willing to live in the stern realities of the desert.

The Separatist Disciples

John the Baptist's disciples interacted with people in the cities, and John himself stayed just a few miles outside Jerusalem, where curious people could take a day trip to hear him.[14] But a group known as the Essenes became so disgusted with the liberalism and spiritual lethargy of the mainstream that they, like Jesus, went into the desert to fight against the devil. This fully monastic and separatist group functioned under extensive rules and very demanding entrance requirements. For example, a two-year trial period included a testing of their knowledge of the Torah, followed by what we now call a communal or peer review. Although some were scholars, their spirituality wasn't simply an academic pursuit. They desired to imitate God and to live in a true brotherhood of love. They saw themselves as the true Israel and they lived, prayed, and worked for the kingdom of God to come to Israel. Eventually, they withdrew to Qumran, where the Dead Sea Scrolls were produced.

The Zealots

Josephus identified several messianic movements that flourished in Palestine, products of the political unrest prompted by harsh economic conditions and the military occupation of the Romans.[15] Usually a group of followers gathered around a leader and acclaimed him as king. Some of these groups wore uniforms, and in one case, even body armor. They didn't study the Torah as much as they sharpened their swords. Jesus attracted many of these Zealots, who desired to make him king.[16] One lesson we can learn from Jesus' refusal to become a political leader is that he didn't see the power of the state as the solution to society's basic problem of sin. While politics can be a noble career, Jesus saw "changing the world" as an internal issue that required inner transformation (see Luke 6:43-45).

∽ ∾

Based on these four groups that practiced discipleship, we can better understand that when Jesus said, "Make disciples," the people around him might have been confused. When Jesus' disciples told others to make disciples, those listening might have thought of the Pharisees, John the Baptist, the separatists, or even political revolutionaries like the Zealots. Wilkins notes,

> Discipleship in the ancient world was a common phenomenon. It primarily involved commitment of an individual to a great master or leader. The kind of commitment varied

with the type of master. The important feature for us to understand is that when Jesus came and called men and women to follow him, not all understood him in the same way. Not all understood the apostles in the same way when they went into the furthest reaches of the known world calling for men and women to become disciples of Jesus. Depending upon the background of the audience, some might have heard quite a different thing than what was meant by Jesus or his apostles.[17]

Now that we understand some of the background of discipleship during the time of Christ, we can examine the tradition that Jesus emerged from and how he built on it.

CHARACTERISTICS OF THE RABBINICAL TRADITION

As we've noted, the common contemporary understanding of Jesus' command to make disciples relates to post-conversion training. We often teach discipleship as an optional and temporary experience, and we keep it within the confines of the church. If we want to correct that understanding so that the church can multiply in a healthy way, we need a fuller understanding of what the disciples heard Jesus say about discipleship.

First-Century Discipleship

The first thought Peter, James, John, and company likely had when they heard Jesus say, "Make disciples," was that they would find and develop other people like themselves. Clearly the apostle Paul believed this years later.[18] All of these men knew that making disciples involved making a serious commitment to follow a leader.

Let's briefly look at five characteristics of first-century discipleship.

1. Deciding to follow a teacher: Young men could join a variety of schools, each led by a rabbi or a teacher. In some cases, students chose their teacher and, of course, teachers could accept or reject a student's application. If a young man hadn't achieved a certain academic and social status by the time of his bar mitzvah at age thirteen, he would instead choose a life of farming, fishing, carpentry, or the like. The fact that Jesus and his followers were laborers explains why the religious establishment didn't accept them.

The disciple of first-century Judaism learned everything from his teachers. He learned his teacher's stories, his life habits, how to keep the Sabbath his way, and his interpretations of the Torah. And when a disciple learned everything his teacher knew, he then taught his own disciples.

A disciple's commitment to follow his teacher lies at the heart of the transformational process. Every disciple must make a commitment of submission to at least one other person. Without this relational dimension, everything that follows is weakened. The teacher-disciple relationship creates a powerful bond that's at least as important and often more crucial than a father-son relationship.

First-century discipleship was expressed as a servant-master relationship (see Matthew 10:24). Once accepted as a disciple, a young man started as a *talmidh*, or beginner, who sat in the back of the room and could not speak. Then he became a distinguished student, who took an independent line in his approach or questioning. At the next level, he became a disciple-associate, who sat immediately behind the rabbi during prayer time. Finally he achieved the highest level, a disciple of the wise, and was recognized as the intellectual equal of his rabbi.[19]

2. Memorizing the teacher's words: Oral tradition provided the basic way of studying. Disciples learned the teacher's words verbatim to pass along to the next person. Often disciples learned as many as four interpretations of each major passage in the Torah.

3. Learning the teacher's way of ministry: A disciple learned how his teacher kept God's commands, including how he practiced the Sabbath, fasted, prayed, and said blessings in ceremonial situations. He would also learn his rabbi's teaching methods and the many traditions his master followed.

4. Imitating the teacher's life and character: Jesus said that when a disciple is fully taught, he "will be like his teacher" (Luke 6:40). The highest calling of a disciple was to imitate his teacher. Paul called on Timothy to follow his example (see 2 Timothy 3:10-14), and he didn't hesitate to call on all believers to do the same (see 1 Corinthians 4:14-16; 11:1; Philippians 4:9). One story in ancient tradition tells of a rabbinical student so devoted to his teacher that he hid in the teacher's bedchamber to discover the mentor's sexual technique. To be sure, this is a bit extreme, yet it demonstrates the level of commitment required to be a disciple.

5. Raising up their own disciples: When a disciple finished his training, he was expected to reproduce what he'd learned by finding and training his own apprentices. He would start his own school and call it after his name, such as the House of Hillel.

These five characteristics describe the institution of discipleship as practiced in the first century.[20] Jesus used these practices with his closest followers. When he called on them to make disciples, he expected them to find others who would make the five commitments. When he said, "[Teach] them to obey everything I have commanded you" (Matthew 28:20), they knew the task would require the kind of dedication found in these five commitments.

Of course, some questions now cry out for an answer: What would this look like for us now? If these characteristics describe what Jesus meant by "make disciples," shouldn't we practice discipleship the same way? How common is this kind of discipleship in the contemporary church?

THE UNIQUENESS OF JESUS' DISCIPLESHIP

Before we answer the questions on page 64, let's look at some unique qualities of being a disciple of Jesus in the first century.

Unique in Whom He Chose

Jesus required certain qualities in the men he chose as his first disciples. He didn't choose Gentiles, because they didn't fit the profile of God's promise to Abraham (see Genesis 12:1-3; 15:1-5). Also, Gentiles had no background or understanding about the kingdom of God and the role of the Messiah. Jesus also didn't choose Hellenistic Jews, who came from the Greco-Roman culture with all its beauty and all its evil. As Doug Greenwald, executive director of Preserving Bible Times, writes, "They still wanted to go to the synagogue on Sabbath and listen to the Torah being read, but they also wanted to go to the theatre, arenas, circuses, gymnasiums and baths and participate in the pleasures of the Greco-Roman culture."[21]

Only one demographic remained: the observant Jew. The world of the observant Jew included the tiny elite strata of the Pharisees. But the vast majority of observant Jews came from the trades: fishing, farming, carpentry, and commerce.

Greenwald lists some of their characteristics:

They had a passion to be pure, purity being defined as doing those things that would honor God as interpreted by their rabbis. Thus they would never:

- Set foot on Gentile land or in a Gentile house.
- Dine with sinners.
- Seek out and fellowship with lepers.
- See disabled people as being "right" with God.

- See anything of redeeming value in a tax collector.
- They were zealous not to be compromised with Greco-Roman Culture.
- They knew the Scriptures incredibly well.
- They were men of prayer, albeit mostly ritualized prayer, and would pray at different times of the day.[22]

Observant Jews also knew their culture. They understood the Scriptures and spirituality through a cultural filter. Most weren't elitist at all. In fact, only the Pharisees considered them unlearned because they had no professional theological training.

Jesus chose men who had the basic raw material to help him rescue the world, starting in Jerusalem. They had passion and spiritual hunger. They were common enough to work outside the religious system. They had a lot to give up, but one thing they didn't have to give up was a religious career; perhaps nothing paralyzes a leader's personal transformation more than the prospect of losing his religious career.

Uniquely Based on Friendship and Common Respect

Jesus reacted strongly to the Pharisees' hypocrisy, which led to a crucial difference in his teaching on how to relate to others. He scolded them for their selfish ambition and propensity for showmanship. Then he sharply explained the difference to his own disciples:

> "They love to be greeted in the marketplaces and to have men call them 'Rabbi.' But you are not to be called 'Rabbi,' for you have only one Master and you are all brothers. And do not call anyone on earth 'father,' for you have one Father, and he is in heaven. Nor are you to be called 'teacher,' for you have one Teacher, the Christ. The greatest among you

will be your servant. For whoever exalts himself will be humbled, and whoever humbles himself will be exalted." (Matthew 23:7-12)

Jesus made the distinction that his disciples were not to raise up new disciples for themselves. The disciples of Jesus were never to take the role of master. Both then and now, Jesus commands his disciples to raise up more disciples for him. Yes, we'll have teachers, mentors, and leaders, but they'll never become our masters. Yes, we submit to authority, but it's voluntary and an act of love and humility. As disciples today, just as in the first century, we're called to follow Jesus and to raise up more disciples for him.[23]

Unique Because It Redefined *Disciple*

The lexical definition of *disciple* is "learner."[24] But in the first century, the cultural understanding of *disciple* was "follower." In addition, disciples display certain characteristics and behaviors (see chapter 1). We generally accept that all who commit their lives to Christ are his disciples. Yet someone can have all these qualities and still miss the key connection required for being a follower of Jesus: following someone who can teach you how to follow Jesus. Again, a disciple is someone who submits to at least one other person in a healthy and appropriate way as a means of support and accountability to develop fully as a follower of Jesus.

People who claim to be followers of Jesus pack our churches. But they're not connected in community; they try to fly solo. The great John Donne's famous utterance "No man is an island" has been secularized as a noble sentiment for membership in the world community. But as dean of St. Paul's Cathedral in London, Donne was speaking of the disciple's need for community.

Solo discipleship occurs in a program. If I try to fly solo, I'll engage only in activities or spiritual exercises that I have time for or that seem attractive to me. In other words, I'll maintain control of Jesus' agenda for me, and I'll keep my distance from anyone who might threaten my autonomy.

But just imagine with me for a moment what would happen if we started teaching and practicing how to be disciples as Jesus described them, submitting ourselves to a more mature, seasoned follower. Unless we're doing this, we're not following Jesus the way he desires. We must adjust our definition of a disciple to fit what Jesus truly meant. He demonstrated what he meant by the way he lived and by what he modeled when he called the Twelve to be with him. And further, he changed his relationship to them when he commissioned them to go make other disciples who would follow him.[25]

A fuller definition: A disciple is a student or follower of Jesus. A disciple has decided to submit to at least one other person under appropriate conditions in order to become like that person as that person follows Christ. Because character develops in community, the disciple's intention is to go deeper with God and to be shaped into the image of Christ.

Unique in How We Should Apply It Now

Let's summarize exactly what a disciple should be.

1. A disciple submits to a teacher who teaches her how to follow Jesus.
2. A disciple learns Jesus' words.
3. A disciple learns Jesus' way of ministry.
4. A disciple imitates Jesus' life and character.
5. A disciple finds and teaches other disciples who also follow Jesus.

If this describes what it meant to be a disciple in the first century, shouldn't we practice it the same way now? I've been accused of being a master of the obvious, and I'm going to display my mastery once again. The answer to this question is yes. I believe that because we've lost the art of making disciples, the kingdom of God is not advancing as planned. I've written on discipleship and disciple-making more than most, yet I feel like I've struck gold! So, resoundingly yes—we desperately need to rediscover this lost treasure.

Is This Kind of Discipleship Common Today?

Sadly, unknown is closer to reality than uncommon, especially when we look for discipleship with all five elements listed on page 68. A lot of ministries contain three of the five, a small minority have four of the five, but almost none—including my church—practice all five. The most common characteristics are numbers 2 through 4:

2. A disciple learns Jesus' words.
3. A disciple learns Jesus' way of ministry.
4. A disciple imitates Jesus' life and character.

These three qualities are the least challenging of the five. People willingly study the Bible, and from that they become acquainted with Jesus' way of ministry and his character. Frankly we can do this without needing to change. Again, we've found ways to be Christian without becoming Christlike. Qualities 2 through 5 are indeed vital, but 1 and 5 make being a disciple and disciple-making work.

The frightening truth is that many Christians don't do 2 through 5 very much. But what scares me even more is that we can practice 2 through 5 alone and be considered mature leaders. The fact that we avoid submitting to others as disciples and that we seldom reproduce by making other disciples is a hideous trait within the body of

Christ. The characteristics found in 1 and 5 are absolutely necessary for the process of discipleship to work. By *work*, I mean that
discipleship results in character transformation and multiplication.
The kingdom of God grows through the principle of discipleship.

Churches should be outposts for God's kingdom, sending centers
for the real work we do in the various parts of life—how our life
affects other lives where we live, work, and play (see 2 Timothy 2:2).
But without 1 and 5, we'll continue to be unable to truly reach others.
Why? Let's look briefly at these two characteristics and how they help
us reach others.

A Disciple Submits to a Teacher

Most people never get to this, and it's the primary reason they don't
grow well or for very long. Yet nothing is more fundamental to spiritual maturity. Character develops in community and that occurs
only with submission. Paul taught that submission was for everyone
(see Ephesians 5:21). This basic trait makes Jesus attractive to us
(see Philippians 2:5-8). God opposes the proud and gives grace to
the humble. God asks for and rewards our humility. Of course, we
can easily dodge this command—I mean, who *isn't* humble before
God. But the New Testament also teaches that we reveal our humility in our relationship to other believers. Submission provides the
proof of humility, and that's why character is built in community.
Submission requires checking my autonomy at the door and allowing the other person to help me keep my commitments to God.

The genius of submission in a discipleship relationship is that
it's a two-way street. No one is master. Both are servants of Jesus and
both benefit greatly from the relationship. Generally one person is
more seasoned and might be considered the lead teacher, the one
who teaches the other person what it means to follow Jesus.

This kind of relationship provides the strength required to hold
us together as we face challenges to our faith. If we don't have this

kind of support, an event or crisis can shake our faith and send us into a destructive downfall. We'll probably emerge later, but much time — even years — is lost. Without submitting themselves to this kind of community, even well-intentioned believers drift and find themselves nearly comatose spiritually, numbed by years of religious activity without transformation.

A Disciple Finds and Teaches Other Disciples

The reason disciple-making often fails is that we don't expect it to reproduce. The next time you go to church, I can almost predict what will happen. You'll see people sitting in the same places, talking to the same people, at about the same time before and after the service. The songs, message, testimonies, and so forth will be about the same each week. And all of you know an awful lot about Jesus! You've spent much of your lives meeting with other believers. You've learned Jesus' words and his ways of doing ministry, and you've dedicated yourselves to imitate his character. Yet there you sit, very much the same this year as last, near the same empty seats in about the same places.

I know, because my church looks the same. Sure we try to witness when we can, when the opportunity arises. But let's face it; we barely have a pulse. And you and I both wonder why our churches aren't doing better. It's because disciple-making has become optional. We've reduced spiritual development to an in-house and non-threatening experience. When we do four of the five dimensions of disciple-making that Jesus taught, we're still just meeting with ourselves. We talk to ourselves, we interact about ourselves, and we address issues about us. We're trapped in a closed system.

Once we're "fully taught," we should be finding and teaching other disciples for Jesus. That's what the Great Commission is about: "I've trained you, now you go do the same thing."[26] Yet most of us would have to admit that we haven't followed Jesus in this way at all.

How would finding and teaching other disciples look in the flow of twenty-first-century life? The answer must be to reproduce—to make new disciples. While all kinds of valid methods exist for evangelizing, the model that penetrates our culture best is the "make disciples" model within our own relational networks.

This tests our commitment. I often wonder if we're more committed to packing our churches than to penetrating our culture. But penetrating our culture is the heart of making disciples. So, what will we do?

Suggested Resources

The Concept of Disciple in Matthew's Gospel, As Reflected in the Use of the Term "Mathetes" by Michael Wilkins (E. J. Brill, 1988). Sets the gold standard regarding the lexical history of disciple/*mathetes*.

Following the Master: Discipleship in the Steps of Jesus by Michael Wilkins (Zondervan, 1992). In this broader, more engaging, and personal treatment of discipleship in the New Testament, Wilkins provides the basic theology needed to give the discipleship movement academic credibility.

Choose the Life: Exploring a Faith That Embraces Discipleship by Bill Hull (Baker, 2004). Additional reading on the nature of faith that transforms and on the destructiveness of a forgiveness-only gospel.

THE STORY
OF DISCIPLESHIP

If you've ever taken a tour at Universal Studios, you know that some people riding the trams ooh and ah over everything they see, while others find the tour disappointing and even cheesy. Often, sweet moms point out the obvious while empty-walleted and sunburned dads click away with their digital cameras. Meanwhile the family's bored teenagers roll their eyes at the phony-looking floods and the hokey mechanical shark from *Jaws*.

For the following tour of discipleship's history, I've put together a route somewhat like a Universal Studios tour. I'm sure it will delight some and disappoint others. However, we need to take this tour because discipleship has a story. This story provides the confidence we need to know that discipleship and spiritual formation have survived through the centuries and that they aren't some relatively recent invention of Americans who decided to program and formulize spiritual growth.

So, where will this tour of discipleship lead us? How do we trace it through the tumultuous and winding road of history? Will we find the intentional development of disciples? Were church leaders in centuries gone by giving spiritual direction to their congregations? Did other generations value submission and relational accountability? Under the radar of history's social-political events, was the church able to focus on the disciple's maturity and journey in imitating Christ?

Before we start the tour, I have bad news and good news. First, the bad news: Because of limited space for our quest, probably 90 percent of my research didn't make the cut. I only wish you could benefit from it as much as I have. The good news: I've arbitrarily strained what I found for your easy access. Still I feel a bit like a criminal for not revealing more of what I've learned. (I encourage you to check out the suggested reading list at the end of this chapter, which lists most of the resources I've used.)

For this tour, I've chosen three early bishops who provided spiritual direction. Then three maverick monks who expressed the need for renewal in the established church. Next, a look at the Middle Ages — a time of poverty, illiteracy, corruption, and disease, but also of rich intellectual development among the aristocracy and clergy. And finally, a quick examination of seven people who shaped discipleship during the Reformation.

BISHOPS AS SPIRITUAL GUIDES

Clement and Constantine serve as bookends of early church history. Clement was an early Roman bishop who lived at the end of the first century. Constantine the Great, who ruled the Roman Empire from 306 to 337, died just after being baptized. He made Christianity legal in the Edict of Milan in 325, ending two hundred years of sanctioned persecution of Christians.

To understand the foundation of what was important to the church during these years, we need to listen to its leaders. After the death of the apostles, the location of authority moved to bishops — a word that simply means "overseers." Each city had a bishop who oversaw the church in that community. Ignatius, often considered the bishop of bishops, insisted on "one city, one bishop, one altar," where the bishop brought the entire church together in worship around the liturgy.

So, what did these early leaders focus on? What did they leave behind for us? How did they disciple the people? These men weren't mystics. They lived practical lives, serving God in the ordinary matters of life, loving their families, doing the slow soul work required as shepherds of God's people. We need to look beyond the robes, special hats, and impossible details of ceremony that surround the image of today's bishops to see these men of the first century who lived for Christ and served others sacrificially.

Clement of Rome

Clement lived at the end of the first century and might be best known for a letter he wrote to the Corinthian church. Most church historians believe that he knew and interacted with several of the apostles and that the apostle Peter commissioned Clement to ministry. He advised the Corinthians on the practice of the spiritual disciplines and stressed the need for unity. Richard A. Burridge, dean of King's College in England, summarized Clement's concerns for the spiritual life of the Corinthian Christians:

> For Clement, prayer, fasting, and almsgiving constituted the regular and essential structure of Christian spirituality. There is no true inner life in the service of Christ that is not marked by them. Such an approach gives Christian spirituality a character of profound "relatedness" to the real world:

care for others and a deep sense of humility are necessary in the believer, even though such a person has received election of the loving God. It was this that kept Christianity, in the early period, from becoming just another elitist spiritual movement concerned with inner purity, or from becoming a mystical individualism disconnected from society.[1]

Very simple and real. Power and mission — the impulse to reach out and serve as Christ did — come out of personal transformation.

We might wonder why Clement didn't call for a discipleship that included Scripture reading, Bible study, Scripture memory, one-on-one work, or a "quiet time." Quite simply, though the Bible was finished, it was still not recognized as we know it. The canon of the New Testament wasn't settled until almost two hundred years after Clement, when the letters of the apostles and bishops were all sorted out in 367.[2] Of course, printing presses didn't exist and neither did books as we know them. Only the elite had access to parchments. Fragments or copies were read during public services because many people couldn't read or write. The poor, common laborers, and the poorly educated made up most of the church. Their spiritual formation occurred within a communal life, the importance of which can't be overstated. They lived in an interdependent society and experienced spiritual formation together, making the altar — the place of communion — central to their worship.

Ignatius of Antioch: The Bishop of Bishops

Ignatius, who lived from 50 to 117, wrote the book on bishops and their work. Fortunately that means he wrote the book on how to disciple a congregation. Toward the end of Emperor Trajan's reign, Ignatius traveled throughout the empire on his way to Rome to be tried for being a Christian. He visited with Polycarp, the bishop of Smyrna, and Irenaeus, the bishop of Lyons, who considered himself

Ignatius's disciple. Ignatius wrote to the church at Rome, begging them not to arrange for his release; he desired to be martyred to prove that he was a disciple. Martyrdom was the *sin e qua non* (or "essential" quality) for being a true disciple during that period.[3]

Ignatius left seven letters to the churches of Asia Minor: Ephesus, Magnesia, Tralles, Rome, Philadelphia, and Smyrna, along with a letter to Polycarp. He believed that the highest function of leadership was leading the gathered church in worship. The bishop served as the chief celebrant of the Eucharist, which brought the church together in unity around Christ. The most important part of a disciple's life was his life in Christ and in the community of Christ, so living in unity with Christ and those in the community was the central task of the leader. As Ignatius's mentor, the apostle John wrote, "If we claim to have fellowship with him yet walk in the darkness, we lie and do not live by the truth. But if we walk in the light, as he is in the light, we have fellowship with one another, and the blood of Jesus, his Son, purifies us from all sin" (1 John 1:6-7).

While living in unity and love with our brothers and sisters in Christ might seem to be an obvious element in basic discipleship, it's at this very point that many disciples falter. In his letter to the Ephesians, Ignatius pointed out both his humility and his commitment to discipleship — even his own:

> I do not command you, as though I were somewhat arrogant. For even though I am in bonds for the Name's sake, I am not yet perfected in Jesus Christ. [For] now am I beginning to be a disciple; and I speak to you as to my schoolfellows. For I ought to be trained by you for the contest in faith, in admonition, in endurance, in long-suffering.[4]

We can conclude that both Clement and Ignatius emphasized the importance of study, prayer, service, worship, unity, and love toward others. In the same letter, Ignatius also urged members of the church to submit to their local leaders in the bishop's absence:

> May I have joy of you always, if so be I am worthy of it. It is therefore meet for you in every way to glorify Jesus Christ who glorified you; that being perfectly joined together in one submission, submitting yourselves to your bishop and presbytery, ye may be sanctified in all things.[5]

Ignatius saw daily submission to a practical authority as critical to spiritual development. This foundational truth takes us back to the very beginning of discipleship and builds our confidence that it remains true now.

Polycarp of Smyrna

Polycarp, who was martyred in 156, believed that a true disciple would be martyred, because it meant to imitate Christ and his suffering. This bishop stressed love for the poor and attacked those who made Christ a mere intellectual symbol. Polycarp's life and death provide another reason to believe in the great strength of character found in the church during this period of persecution.

The historian Jerome wrote of him:

> Polycarp, disciple of the apostle John, and by him ordained bishop of Smyrna, was chief of all Asia, where he saw and had as teachers some of the apostles and others who had seen the Lord. He, on account of certain questions concerning the day of the Passover, went to Rome in the time of the emperor Antoninus Pius while Anicetus ruled the church in that city. There he led back to the faith many of the believers who had been deceived through the persuasion of Marcion and Valentinus, and when Marcion met him by

chance and said, "Do you know us?" he replied, "I know the firstborn of the devil."

Afterwards during the reign of Marcus Antoninus and Lucius Aurelius Commodus in the fourth persecution after Nero, in the presence of the proconsul holding court at Smyrna and all the people crying out against him in the Amphitheater, he was burned. He wrote a very valuable Epistle to the Philippians which is read to the present day in the meetings in Asia.[6]

Polycarp's contact with the apostle John and others who had seen Christ impressed Jerome, the early historian. As a great teacher and debater, Polycarp also won back many disciples who had gone astray in their theology.

Polycarp's epistle to the Philippians contains interesting information. He filled this short letter with practical advice and many quotations from the apostle Paul. Polycarp also addressed the ordinary issues of temptation, faithfulness in marriage, the care of widows, the danger of false teaching, and the importance of regular Scripture reading and prayer. After his martyrdom, he was best remembered for his encouragement of self-control, prayer, and fasting as means of not falling into temptation.

The members of Polycarp's congregations in Smyrna needed to be together to help each other keep their commitments to God. It takes a community to disciple one person, and early leaders like this bishop began a tradition of speaking directly and firmly about the ongoing battle of the flesh and the Spirit. Through Polycarp's life, death, and ministry, we can conclude that the life of a disciple has always been a life of discipline. Often that needed discipline only touches a life when a community of believers works together under the authority of its leaders. It's comforting to know that for the past two thousand years, spiritual leaders have addressed the same human issues.

Summary

The apostle John either mentored or at least spoke to all three of these bishops. Simplicity and reality describe their prescription for the church and disciples. They encouraged prayer, fasting, giving, and connectivity. In particular, Ignatius said bishops should provide corporate spiritual direction through the leading of community worship around the Lord's Table.

These men were willing to die for their faith, and Ignatius and Polycarp actually did. But they also desired to live for Christ in a daily sacrificial way to be good examples to the people they led. In all the best ways, they represented what being witnesses for Christ includes. By practicing the same disciplines as Christ, they became godly and disciplined men.

The power of one life to influence another is the beginning of discipleship. As Jesus said, when a disciple is fully taught, he "will be like his teacher" (Luke 6:40). These three early bishops set the standard for others, and they're worthy of imitation.

WHEN WE WERE ALL CATHOLICS

Christianity became legal in 325 and was the state religion of the Roman Empire. During the next four hundred years, the church morphed into Christendom.[7] After the defeat of Rome in the fifth century, the church continued.

Catholic means "universal." The church was unified under bishops and eventually the bishop of Rome emerged as the bishop above other bishops. In turn, he became the pontiff, or pope. We just covered several hundred years of history with 130 popes, but in reality, it didn't progress in a straight line. The validity of the popes and the veracity of their personal lives zig-zagged across the rural and political landscape.

By the Middle Ages, popes had sons they called nephews and they had armies. Many were thoroughly corrupt. They weren't at all like Clement, Ignatius, or Polycarp, who provided spiritual direction for their people. They became more like a crime syndicate, using evil means to maintain control of power and wealth.

Julius II, from the early 1500s, is an example of a corrupt pope. He was primarily consumed with having Michelangelo sculpt his tomb, but somehow stumbled into having him paint the Sistine Chapel. Julius also went off to war with a marching band, servants, and three thousand horses, stopping on the way to visit his daughter —yes, his daughter and her husband. The war concluded without any fighting, and Julius returned home as the victor to carry on his papal rule. This definitely didn't reflect the way of Jesus.

While it took a long time for the one true church to fall from grace, it didn't take much time at all for some of its members to grow dissatisfied with what they saw as a compromised church.

MONKS AND MAVERICKS

When most of us think of monks and monasteries, the words *maverick, innovator, entrepreneur, daring,* and *adventurous* don't come to mind. Yet the first monks, fed up with the numbing routine of church activity without transformation, rebelled. We might think of them as "dropping out" of the church to lead a movement that dramatically changed the church.

Origen of Alexander (185–254), a great scholar and the creator of what we now call biblical interpretation, believed that the human spirit could ascend to the presence of God only if the turbulent desires of the physical body were brought into check. He was an ascetic[8] thinker, seeing the body, mind, and soul as so intimately related that spiritual progress could take place only following discipline of the body and purification of the mind through study. His writings became highly influential in the century following him, when the movement of the ascetics, later called monasticism, began.[9]

The first known monk (solitary person) was St. Antony the Hermit. He lived about the same time as the great scholar, bishop, and courageous leader Athanasius (296–373). Antony was among the first of the Desert Fathers, a group that reacted to the spiritual slackness in the church and determined to seek God in solitude. In the spirit of Jesus, they went to the desert to fight the Devil. Antony sold all his property and gave it to the poor. As he attracted disciples, a monastic order resulted. He and the other Desert Fathers gained so much influence that, by the fourth century, Christians were leaving cities and searching for places of solitude.

The hermit ministry eventually died out, in some cases due to harsh weather, disease, and attacks from animals. This led monks to move into walled communities, where they could be protected from the elements and be alone — together. The older teachers became abbots (fathers) and were like bishops for monastics. By the fifth century, their influence grew to the point that the most power-ful bishops in the Catholic Church were chosen from the monks. Virtually every important writing of the church was done by and in the context of the monastic life, so the life of "great pains" — disci-pline and abstinence from sex, marriage, or wealth — became domi-nant among Christian lessons.

Characteristics of Monks

Monks were courageous, very tough, legalistic, and extreme. We might conclude that they tried too hard and went too far. But if we look past the celibacy, hair shirts, self-flagellation, living in marshes, and abuses of Scripture, we can examine what relates to us now. For instance, we can learn a lot from their reaction to Christendom. In fact, Dietrich Bonhoeffer said, "The renewal of the church will come from a new monasticism, which will be nothing like the old."[10] What could this new monasticism without walls be like? What qualities did the monks of history possess that we could have now?

- They chose a definite pattern of life—a life of humility, sacrifice, submission, and service.
- They saw the road to godliness as one of discipline.
- They saw value in living by a rule, sharing an agreed-upon life. They desperately needed each other to remain faithful.
- They practiced the disciplines that Jesus modeled—disciplines that freed them from slavery to their own body's appetites and that connected them to God and reformed them spiritually.
- They applied themselves to serving others.

The monastics committed themselves to restoring the way of Jesus to the church. As it matured, the movement formed great forces for good and improved the lives of both the monks and countless others.

If we could recapture all of these characteristics, today's church would experience new energy. However, because that's counterintuitive both to human nature and to American culture, I agree with Bonhoeffer. While the new monasticism will be unlike the old in structure, it must be just like the old with its emphasis on sacrifice. Every church on the planet would benefit from following the commitments detailed above.

Because the church today needs to rediscover these qualities, let's quickly look at three monks and their succeeding monastic orders to see how they practiced following Jesus.

God in the Ordinary: Benedict and the Benedictines

As the son of a wealthy landowner, Benedict of Nursia (480–550) studied in Rome, where he discovered a community of ascetic believers that had been active for many years. Benedict rejected urban life and moved to the village of Affile, where he pursued a life of seeking God. A translation of his writings, *The Rule of St. Benedict*, has become increasingly popular and can be found today in bookstores.

Benedict believed that the path to spiritual maturity came from a balance of study, prayer, and work. Thus the Benedictine monks became known for their balanced approach to life. They believed in finding closeness to God in an ordinary life involving a daily pattern of meditation, reading, and doing regular tasks. They also believed that knowing God entailed more than the religious rituals found in the church and that intimacy with God wasn't reserved for just the elite. The Benedictines melded the secular and the spiritual into one life — the life of God.

As present-day disciples, we can learn from the Benedictines to seek and serve God each day in study, prayer, and at our place of labor. Further, we can realize that serving our spouse, giving our time to others, and sacrificing our material wealth all constitute discipleship.

Live Like Christ and Love the Poor: Francis of Assisi and the Franciscans

Most people remember Francis of Assisi (1181–1226) as the strange man who preached to the animals, providing today's animal rights advocates with their own patron saint. People who don't want to evangelize verbally often quote Francis of Assisi: "Preach the gospel at all times and, if necessary, use words."

Francis, the son of a wealthy Italian cloth merchant, is probably the most popular of the medieval saints.[11] His goal to live the life that Jesus lived sounds familiar — because it lies at the heart of salvation! This impulse to imitate Christ provides the proof that, indeed, Christians experience regeneration — the new birth. And

Francis wanted to live the life that Jesus lived in poverty.

By the way, poverty seems to be a thread running through all monastic orders, in spite of the many godly people in Scripture who possessed wealth: Job, Abraham, Joseph, Saul, David, and Solomon. Many in the monastic movement carried the desire to be like Jesus too far. For example, Jesus wasn't married, so we won't be married. Jesus didn't own anything but his robe, so we will also get rid of material wealth. Their well-intentioned actions were meant to eliminate temptation and sins that so easily entangle (see Hebrews 12:1-3). However, we can certainly conclude that in spite of their overreaction, Francis and his followers did a much better job of becoming like Jesus than many of the church's leaders did.

To what extent should present-day disciples give up material wealth? That question created bitter battles even among Francis's own disciples. However, we should be willing to admit that materialism, probably more than any other factor, clouds the judgment of American Christians (see 1 Timothy 6:6-10). It dulls our appetite for God and the need for his grace in our daily life. The accumulation of stuff creates its own anxiety and busies us with its care and growth. It creates a consumer mentality, driving churches to build bigger buildings and make numerical growth the goal. It taints the gospel, creating the monster of competition that we must continually feed.

Thus I draw from Francis of Assisi the reality of loving the poor, but not necessarily becoming poor on purpose. The Franciscan monastics remind us to live simply so that we can use any wealth we have for the benefit of others. When you glance through most of the contemporary literature on discipleship, this aspect is shamefully absent.

Intellectual Life: Dominic and the Dominicans

Benedict emphasized balance in work, study, and prayer. Francis focused on the poor. Dominic (1174–1221), an Augustinian monk, stressed the importance of effective preaching.

A highly educated Spaniard, Dominic favored a severe ascetic pattern. He started preaching academies for both men and women during a time when common priests didn't have the education to combat the heresy being taught at the time. Dominic set out to battle the false teaching that had captured much of the upper class and local rulers.

Dominic founded an order of preachers and sent them two by two into the jaws of the enemy. The Dominicans renounced the world and all its pleasures. These brave men and women went into Paris, Bologna, and other hotbeds of heresy. With the blessings of Pope Innocent III, the Dominican order and its message spread quickly. "Dominic stressed the importance of a strong intellectual life, not only for refuting heresies but also for building up a sound, well informed spirituality."[12] Among their number was Thomas Aquinas, perhaps the greatest mind of the Middle Ages, whose integration of philosophy and theology set a new standard of thought that remains to this day.

The contemporary church has already seen a time similar to Dominic's. In the early part of the twentieth century, theological liberalism challenged the authority of Scripture, the divinity of Christ, the need for world missions, and other foundations of orthodoxy. The response came from a group who stressed the fundamentals (and who were labeled "fundamentalists"). This responding group started seminaries such as Westminster in Philadelphia, Fuller in Pasadena, Trinity in Chicago, and Dallas Seminary. Like Dominic's new order of preachers, these schools took up the cause of defending the faith and enhancing the intellectual life of the preacher. These schools, along with Billy Graham and others, created *Christianity Today* magazine and founded the National Association of Evangelicals and the Evangelical Theological Society, and elevated the intellectual prowess of young men and women.

Looking forward to the present, we find the evangelical movement disorganized, but in a good way. Individuals and organizations who identify themselves as evangelicals retain a common commitment to the orthodox faith. And the movement possesses plenty of intellectual firepower.

At the Christian street level, however, there still exists what Mark Noll, a church historian at the University of Notre Dame, called the "scandal of the evangelical mind" — a lack of evangelical scholarship. Disciples need a balance of reason and faith. Like an airplane, both wings are needed. Sadly, many Christians try to fly with just the faith wing. This concerned the Dominicans regarding the clergy in the twelfth century, and it concerned English writer Harry Blamires for the layperson in the twentieth century. He wrote,

> We speak of "the modern mind" and of "the scientific mind," using that word mind of a collectively accepted set of notions and attitudes. On the pattern of such usage I have posited a Christian Mind, chiefly for the purpose of showing it does not exist. There is no longer a Christian Mind. . . . The Christian Mind has succumbed to the secular drift with a degree of weakness unmatched in Christian history.[13]

Diplomat and Christian philosopher Charles Malik agreed, warning in 1980, "I must be frank with you: the greatest danger besetting American Evangelical Christianity is the danger of anti-intellectualism. The mind as to its greatest and deepest reaches is not cared for enough."[14]

As disciples, along with loving God with our whole heart and whole soul, God calls us to love him with our entire mind (see Matthew 22:37). God wants us to be good stewards of our intellectual ability and to use it to the fullest for the purpose of his kingdom.

Summary

Dietrich Bonhoeffer, who said renewal would be birthed by a new monasticism, is right some sixty years later. The monastic movement infused the slow-moving and corrupt machine called the church with fresh ideas and spiritual energy. The monastics attacked by retreat. Benedict taught that we find God's power in the ordinary things of life. Francis taught that we imitate Christ when we love those in need. And Dominic stressed the importance of the intellect and the ability of the church's leaders to articulate the faith.

These mavericks of their time taught us that the journey outward includes the journey inward. They taught us to base discipleship—imitating Christ—on a foundation of inner strength. Discipleship involves the quest of going deeper with God, positioning ourselves to undergo a transformation of character. From these men, we understand that the Great Commission first must be about depth before strategy. They taught us that true conversion means discipleship, and further, that discipleship means discipline. We can experience great freedom when life's appetites serve God's kingdom rather than dominate our own lives.

THE MIDDLE YEARS

The Middle Ages, the Dark Ages, Medieval times—all label a rather distasteful time for humankind, with decadent church leadership, high illiteracy rates, and frequent wars and famines. During that time, the Black Death killed 40 percent of Europe's population. Yet Wycliffe, Anselm, Bernard of Clairvaux, Thomas à Kempis, Thomas Aquinas, Dante, and other giants of literature and thought also came out of this era.

The major factor affecting people's spiritual formation was illiteracy. The vast majority couldn't read or write. Few books existed and only the elite could afford or read them. The elite included the clergy, who were among the best educated. In fact, because the clergy had a near-monopoly on literacy and dominated society, little history exists that describes the life of ordinary people; most of the recorded history of the time tells the story of the literate and wealthy. However, we do know that three primary influences affected the intentional discipling of the common person: the Eucharist, community life, and art.

The Eucharist

Eucharist is the English translation of the Greek word for thanksgiving. We shouldn't think of this as the contemporary Catholic Mass, but as a simpler and more straightforward celebration of the gathered congregation around the sacrifice of Jesus. Ignatius of Antioch gave basic instructions on the church in worship and the Eucharist.[15] The "Great Thanksgiving," or Eucharist, is built on the Last Supper, which was built on the Passover meal. Of course, the Last Supper had no bells ringing or choirs singing, no vestments, no smoke in the air, and no formal liturgy.

For many years, the church was Catholic, or universal, and was built around the bishop of Rome and a descending hierarchy of bishops, some of whom eventually became archbishops and cardinals. The Great Schism (1378–1417) occurred as these church leaders fought about who the bishop of Rome, the pope, should be. The Great Division occurred in 1054, when the church split between East and West, Constantinople and Rome. This created the Roman Catholic Church and the Eastern Orthodox Church, and meant that the church was no longer universal.

Yet through every twist and turn of history, through all the persecutions, the famines, the wars, the church councils, and the madness and blessings of everyday life, one thing was constant: The people of God, rich and poor, professionals and peasants, royalty and commoner, all gathered as one around Christ and his sacrifice. In that moment at the altar, it all came together: the confession of sin; the forgiveness of sin; the celebration of Christ's life, death, resurrection, and promise to come again. It all converged in that moment of the Eucharist, when Christ was present with his people.

Over the years, the church divided further as it quibbled over the details of this holy moment, but the Eucharist remains at the core of what all Christians share. The basic liturgy that developed remains one of immense holiness. In that moment, the saved sinner kneels before God, experiences fresh relief of her sin through a prayer of confession, takes the bread and the cup where—in some mysterious way—Christ becomes present through the Holy Spirit. During the Eucharist, the child of God remembers the past in thanksgiving, experiences the grace of God in the present, and looks forward to the great feast promised in heaven. Each day before work, cobblers, farmers, kings, and servants—brothers and sisters in Christ—would all kneel before God, then stand to their feet and face the day renewed and refreshed as ambassadors of Christ.

> BREAD OF THE WORLD IN MERCY BROKEN,
> WINE OF THE SOUL IN MERCY SHED,
> BY WHOM THE WORDS OF LIFE WERE SPOKEN,
> AND IN WHOSE DEATH OUR SINS ARE DEAD;
> LOOK ON THE HEART BY SORROW BROKEN,
> LOOK ON THE TEARS OF SINNERS SHED;
> AND BE THY FEAST TO US THE TOKEN
> THAT BY THY GRACE OUR SOULS ARE FED.[16]

Community Worship

Primitive life in the Middle Ages demanded interdependence. Living in community—sharing homes, bedrooms, food, water, and tools—was simply the life they lived. The people came together for worship and wouldn't have thought of it as an individual exercise. In addition to the celebration of the Eucharist, they also spent some important formational moments to prepare for the altar.

Remember, most people didn't have Bibles, because there were no printing presses. Even if people had Bibles, they wouldn't have been able to read them. However, the reading of Scripture and saying of prayers took place in community worship. And the clergy delivered sermons to explain the gospel message and to help worshipers apply the Scriptures.

Personal devotions, or "quiet time," weren't personal. They were communal out of necessity because the people couldn't read or write. During any time they spent alone with God, they might pray based on memory and meditate on what they'd been taught in community worship. But the common people of the Middle Ages wouldn't have had a daily personal devotional life as we think of it. Daily devotions were communal. The people gathered daily—early in the morning to pray, to hear the Word of God, to confess their sins, to wish their brothers and sisters the peace of God, and then to move on to face their day.

Because spiritual formation of disciples during that time was based on a communal approach, people knew the liturgy. They memorized it and could meditate on its richness. While we don't want to idealize the people who lived during those days, we certainly should look at how discipleship was alive and well in that process. And we should be brave enough to admit that perhaps one reason so many present-day disciples struggle to do devotions alone is that they are best done in community.

Art

Artists of the Middle Ages knew their work would illuminate stories for the common, illiterate people of the day. Probably the best-known artist of the time, Michelangelo, painted the ceiling of the Sistine Chapel from 1508 to 1512, just prior to the Reformation. Although literacy was rising, less than half of the population could read. He knew his work at the Sistine Chapel would assist worshipers.

> Michelangelo would have expected that pilgrims filing into the Sistine Chapel for Mass to recognize the scenes on the medallions. But even the illiterate, who had never seen the Malermi Bible,[17] would no doubt have been familiar with many of the scenes from depictions of them elsewhere — just as, of course, they would also have recognized The Flood and The Drunkenness of Noah.[18]

Frescoes such as Michelangelo's ceiling paintings served much the same purpose as the *Biblia pauperum*, or "poor man's Bible," a picture book used by the illiterate. Masses sometimes lasted for hours, giving worshipers plenty of time to contemplate the artwork around them.[19]

Today we certainly understand the power of images. Images empower ideas and evoke emotions. Why do today's tourists make pilgrimages to the Louvre in Paris or the Uffizi in Florence? Sure, it might be "the thing" to do — go to Europe and look at art you don't understand and eat great food you do understand. However, the works of artists such as da Vinci, Michelangelo, Raphael, and scores of other masters evoke powerful emotions. Even though most viewers stand in line for hours and don't understand the history of the images, they're moved by the stories, the colors, and the extraordinary ability of the artists.

I recall standing at the feet of Michelangelo's *David*, moved by its power and beauty as I reflected on the man who was after God's own heart. Raphael's *The Transfiguration* and his work in the Vatican Museum papal apartments have moved many to tears, transporting them emotionally to realms of praise and thanksgiving beyond their normal experiences. A painting that particularly moved me, Caravaggio's *The Deposition*, depicts Jesus' disciples and friends taking him down from the cross in preparation for burial. Somehow this image took me to that moment, where I felt their despair, their sense of failure. I began to feel what they might have felt when they thought all hope was gone.

And no painting moves me more that Rembrandt's *The Return of the Prodigal*. The original hangs in the Hermitage in St. Petersburg, Russia, and a copy hangs just over my right shoulder in my study. This image depicts the passion of the grateful father, the relief of the returned son, the angst of the faithful son, the appreciation of the father's friends. It evokes healing, comfort, thanksgiving, a sense of consummation, and relief. It calls on all of us to be like the father—forgiving, always waiting, always hoping for our beloved to return home.

One of the most memorable worship experiences of my life was a Sunday worship service at St. Paul's Cathedral in London. I wasn't moved as much by the excellent choir or the elaborate processional as I was by the story of redemption painted on the dome. These images transported me to a place of praise and adoration as I drank in their beauty.

What's the role of art as part of spiritual formation in contemporary life? Most of us are products of the Reformation, which reacted to the images of medieval Christianity by removing the altars and moving the pulpits to center stage in order to give the proclamation of God's Word a central place. However, this brought a rejection of art and caused the loss of a tool that God uses to speak to people and move them to praise and service. In addition to the loss of sacred art, most of us face a daily confrontation with other images via television, films, printed media, and our computers. Our challenge is to filter out the vast barrage of images that can damage our souls and then find images that foster the process of following Jesus.

In the Middle Ages God used art to form people spiritually. He does the same in our postmodern age. Discern and enjoy.

Summary

Spiritual formation during the Middle Ages took place by stimulating all the senses. With the Eucharist, each person held in his hands and tasted with his tongue elements that stimulated memory and praise of Christ's finished work. As writer and former pastor Eugene Peterson says, "Just as Sabbath-keeping protects creation from the sacrilege of being taken over by us, so the Eucharist protects salvation from being dominated by our feelings and projects."[20]

The people worshiped as a community—many times on a daily basis—and shared life because they depended on each other. Because books were rare and most people were illiterate, the people related to God as a group. Frescoes and other art forms in the sanctuary caused worshipers to lift their heads to the heavens. These images provided beauty and inspired the people to live for a higher purpose than what they saw in the filth and squalor of their daily existence.

We can learn much from the church of the Middle Ages. Even now, half of the world's population is illiterate and lives in poverty, yet God continues to change them through the same appeal to all their senses. Modern technology provides a fast and portable means of speaking their language. All of us need to touch, hear, see, smell, and speak in our own language a liturgy of confession and praise to God.

Every household in America owns four Bibles, and we have wonderful Bible teaching, while artful music and drama wait at our fingertips. A glut of images can stimulate in us the vilest action or inspire the most glorious praise of God. May God give us the discipline to use all that we have for our own discipleship and for the making of other disciples.

THE REFORMATION: NEW LIFE

One of the most significant developments of the historical era of the Renaissance was the invention of the printing press. Printing with moveable type made it possible for ideas—including religious ideas—to reach across Europe. With the invention of the printing press some fifty years earlier, news of Martin Luther's ideas spread quickly after he nailed his 95 Theses on the Wittenberg Castle Church door in 1517.

The church was ripe for this message of justification by faith alone, in the work of Christ alone. Historian Herman J. Selderhuis summarized:

> On the eve of the Reformation the experience of faith was, for many, dominated by fear—the constant fear of being eternally damned, of ending up in hell, or at least spending many years of agony in purgatory. What this fear amounts to can best be illustrated by the collection of almost 19,000 relics[21] owned and cherished by Ellector Frederic of Saxony. Everyone reverently visiting these relics would receive a reduction in punishment of almost two million years.[22]

In contrast, Luther's message from the Scripture was this: God is first your Father before he's your Judge. This lifted the weight from the shoulders of millions of people, drawn to the idea that a regenerate person could be set right with God by faith alone in what Christ had done, rather than by striving to please God and earn his favor.

Candles and statues began to disappear from churches, and pulpits took center stage. The Eucharist changed from the mystery of transubstantiation[23] to a remembrance of Christ's sacrifice. The primary message also changed, emphasizing that Christ comes to his people through the Word of God as revealed in Holy Scripture and that every person is a believer-priest and can go directly to God through the one mediator, Jesus Christ.

Of course, the big names of the Reformation included Martin Luther, John Calvin, and Thomas Cranmer. Volumes upon volumes have been written about the vast sweep of the Protestant Reformation, but here we'll focus on discipleship; some of the most important aspects of following Jesus arose from this movement. The Reformation shaped just about everything most of us know about Christianity.

Courage: Martin Luther

In the fall of 1510, two Augustinian monks traveled seven hundred miles to Rome. One was a twenty-seven-year-old named Martin Luther, a witty and spirited son of a miner. When Luther (1483–1546) arrived in sight of the Porta del Popolo (what we call Vatican Square), he threw himself on the ground and shouted, "Blessed be thou, holy Rome!" His enthusiasm was short-lived.[24]

Not long afterward, Luther's mentor asked him, "Martin, have you ever read the New Testament?" A guilt-ridden and angry Luther answered, "No." Here stood a brilliant Augustinian monk who had studied every major discipline, yet he'd never cracked the Gospels. However, once he did, he certainly made up for lost time! Luther's displeasure with the church simmered for years and came to a boil through his disgust at the practice of indulgences. This practice involved individuals paying the church and clergy in an effort to gain salvation.

In 1517, Luther nailed his 95 Theses — more accurately, his protests against the church — to the church door at Wittenberg Castle. As a result, he stood trial for heresy. However, he refused to recant, and in 1521, at the Diet of Worms, he was excommunicated. This is when he spoke the famous words, "Here I stand; I can do no other."

Luther soon left the Augustinian order and married. God used his courage to free millions from the oppression of a corrupt church dominated by clergy who planned to continue their regime of guilt and control over people.

The Reformation essentially began when the truth spread that if individuals went directly to God through Jesus Christ and, by faith, received God's free gift of salvation, their lives would be transformed. Conditions were just right for Luther's action. His ideas made common people realize their importance to God. And German princes, who were ready to challenge the pope's authority, took notice.

Martin Luther stood up and put his life and work on the line. And he stood alone. He still stands as the example of courage for contemporary disciples. May each of us be willing to step forward when our time comes.

Spiritual Basics: John Calvin

Before long, Frenchman John Calvin (1509–1564) announced that he agreed with Luther. Forced to flee a very intolerant Catholic France, Calvin found himself in Geneva. From there, he wrote back to his fellow clergy what now is known as *The Institutes of the Christian Religion*, which first appeared in 1536. Calvin's *Institutes* became the most influential writing of that period, providing the basic theology for people as they grasped for a mooring in the theological storm. Calvin wielded massive influence, becoming the most widely published author in England for a hundred years.

Calvin wrote, "By imitating Christ we are drawn into union with him, a union which is 'a sacred marriage by which we become bone of his bone, and flesh of his flesh.'"[25] We should note that although Calvin became known for what we call Calvinism—the emphasis on God's sovereignty regarding salvation—this was not his focus. Instead he was a practical, back-to-basics leader, as seen through his years as a pastor in Geneva and his work on the city council.

While Luther started the Reformation, Calvin put feet on it. He organized it and sent it walking down the main street of life. In our discipleship, we can do what both Luther and Calvin did: possess the courage to take a stand and the dedication to develop the imitation of Christ for people in practical ways.

Personal Devotions for Every Person: Thomas Cranmer

Although Thomas Cranmer (1489–1556) acquiesced to Henry VIII's divorce and other lawless desires, he played an important part in extending spirituality to the common person. In fact, as Archbishop of Canterbury, Cranmer failed in almost every major crisis he faced. He stands in contrast to the great Thomas More, who was executed for not giving in to Henry VIII's wishes.

Cranmer deserves mention for his introduction of *The Book of Common Prayer* in 1549. *The Book of Common Prayer* was a devotional guide for the common person, just as the title indicates. The rapid rise in literacy among the English people along with the production of books made it possible for the average person to practice a personal devotional life. However, as Gordon Mursell, Dean of Birmingham Cathedral, explains, priests insisted on remaining part of the individual's devotional life:

> Parishioners were to hear the Scriptures read aloud in church twice every day, when the parish priest rang the bell and summoned them to join him for Morning and Evening Prayer. Cranmer took the old sevenfold monastic rhythm of common prayer and reduced it to just two daily services, Morning and Evening Prayer, both of which were to be recited not just for the people but *by* them—and in their own language.[26]

The Book of Common Prayer was the first time common people had a book in their hands that gave them a daily structure, the church calendar, special days, along with plenty of Scripture and prayers. This book remains a rich resource for millions of members of the Catholic Church, as well as the worldwide Anglican Communion and its counterparts in other denominations.

I probably can't overstate the impact of such a book at that time. If they could afford their own copy, families, small bands of believers, and individuals could meditate on the Scriptures and spend time in prayer with some guidance. *The Book of Common Prayer* nourished a nation then and still feeds the world today. We might think of it as something like the first study Bible, but far more crucial in its effect. Discipleship is more difficult when disciples can't have their hands on Scripture. So, in spite of his weaknesses, Cranmer should be honored for his role in giving common people a real shot at personal spirituality.

Disciplines of the Inner Life: Philip Jacob Spener

Philip Spener (1635–1705), a young pastor born and raised during the Thirty Years War, voiced a plea for reform in the German Lutheran church in his classic work *Pia Desideria (Pious Desires)*. A lifelong friend of philosopher Gottfried Leibniz, Spener significantly influenced the next leader of German Pietism, August Hermann Francke. Spener also sponsored the baptism of Nicholas Ludwig von Zinzendorf, a founder of the Moravian church, whose members played a crucial role in the life of John Wesley.

Spener is the father of Pietism, best defined as an emphasis on the heart and passion of spirituality. He lived a hundred years after Luther, when the German church was orthodox, cold, detached, in need of resuscitation. His *Pious Desires* had several dimensions, including passion toward God, a focus on loving one's neighbor, and a healthy focus on self. Because of his belief in the practice of spiritual disciplines, Spener would fit in today's spiritual formation movement.

Spener noted that "in Pietism the Bible is not only read and studied, but also meditatively discussed in groups of believers."[27] He urged people to get together in small groups and, as believer-priests, to minister to one another—a new and radical concept in that time. Spener saw that a systematic plan for renewal would bring new life to the entire church. He called for private meetings called *collegia pietatis*, gatherings of the highly motivated. Spener prescribed the following:

- To encourage a more extensive use of the Word of God, it should be read and discussed in the *collegia pietatis* or small group.
- To encourage members to read the Scripture privately.
- To read books of the Bible from start to finish so they could be understood the way they were written.
- To conduct one's group much like the Scriptures instruct in 1 Corinthians 14:26-40.
- To minister to one another as believer-priests.
- To hold each other accountable to live out the truth of God's Word with integrity.
- To help each other keep their commitments to God.
- To conduct themselves well, even among those they disagree with.[28]

As we explore these leaders of the Reformation, we can see clearly that God continued to provide his people with what they needed to grow spiritually: Luther, courage to call for reform; Calvin, practical and back-to-basics teaching; Cranmer, spirituality for common people. And as the fires of the Reformation began to flicker, Spener fanned the embers and sparked a surge of personal spirituality.

Through these leaders, we see a pattern for successful discipleship: courage, instruction, access to God's Word, and accountability in living it out. We need all of these now, perhaps more than ever.

Community: Count Nicholas Ludwig von Zinzendorf

Nicholas Zinzendorf (1700–1760), born into a noble family and raised in a grand castle by his Pietistic grandmother, became a part of the Pietist movement and was baptized by Spener. Zinzendorf struggled with a call to vocational ministry, but finally decided to fulfill his role as a count. He was very motivated spiritually, even to the point of forming a society for study and prayer that included the king of Denmark, the Archbishop of Canterbury, and the Archbishop of Paris.

In 1722, Zinzendorf allowed a communal sect called the Moravians to live on his land. They settled in a small town called Herrnhut ("the Lord's watch"). Although they lived in community, the Moravians were divided and in trouble. In 1727, Zinzendorf left public life to spend his time working with them. From his work, the group formulated a covenant called the Brotherly Agreement, which set forth the basic tenets of Christian behavior. An intense renewal followed, often described as the Moravian Pentecost. John Jackman, director of the *Zinzendorf* documentary film series, describes this experience: "During a communion service the entire congregation felt a powerful presence of the Holy Spirit, and felt their previous differences swept away. This experience began the Moravian renewal, and led to the start of the Protestant World Mission movement."[29]

Herrnhut became well-known as an example of Christians choosing to live together in intentional community. Like any true spiritually, it moved beyond self and existed for others. In 1727, Zinzendorf addressed the community:

> Herrnhut . . . must remain in a constant bond of love with all the children of God belonging to the different religious persuasions. They must judge none, enter into no disputes with any, nor behave themselves unseemly towards any, but rather seek to maintain among themselves the pure evangelical doctrine, simplicity and grace.[30]

The Moravian group's willingness to reach outside their community explains why William Carey, who many call the father of world missions, gave credit to Zinzendorf as the true father. Zinzendorf coached people in living in covenant relationships and helped them avoid the usual pitfall of self-absorption.

Every faith community needs to seek this balance as its members walk the tightrope of devotion and mission. Zinzendorf represents the kind of leaders who can shape a faith community and mobilize a naturally fragmented people into a passionate unit. The call to discipleship involves much more than our personal devotion to Christ. It extends to others around us as well. People often think they're spiritual, but they can't get along or work with others. The inability to live together with others provides pretty compelling evidence that we're not living with the humility and grace that Jesus called us to.

Zinzendorf's skills and heart created a community fired with a power that comes only from unity. The Moravians became the originators of world mission rather than a blot on the name of Christ. As Jesus himself said, "Blessed are the peacemakers, for they will be called sons of God" (Matthew 5:9).

Discipleship Done Right: John Wesley

No other person from post-Reformation history developed discipleship more than John Wesley (1703–1791). Wesley didn't start out to form the United Methodist Church; he was a committed Anglican and meant to bring new life to its sagging spirituality.

The ministry of John Wesley: Of all the figures in the history of Christianity, perhaps the one who still speaks most to us as God's people is John Wesley. He lived at the close of the Agrarian Revolution and the beginning of the Industrial Revolution. Wesley stood as part of the Reformation with his emphasis on the central doctrines of salvation by grace and through faith alone and of the authority of a fully inspired Bible (yet he was aware of the attacks on the authority and reliability of the Bible).

The Revival, the First Great Awakening, grew so fast that lay-people were needed to preserve its results. Wesley managed a remarkable balance in encouraging and supporting their participation yet maintained the biblical role of pastor. His use of class meetings and lay preachers changed people and their society, resulting in social reform. Without question, Wesley's greatest contribution in the field of church growth was his ability to harness the laity.

Wesley's major contribution in the realm of theology was his teaching about holiness, which Scripture teaches is possible in this life. He maintained a balance between faith and works, between God's part and ours. The godly lives of those who followed his teaching inspired even their critics.

The place of small groups in the life and ministry of John Wesley: Both of Wesley's parents came from the Puritan stream of English Protestantism, and his grandparents would have spoken of the Great Ejection (1662), when the established church excluded non-Anglicans.

In a very real sense, Wesley's concepts of spiritual discipline probably have their beginnings within his family.[31] His mother, Susannah, began a regular, informal study meeting in their home when John was only nine. She claimed in a letter to her husband Samuel that this caused church attendance to increase from twenty-five to more than two hundred.[32] After John completed his studies, he joined a society that his younger brother Charles had formed with two friends in 1729 at Oxford University.

This brings us to the Holy Club, which was given several other titles, such as the Bible Moths, the Reformers' Club, the Godly Club, and The Enthusiasts. But the title people remember is Methodists.[33] Holy Club meetings included prayer, Bible reading, sharing the experiences of the day, and encouraging one another. Their activities focused on three areas: the imitation of Christ, evangelism, and doing good to those in need, especially those in prison.[34]

The Holy Club was really the first Methodist fellowship meeting,[35] and its pattern was reproduced wherever Methodism went. James Hervey, part of the group at Lincoln College, Oxford, encouraged some boys in a school near his home to form a group. He gave the following reasons:

1. Because we are ignorant and short sighted . . . and often unable to discern things that are excellent. But God reveals to one what is good for another; so that, in a multitude of counsellors there is wisdom.
2. Because we are lovers of ourselves . . . unwilling to see our own errors, therefore unlikely to amend them. Whereas our friends will, with a meek and impartial spirit, show us our faults.
3. Because we are weak and irresolute . . . let go our integrity upon any opposition. But a band of friends who are like-minded, inspire us with courage and confidence.
4. Because we are lukewarm in religious duties. But a holy fellowship will kindle and keep alive a holy fervour.[36]

Today we can apply much from Wesley's life and ministry — including the role of laypeople both in ministry and in sparking social reform. This springs from pursuing a life of holiness. In addition, small accountability groups provide a foundational place to focus on study, to encourage each other, and to reach out to people beyond the group.

A Gospel That Embraces Discipleship: Dietrich Bonhoeffer

Dietrich Bonhoeffer (1906–1945) grew up in a suburb of Berlin, the son of a famous physician. He and his twin sister were two of eight children. His family didn't attend church, but they had a cultural attachment to the German Evangelical Church. At the age of eleven, Bonhoeffer decided out of nowhere to become a theologian. Several years later, he entered the University of Berlin and earned a Doctor of Theology degree at age twenty-one. Ironically, except for formal occasions, Bonhoeffer remained a nonchurchman.

Bonhoeffer possessed a brilliant mind, but his commitment to truth separated him from others. He had the heart of a lion. When older and more experienced men around him were capitulating to the theories and laws of the Nazi party, Bonhoeffer wouldn't move an inch. His position was that the infamous Aryan Clause that eliminated all Jews from the church was anti-Christian. He wrote a pamphlet of protest, viewing his opposition as an act of solidarity with the gospel.

A series of events over a ten-year period shaped Bonhoeffer's life. First he studied at New York's Union Theological Seminary, where he learned more at the feet of friends than he did at those of Reinhold Niebuhr. His European sense of superiority plus the liberalism at Union became a major impediment to his assimilation of their views. Being a follower of Karl Barth, Bonhoeffer was in the process of becoming more conservative. He learned about the power of the gospel from Jean Lasserre and the joy of worship at the Abyssinian Baptist Church in Harlem, pastored by Adam Clayton Powell.

During this period, Bonhoeffer made a personal commitment to Christ. He decided to return to Germany, believing that if he wasn't present for the trouble, he had no right to participate in the country's rebuilding. During this ten-year period, he spent two years pastoring a church in London and had many opportunities to escape Germany, but he resisted them all. He helped build a coalition via the Barman Declaration, The Bethel Confession, and the starting of the Confessing Church. These bold stands against the deteriorating German Evangelical Church and against the oppression of the church and especially of the Jews led Bonhoeffer to open a maverick seminary for the Confessing Church, first at a seaside community called Zingst and later at Finkenwalde. During this time, Bonhoeffer also finished his two most-read works, *The Cost of Discipleship* and *Life Together*.

Bonhoeffer became involved in a plot to kill Hitler, was found out, and was imprisoned. He spent the last two years of his life in Tegal Prison before he was hanged in a courtyard in Flossenburg. The prison doctor described the last moments before Bonhoeffer's execution:

> Through the half-open door in one room of the huts I saw Pastor Bonhoeffer, before taking off his prison garb, kneeling on the floor praying fervently to his God. I was most deeply moved by the way this lovable man prayed, so devout and so certain that God heard his prayer. At the place of execution, he again said a short prayer and then climbed the steps to the gallows, brave and composed. His death ensued after a few seconds. In almost fifty years that I worked as a doctor, I have hardly ever seen a man die so entirely submissive to the will of God.[37]

The Cost of Discipleship remains the classic of classics on what commitment to Christ requires. Bonhoeffer's actions make his writing about discipleship so captivating. His life—with its power, passion, and reality—reaches out again and again and moves men and women to action. The cost of discipleship for him involved giving his all, just as his Lord had. Bonhoeffer taught a number of truths that reach across the ages and speak to us today with a power unlike anything we now hear.

"Christianity without discipleship is always Christianity without

Christ"[38]: I chose these words of Bonhoeffer to be the first in this book because the essence of the Christian life and of discipleship is following and becoming like Christ. Jesus defined what it means to be his follower — to be a Christian — when he said,

> "If anyone would come after me, he must deny himself and take up his cross daily and follow me. For whoever wants to save his life will lose it, but whoever loses his life for me will save it. What good is it for a man to gain the whole world, and yet lose or forfeit his very self?" (Luke 9:23-25)

Believing in Christ starts with self-denial, then answering his calling. That's what it means to take up our cross.

This journey of following Christ as his disciple is a lifelong one. Anything less is a Christless Christianity. Without the reality of following Jesus, Christianity is just a religious philosophy.

Bonhoeffer's radical nature compelled him to believe these words and act on them. Further, he made his statement in the context of thousands of professing Christians who denied the gospel and their Lord's example by capitulating to the Nazis. Their faithless response was tepid, the kind of thing to spit out (see Revelation 3:16). Bonhoeffer urged Christians to read the Sermon on the Mount and then live it. That would be discipleship, because it is a Christianity with Christ.

"Faith is only real in obedience"[39]: James, the first writer of the New Testament, said it so well: "Faith without deeds is dead" (James 2:26). In other words, faith without action isn't really faith at all. James wasn't talking about works as a way to be made righteous; rather he was talking about the nature of faith.

The word *spirit* — *ruah* in Hebrew and *pneuma* in Greek — means wind or something that moves and changes what it touches. During the time of mystics in the Middle Ages, the term *spirituality* was coined. This changed the meaning of the word *spirit* to mean a state of being found in a person, rather than the actions of that person. As defined by the New Testament, a spiritual person is a person of action.

Similar damage has changed the word *faith* to mean what a person agrees with. The church is up to its eyeballs in agreement, but that moves nothing and poses a threat to no one. Bonhoeffer wanted to restore the robust original meaning of faith to mean *that mysterious attribute that creates action.* Restoring faith puts the power back in the gospel—a gospel that naturally makes disciples. He believed that discipleship wasn't just an option, because Jesus didn't allow for that kind of faith.

"Cheap grace": Bonhoeffer described the Christian experience as a life of costly grace rather than cheap grace. "We Lutherans have gathered like eagles round the carcass of cheap grace," he wrote, "and there we have drunk of the poison which has killed the life of following Jesus."[40]

The cost of discipleship demands our willingness to leave all things behind and follow Jesus wherever he leads. Cheap grace serves as discipleship's bitterest foe, which true discipleship must loathe. Cheap grace is our enemy because it makes a life of transformation optional. Bonhoeffer said, "We must never make cheap what was costly to God."[41] No tepid responses to what cost everything to Christ! Our response should be discipleship—our lives, our all.

Bonhoeffer expressed this discipleship beautifully in his well-known poem "Who Am I?"

WHO AM I? THEY OFTEN TELL ME I WOULD STEP FROM MY
    PRISON CELL
    POISED, CHEERFUL AND STURDY,
    LIKE A NOBLEMAN FROM HIS COUNTRY ESTATE.
WHO AM I? THEY OFTEN TELL ME I WOULD SPEAK WITH MY
    GUARDS
    FREELY, PLEASANTLY AND FIRMLY,

AS IF I HAD IT TO COMMAND.
WHO AM I? I HAVE ALSO BEEN TOLD THAT I SUFFER THE
    DAYS OF MISFORTUNE
WITH SERENITY, SMILES AND PRIDE,
AS SOMEONE ACCUSTOMED TO VICTORY.

AM I REALLY WHAT OTHERS SAY ABOUT ME?
    OR AM I ONLY WHAT I KNOW OF MYSELF?
    RESTLESS, YEARNING AND SICK, LIKE A BIRD IN ITS
        CAGE,
    STRUGGLING FOR THE BREATH OF LIFE,
    AS THOUGH SOMEONE WERE CHOKING MY THROAT;
    HUNGERING FOR COLORS, FOR FLOWERS, FOR THE
        SONGS OF BIRDS,
    THIRSTING FOR KIND WORDS AND HUMAN CLOSENESS,
    SHAKING WITH ANGER AT CAPRICIOUS TYRANNY AND
        THE PETTIEST SLURS,
    BEDEVILED BY ANXIETY, AWAITING GREAT EVENTS
        THAT MIGHT NEVER OCCUR, FEARFULLY POWER-
        LESS AND WORRIED FOR FRIENDS FAR AWAY,
    WEARY AND EMPTY IN PRAYER, IN THINKING, IN DOING,
    WEAK, AND READY TO TAKE LEAVE OF IT ALL.

WHO AM I? THIS MAN OR THAT OTHER?
AM I THEN THIS MAN TODAY AND TOMORROW ANOTHER?
AM I BOTH ALL AT ONCE? AN IMPOSTER TO OTHERS,
    BUT TO ME LITTLE MORE THAN A WHINING, DESPI-
        CABLE WEAKLING?
    DOES WHAT IS IN ME COMPARE TO A VANQUISHED ARMY,
    THAT FLEES IN DISORDER BEFORE A BATTLE ALREADY
        WON?

WHO AM I? THEY MOCK ME THESE LONELY QUESTIONS OF
MINE.

WHOEVER I AM, YOU KNOW ME, O GOD. YOU KNOW I AM
YOURS.[42]

SUGGESTED RESOURCES

ON THE HISTORY OF DISCIPLESHIP

*The Story of Christian Spirituality: Two Thousand Years from,
East to West*, Gordon Mursell, ed. (Fortress, 2001). Provides
a treasure of various veins of spiritual history, good art, and
special pages or articles on key figures. Also provides quick
access and has a good sense of story.

Christian Spirituality by Alister E. McGrath (Blackwell
Publishers, 1999). More pedagogical than the above work, but
straight to the point. Covers theological schools of thought and
the history through figures from Gregory of Nyssa to J. I. Packer.

*Streams of Living Water: Celebrating the Great Traditions of
Christian Faith* by Richard Foster (HarperSanFrancisco, 2001).
Provides a very helpful look at six major streams of spiritual
thought: the contemplative, holiness, charismatic, social
justice, evangelical, and incarnational traditions.

Spiritual Theology: A Systematic Study of the Christian Life by
Simon Chan (InterVarsity, 1998). Excellent summary of the
theological and practical aspects of the spiritual life. Takes into
consideration the history of spirituality and how that applies
now.

ACCESS TO HISTORICAL FIGURES

In addition to the following books, if you want to know more about any historical figure in this chapter, I recommend that you do a search with his name using your favorite Internet search engine.

Pia Desideria (Pious Desires) by Philip Jacob Spener (Wipf & Stock, 2002). Originally published in 1635, a must-read for those who want to hold something so near the Reformation in hand. Most exciting are the practical applications via small groups Spener proposed, which are much-needed today.

The Rule of St. Benedict: by St. Benedict (Random House, 1998). The word *rule* comes from Latin *regula*, meaning "way or pattern of life." For those who want to discover the way of life of a famous leader and his religious order.

CHAPTER 4

THE DISTINGUISHING
MARKS OF A DISCIPLE

IN THIS CHAPTER
- THE IMITATION OF CHRIST
- THE CALL TO DISCIPLESHIP
- THE SIX-FOLD DEFINITION OF BEING CONFORMED TO CHRIST'S IMAGE

Most of us have been through times so hectic that we wish we had a double—a clone who could help us multiply our efforts. Maybe you remember the 1996 movie *Multiplicity*. Unable to strike a balance between home life, career, and having fun for himself, Michael Keaton's character, Doug, takes up a scientist's offer to Xerox him.

The first clone gets an extra dose of Doug's aggressive side and solves most of Doug's troubles at work. The second clone seems to get a dose of Doug's more . . . uh . . . feminine qualities. He ends up helping Doug's wife, who doesn't realize she's dealing with a clone and is pleased that Doug suddenly understands her needs. When the two clones decide that Doug could use even more help, they make a copy of the first clone, but it ends up embodying Doug's childish qualities.

When the original Doug asks what the first two clones have

done and, more importantly, what's wrong with number three, they answer, "You know how when you make a copy of a copy, it's not as sharp as . . . well . . . the original?"

Of course, this was just a movie created to help us escape. The apostle Paul urged us to become copies in a different way: "Imitate me, just as I also imitate Christ" (1 Corinthians 11:1, NKJV). With these words, he identified that imitating Christ should be our primary goal in discipleship. Certainly we'll never be exactly like Jesus, but we can aim to take on the same characteristics as him. Scripture says that when we do, we'll exhibit the fruit of the Spirit: "love, joy, peace, patience, kindness, goodness, faithfulness, gentleness and self-control" (Galatians 5:22-23).

THE IMITATION OF CHRIST

Even before Thomas à Kempis, author of *The Imitation of Christ*, drew a breath, the idea of imitating Christ was the focal point for followers of Jesus. Of course, imitating Christ never meant trying to become equal with God or to take on God's essential nature. Instead, as Christ's disciples live the way Jesus lived, they should affect others in the same way he did.

The first thing—and we could argue, the only thing—that really matters in following Jesus is the process of getting God into men and women. If this doesn't happen, then nothing important happens. By neglecting first things first, we've damaged the reputation of Christ, his church, and the discipleship process.

So how do we proceed to get God into people?

"Imitate Me"
When Paul addressed the Corinthian church and wrote, "Imitate me," he provided himself as a human example that he wanted them

to mimic or copy. Knowing that he wouldn't be perfect, he added, "as I also imitate Christ."

In just a few words, Paul set up two primary goals of discipleship. The first: Imitate Christ. The second: Although other disciples make for earthly and imperfect examples, imitate them. In fact, experiencing the Christlike qualities of someone close to us provides a powerful illustration of what God in a person looks like. Paul believed so strongly in this principle that he believed Timothy's transformation demonstrated it. Earlier in this letter, he wrote, "I urge you, be imitators of me. For this reason I am sending you Timothy, who is my beloved and faithful son in the Lord; he will remind you of my ways in Christ, just as I teach them everywhere in every church" (1 Corinthians 4:16-17, NEB). Timothy will remind people of Paul's way in Christ, which in turn will remind people of Christ.

Before all the programs and philosophies we have today, Scripture's writers clearly sounded the call to follow Christ's example. The apostle Peter wrote, "For to this you have been called, because Christ also suffered for you, leaving you an example, that you should follow in his steps" (1 Peter 2:21, RSV). When we reach back over the centuries, only one trend emerges from all traditions: to follow or imitate the person of Jesus. Paul considered everything else "dung" in light of knowing, experiencing, and loving Christ (see Philippians 3:7-11).

Why Imitate Christ?

Paul saw the formation of Christ within the disciple as his main work, so he poured himself into it: "Him we proclaim, warning every man and teaching every man in all wisdom, that we may present every man mature in Christ. For this I toil, striving with all the energy which he mightily inspires within me" (Colossians 1:28-29, RSV). He also wrote to the Galatians, "My little children, with whom I am again in travail until Christ be formed in you! I could wish to be present with you now and to change my tone, for I am perplexed about you" (Galatians 4:19-20, RSV).

Striving and travail, working to the point of exhaustion with a high dose of perplexity—ah, the life of a teacher. Yet Scripture tells us that the process of the person of Christ being formed in us is worth working for. It's worth all the pain and anguish, because it's the only thing that really matters. This spiritual formation should be the church's primary and exclusive work. So we should make it our guiding principle and measure every effort of the church and ministry with it. The imitation of Christ provides the scale, and we measure how a ministry spends its money, how it uses its time, how the best and brightest people serve with this scale.

THE CALL TO DISCIPLESHIP

Therefore, my dear friends, as you have always obeyed—not only in my presence, but now much more in my absence—continue to work out your salvation with fear and trembling, for it is God who works in you to will and to act according to his good purpose. (Philippians 2:12-13)

How do we know God lives and works in us? I think the answer comes from Jesus' basic call to discipleship in Luke 9:23-25, which I've quoted several times: "If anyone would come after me, he must deny himself and take up his cross daily and follow me. For whoever wants to save his life will lose it, but whoever loses his life for me will save it. What good is it for a man to gain the whole world, and yet lose or forfeit his very self?"

To understand the call to discipleship, let's explore the many facets of these verses.

The Urge to Follow Jesus

First, if you don't feel an urge to follow and become like Jesus, God isn't at work in you. And if God isn't at work in you, he's not in you. You'll know he's at work and in you when he moves your will, and a moved person will always act. You can respond to God's call only when he gives you the will to do so. When you hear the words of Jesus, "Follow me," and the urge to obey rises up within you, then you can be assured that God is at work.

A practical point should be noted here. As a leader, when you call people to follow Jesus, don't fret over those who say no. Far too many professing Christians have decided not to follow Jesus. They make this choice either because they never repented and turned to Christ in the first place or because they've been misled and think of discipleship as optional.

The Call to the Life

Beyond calling us to follow, Jesus also described the nature of the commitment that we need to follow him. My whole life is the answer to Jesus' call to follow him. He calls and I answer, not just in words, but in the action of following. George MacDonald noted, "Instead of asking yourself whether you believe or not, ask yourself whether you have this day done one thing because he said, 'Do it,' or once abstained because he said, 'Do not do it.' It is simply absurd to say you believe, or even want to believe in him, if you do not do anything he tells you."[1]

When I answer Jesus' call with my whole life, I make myself his disciple at once. Bonhoeffer said, "Only those who are obedient believe and only those who believe are obedient. Faith is only real in obedience."

When God calls us, he invites us to die. And ironically, we'll never be more alive. This is why it's time for a clarion call for the church to return our ministries to the kind of disciple-making that

Jesus taught and that his disciples practiced. It's time to commit to going deep with God and to believe that depth of personal transformation will bring fulfillment of the Great Commission.

Still many resist Jesus' call to discipleship. We've been taught that discipleship is optional or that it only involves establishing new believers. The cost to God's kingdom that our resistance has caused is incalculable and inexcusable. Yet it's not unforgivable or unchangeable. We must change, and I'm happy to say that transformational discipleship — the disciple-making that Jesus taught and that his disciples practiced — is being restored to the church.

The call to live differently: Only Jesus can call us to choose "the life." The church's cardiovascular system is clogged with immature disciples who agree with all we've said about discipleship, but who answer no to the life. Yet Jesus' clear and unequivocal words reach across the centuries to describe precisely what he wants from us. They penetrate our minds and hearts and have a cleansing affect.

In our culture, spiritual greatness is all about size: size of churches, size of book sales, size of crowds at special events. Evangelicals have produced best-selling books, and the media even gives homage to prominent evangelical personalities. Yet at the same time, church attendance has stagnated, the evangelical population has decreased, and only half of evangelicals believe it's their responsibility to tell others about Christ.[2]

It's time for an intervention — to listen to Jesus' words and do the right thing. Jesus calls us to live differently — to step out of where we are and step into the life he provided for us on the cross and planned for us in eternity past.

The operative word — Follow: When Jesus said, "Follow me," he defined faith. Faith goes much deeper than just believing that Jesus is the Christ; the proof of faith is following him.

Allow me once again to employ my mastery of the obvious. If Jesus calls us to follow him, he must be our leader. So we all should be in some distress when we realize that Jesus has largely disappeared as leader. Yes, we rightly acknowledge him as Savior of the world, the Lamb that was slain, our resurrected Lord, and our soon-coming King, yet we don't treat Christ as our leader. We seem to have forgotten his way of teaching, training, and doing works of power. With this oversight, we've sterilized his personality, taking all the spice, humor, and straightforwardness from him. Even more fundamental to following him is submitting to his leadership.

Anyone Can and Should

The first two words of Luke 9:23 immediately stand out: "if anyone." The word *if* leaves room for doubt. You certainly can choose someone or something else to follow. But if that's your decision, the promise of finding yourself with meaning and purpose doesn't apply. *If* also indicates that every convert or new disciple must make the choice to follow Jesus. While we make that decision at the point of repentance and salvation, we also make it at crucial times in our lives and make it every day. That's why Jesus used the word *daily* in verse 23.

Choosing "the life" that Jesus offers also involves choosing a way of life — a life of self-denial and submission to others. We don't just amble our way into discipleship. We make a conscious decision to live by faith. We agree to join others who've committed to follow Jesus rather than try to lead Jesus. We fundamentally give up the right to run our own life. In other words, you can follow your heart, your dreams, your gifts, your personality profile, and seek the right fit. But all that's inferior to following Jesus.

Discipleship evangelism: I recall a number of years ago when conservative pastors moving to liberal churches felt the need to evangelize their new congregations. I've unashamedly confessed to congregations that I'm engaged in evangelizing them to choose "the life," a life of discipleship. I want people to forsake non-discipleship Christianity with its individualism that protects their accountability, stunts their growth, and robs them of joy and personal accomplishment. They lock themselves out from God's plan and dream for their lives. This tiny word *if* jumps off the page and cries out to men and women everywhere. "Following Christ isn't automatic; you must choose" (see Luke 9:23).

"Anyone": While Jesus was probably speaking only to his closest followers when he issued the call to the life, thinking that this is just a message for the select few has done much damage. Yet this perspective has stuck to the church like tape you can't peel off.

Often pastors and leaders are the culprits. We make it acceptable to be Christian without becoming like Christ. We teach that a serious and devout life is optional—that it's not evidence of salvation. I'm grieved that I've been part of this deception. Even when we teach high commitment as the norm, in practice we give people a pass by accepting casual Christianity as normal and making discipleship the bastion of the brave and the elite.

Let Jesus define normal. Obviously, *anyone* means everyone. Discipleship applies to anyone who chooses the life. Even if Jesus only spoke these words to a select few, his use of *anyone* defines the parameters of his intent. One of Satan's greatest lies is that spiritual greatness belongs to the few. He convinces most of us to simply react to life and hang on. We struggle along. We can't be expected to go full throttle after Jesus. We can't live up to the kind of commitment Jesus calls us to. That's just for the super-saints, those we write the books about, those we ply with honorary degrees.

I have a novel idea: Instead of listening to the Enemy, why don't we let Jesus define normal. Clearly, following Jesus is what a disciple does. It's the norm, while anything else is wrecked and in need of repair. Normal means that following Jesus is for the person who hasn't read a book in thirty years, for the homemaker with four children underfoot, for the seasoned saint who has all the information but needs stimulation, and for the teenager who just committed his life to Christ. It doesn't matter if you're young or old, if you're healthy or you have to call 911 for paramedics to help you out of bed. Jesus calls us to follow him. Why would we choose anything else?

Self-Denial Is Essential

Four words in Luke 9:23 make the strong tremble: "He must deny himself." We all admire self-denial in others, but we seem to detest it in ourselves. But we misunderstand what Jesus asks for and what he doesn't ask for.

C. S. Lewis provided important insight here. He believed that self-denial in and of itself isn't a virtue. In fact, denying life's pleasures just to say we did would be the apex of arrogance. This view of self-denial is rooted in the ascetic world of hair shirts and simulated crucifixions. An ascetic lives a life of rigorous self-denial. For example, Father Athanasius Anthony, the founder of Christian monasticism, never changed his vest or washed his feet. Simeon Stylites spent the last thirty-six years of his life atop a fifty-foot pillar.

I love the words of nineteenth-century Scottish preacher Alexander McClaren: "Any asceticism is a great deal more to men's taste than abandoning self. They would rather stick hooks in their backs and do the swinging poojah than give up their sins and yield up their wills."[3] I recall a passage from *The Spiritual Exercises of St. Ignatius* in which he recommends opening a window in foul weather to identify with the sufferings of Jesus. But I like C. S. Lewis's perspective better: "There's no way one should throw out a good bottle of Port and the cigars! We don't need to suffer without purpose. When Jesus said, 'he must deny himself,' he was asking for something very specific."

Say no to self in order to say yes to God. The only righteous role of self-denial is to eliminate any obstacle that blocks saying yes to God. When my will conflicts with his will, self-denial makes following his will possible. Jesus wants me to deny myself the right to be in charge of my own life. He wants to lead and he asks me to follow. That drives a stake through the heart of my will, my ego, and my desire to control.

Of course, denying self in this way can be just as difficult as what the ascetics practice. When we follow Jesus, we deny ourselves the right to justice in human relationships. We deny ourselves the right to a good reputation and immediate vindication. That's what Christ's life was like: he was rejected, slandered, and killed. He gave up his rights as God, meaning he surrendered the opportunity to be worshiped and be successful in the judgment of the world.

I've been in spiritual work for more than thirty years. I know people who hold false opinions about me. If my name entered their conversation, they would say that I'm aloof and uncaring, or that I misled them or even lied. And they will take these opinions to their graves. I hope that someday they'll know the truth, but I should not and will not fight for vindication. That's the heart of self-denial — not insisting on controlling every opinion that others have.

In practical terms, Jesus wants you to deny your self-reliance on that ten-year plan you worked out with a battery of psychological tests and a financial advisor. He wants you to deny yourself success as the world defines it, as the church defines it, and as you define it.

A young man writing a paper on pastoral ministry came to interview me. I'd never been asked the question he started with, and it penetrated me to the core. He asked, "What has been your greatest sacrifice as a pastor?" I just sat for a moment, relishing the opportunity to answer. Then it came to me clearly: "I think it's the discipline to treat certain people better than they deserve to be treated." Some people should be told off, rebuked, and straightened out. But I find myself being careful how I treat them and holding my tongue. I let them shoot at me and accuse me and blame me for their problems. I let them hold me to a higher standard than they have for themselves.

Sometimes I just don't know if I can take it anymore. But then I realize that treating people better than they deserve is the gospel, the kingdom of God, the heart of Jesus, and the essence of love. I must deny myself the freedom to speak my mind and let people have it. Interestingly that's still not my greatest act of self-denial.

The greatest denial is giving up control. For me, the greatest denial has been giving up the right to control my future, to direct the way my life should go. I decided that Jesus will lead and I will follow. While some people might find this easy, it's one of the toughest things I've had to do. I've always been a high achiever and aggressive—a go-for-it type of guy. For much of my life, I created opportunities based on my ideas and then took those opportunities. "Create a door and then walk through it" is another way to say it. So it's a titanic and daily struggle for me to allow Jesus to lead. My natural bent is to follow my vision, my dreams, my heart—and then periodically check behind me to make sure Jesus is blessing what I've chosen.

When I tried to lead Jesus, I would simply "go for it." I'd start making phone calls, writing e-mails, and diving headlong into any project. But now I pray and ask God to provide confirmation through others. I also pray for God to supply the resources in people and funds. Most importantly, I now force myself to question deeply my motives and what's really going on inside me.

I have a friend who says he's committed not to make anything happen on his own. At first, I questioned his commitment as too passive, but I've grown to agree with his position. This doesn't mean I'm a student at the "pray and wait" school. I believe that "pray and wait" is as wrong as "plan and go." The balance needs to be pray, plan, and then go. What my friend meant—and I agree with—is that we need to give God time to prepare the way, to provide prepared hearts, and to show us the resources for the challenges ahead.

Heeling to the hand of my Leader means that I must give

up control of the timing and method of my actions as well as the impetuousness of my nature. I now submit my dreams, visions, and breakthrough ideas to God's leadership and deny myself the right to run my own life. I deny myself in order to say yes to God.

Take Up Your Mission

The cross, central to Jesus' mission, provides a metaphor for ours. How many of us live with the perpetual question, "Lord, what do you want me to do; what's my mission?" The level of angst this question causes is much too high because many of us seek the answer before we're willing to walk the path of obedience. In fact, we step off the path of obedience to try to figure it out. I'm convinced that when we choose the life and deny ourselves the right to run our own lives, then we'll find our cross waiting on the path of obedience. That's when we "take it up."

What does it mean to walk the path of obedience? People often make the mistake of waiting for a clear answer before they start walking. They attend church a couple of times a month, throw something in the offering below 2 percent of their income, and hope to hear something that will get them through the week. They don't see themselves as disciples, learners, or followers of Jesus. They think Jesus' call to be disciples is for monks, missionaries, and ministers. They go through life being Christian without being Christlike. They never pick up their cross because they never place God as their Leader and submit themselves to him. Sadly, in fairness to the people who do this, no one has taught them what following Jesus means.

The way it works: First we choose the life. We set aside any competing priorities and follow Jesus. Then he reveals our mission en route. Jesus taught, "Whoever has my commands and obeys them, he is the one who loves me. He who loves me will be loved by my Father, and I too will love him and show myself to him" (John 14:21).

Obedience provides the evidence of love. Love is the will to benefit others or to respond to their love for us. We know that Jesus loved us first (see John 3:16; Romans 5:8; 1 John 4:19). So the natural response, Jesus says, is to love him back through obedience. That means walking down the path of obedience; as we go, he reciprocates by revealing more and more of who he is.

Many of us are fascinated with Israel. We'd love to go there. We've studied the Bible and know a great deal about its history and places. But until we stand on the Mount of Olives or before the Place of the Skull, we can't truly *experience* Israel. In the same way, many people have studied the Bible and considered following Jesus. But until they "go there," they can't experience the transformation of their character.

When we follow Jesus, we embark on a treasure hunt where we learn about him and about our mission. When we wait at the entrance to the path of obedience for full instructions before we start walking, we can never find our mission. That knowledge is found only en route.

By accepting non-discipleship Christianity, many people don't have a mission. So they sit in the pew and wait. All those missions never completed—what a tragic loss to people's lives, and how much poorer it has left the church and the society we live in.

Know your mission by following Jesus. Discovering our gifts and talents has become more technical in recent years. Thirty years ago, no spiritual gifts tests or curricula existed. Not as many psychological tools were available to measure our temperaments and to create personality profiles. Yet I think people knew as much about their gifts and calling then as they do now.

The fact that I know I am a driver type, a thinker, and a results-oriented creative developer testifies to the deluge of self-indulgence that has swept over the church. We love to soak up all the interesting and complementary findings of such analyses about ourselves. But Jesus didn't have these tools and neither did his disciples. While these tools can be useful if we avoid the psychological orgy, we can also follow a simpler way.

What are my strengths? If you want to know how people experience you, ask five of your friends, "What am I good at? What strengths would you affirm in my life?" They'll be the most accurate tools at your disposal, so valuable that money can't buy you better truth.

The second recommendation, almost as airtight, is to ask, "Where's the fruit or impact of my work?" I like Paul's thinking on this: "I will not venture to speak of anything except what Christ has accomplished through me in leading the Gentiles to obey God by what I have said and done—by the power of signs and miracles, through the power of the Spirit" (Romans 15:18-19). God called Paul to take the gospel to the Gentiles, but he was willing to talk only about the fruit of his work—the efforts that God had blessed.

So, where has God blessed you? Where's the fruit? The answer to that question is the key to finding your ministry "sweet spot." That's the place where your talents and gifts, God's timing, and his personal mission for you converge.

When Paul found his sweet spot, he sought even more: "It has always been my ambition to preach the gospel where Christ was not known, so that I would not be building on someone else's foundation" (Romans 15:20). God gave Paul the mission to create new outposts for the kingdom, not to manage ministry. His calling matched his ambition, and that fit his gifts. Every active disciple of Jesus longs for the sweet spot. Finding it is like a hitter on a hot streak, a stockbroker who makes all the right decisions, or a concert pianist whose training and passion converge to create bliss.

So taking up our cross almost always matches our ambitions. Ambition isn't a sin. Nothing would happen for good or ill without it. God condemns selfish ambition (see James 3:14-16), but healthy ambition is essential to accomplishment. Once you experience fruit, go harder after that area. Fruitfulness is one way that God leads in our lives; it's the treasure on the path of obedience we've been looking at.

The Torment of the Daily

Wouldn't it be grand if Christ's call to the life and to finding our mission involved a one-time decision followed by ceaseless joy and success? Paul's life provides evidence that following Jesus is a tumultuous road (see 2 Corinthians 4:9-16; 11:23-29).

Okay, so we've made a decision and chosen the life. We've rejected non-discipleship Christianity and made a firm, lifelong commitment to follow Jesus. Yet we must still live it out daily in the middle of temptation, weakness, illness, opposition, and the appearance of failure. Every day we must again say, "Yes, Jesus, I'll follow you today. I'll resist heading out on my own just because I don't like the results you gave me yesterday. I won't bail out even though others are abandoning ship like rats. And I'll follow you today even though I feel I've misunderstood your mission for me and that's why I'm depressed."

Choosing the life involves both attitude and action, and the battle is waged as we live out the life each day.

Gaining Your Soul

Life is full of paradoxes. Golf provides a good example. The first lesson I learned in golf was that trying to "kill" the ball in frustration doesn't work like it does in other sports. In football or basketball, anger and adrenaline can improve your game. But on the golf course, hacking at the ball out of frustration causes sweating, the ball doesn't go any farther, and you start talking to yourself. The paradox is that if you want to hit the ball farther, you must swing easily and smoothly. If you want the ball to go left, hit it to the right. If you want it to go right, hit it to the left.

God has created a paradox, counterintuitive to the human

condition, about how we gain our souls. Or to put it another way, how we find everything we really want.

God's paradox: If you want to save your life—put your own agenda first and control conditions and results—then you'll lose your life. In this context, gaining and losing refers to the basic choice of salvation. Jesus didn't box up salvation into a neat formula. He defined it in terms of action rather than doctrine, because faith is action based on belief. So faith defined by Jesus includes following, self-denial, taking up your cross daily, and obeying him. This doesn't violate our concepts of grace; it simply defines the nature of faith.

Jesus' statement is clear: "For whoever wants to save his life will lose it" (Luke 9:24). Our most natural impulse is to set a goal, develop a plan, and go after it. However, this ultimately backfires, because if we insist on directing our own lives, we never enter into the joy and fulfillment of God's dream for us. God has a dream for us that makes our dreams seem small and drab: "For we are God's workmanship, created in Christ Jesus to do good works, which God prepared in advance for us to do" (Ephesians 2:10).

Jesus knows where we need to go. Just as he promised to prepare a place in heaven for us (see John 14:1-3), he also prepares a *right-now-life* of meaning and purpose. When we try to control it, we don't have enough wisdom or knowledge to find that ministry sweet spot. Even as I write these words, I'm not sure what to do next or where to invest my time. I'm asking Jesus to lead me, to organize it for me. I must discipline myself not to jump ahead, to make phone calls and raise money, and all the other stuff. I need to give up my understanding of how I'd like my future to fall into place for a much better and sweeter plan that God reveals. This is counterintuitive, and my flesh is rattling its cage as I write.

So hold your life loosely, forget yourself, follow Jesus, and let him take you where you need to go. Lose yourself in the mission. That's the joyful wonderland of his plan for every follower. If you have plans and strategies that aren't working — and you don't see any sign of God's blessing — retreat to the certainty of his leadership.

I often pray, "Lord, I'm your servant. I'll follow you even if it's into apparent failure, because I have no rights to success as I define it, or as the church defines it, or as my culture defines it. I'm only interested in pleasing you and being successful as you define it."

You might protest that this seems like abdicating responsibility, but I disagree. As a servant, my first responsibility is to follow and to do my Master's will. Jesus tells me to lose my life in the mission, to relinquish control of my life to him. When I do this — and only when I do this — I find all that I've ever wanted.

The rewards: When we answer the call of Jesus, join that order of disciples who follow him wholeheartedly, we experience great rewards. We know the joy that our lives are on target with God. We have the comforting knowledge that one day we'll hear what every servant desires, "Well done, good and faithful servant!" (Matthew 25:21,23).

We can also echo the inspiring words Paul issued near the end of his life:

> For I am already being poured out like a drink offering, and the time has come for my departure. I have fought the good fight, I have finished the race, I have kept the faith. Now there is in store for me the crown of righteousness, which the Lord, the righteous Judge, will award to me on that day. (2 Timothy 4:6-8)

Every disciple dreams of living a life with great meaning and fulfillment. But that life doesn't come to people who drift about as immature converts. It only belongs to those who choose the life of transformational discipleship.

God is raising up men and women who are hungry for him, leaders who want to be the revolutionaries that Christ intended us to be when he told us to make disciples of the world and to teach them everything that Christ commanded. But first we must teach ourselves what Christ commanded. First we must commit to allowing him to transform our spirits. First we must make it the exclusive task we take on.

The revolution can begin when passion and power return to the people filling our churches. In fact, I think all that's really needed is for the transformation to reach the leaders of our churches — then the revolution can begin. I think it already has started.[4]

THE SIX-FOLD DEFINITION OF BEING CONFORMED TO CHRIST'S IMAGE

Now that we've looked at how we must answer the call to follow and to become like Jesus, let's define what that means. Based on the life of Jesus, I believe becoming like him includes six issues of transformation. Living this way leads to being formed then conformed, and that leads to transformation:

1. transformed mind
2. transformed character
3. transformed relationships
4. transformed habits
5. transformed service
6. transformed influence

1. Transformed Mind: Believe What Jesus Believed

It's one thing to believe in Jesus. It's quite another to believe what Jesus believed. And the first can't be what it should be without the second. Acquiring the mind of Christ — thinking and feeling what Jesus does — that's transformation. What did Jesus believe about life? What was important to him? How did he define the good life? What is good and evil? How do we conduct our life? And in the end, what really matters?

The Gospels contain stories of how Jesus confronted life, how he handled the poor, the sick, the unforgiven, and the self-righteous. As disciples, our quest should be to believe what he believed so we can live the way he lived. Paul told the church in Rome that we're transformed by the renewing of the mind (see Romans 12:2). Because the mind provides the base of operations for humans, we can't establish our life on a concept we can't grasp.

Great leaders have found what Jesus believed from the Sermon on the Mount, a fifteen-minute sermon that changed the world. Albert Schweitzer, Mahatma Gandhi, Leo Tolstoy, Dietrich Bonhoeffer, and Martin Luther King Jr., to name a few, have all pointed to the Sermon on the Mount as a seminal and transformational passage in their lives. So, what did Jesus say and believe that these leaders found so radical and life-changing?

What the good life is not: Notice that a life of pride, self-assuredness, and complacency, and a focus on competence aren't on the list of qualities in the Sermon on the Mount. Jesus didn't advise us to look out for number one, to fight for our rights, to avoid suffering and hardship, and to stay out of the line of fire of those who attack Christians. The good life doesn't mean living under the radar or expecting an absence of external conflict. None of this has high value in God's kingdom; the kingdom of God is not of this world.

What the good life is: Being a disciple is an attitude (see Matthew 5:1-12). An attitude is a "manner of acting, feeling, or thinking that shows one's disposition or opinion."[5] The Beatitudes provide the inner core for how to live from our satisfied spiritual center. The foundational trait is humility. We develop a different worldview that believes that character and its influence are of the highest value and worth suffering for. We choose to "rejoice and be glad" (5:12). We discover that the blessings from the Sermon on the Mount come when we position ourselves for an obedient lifestyle. Like a well-trimmed aircraft in flight, we choose the right attitude.

Influence is based on character. Jesus didn't say, "Let everyone see your wonderful ideas and nuanced vocabulary and persuasive speech." Instead he delivered a simple but penetrating commission: Let them see your good deeds.

> "You are the salt of the earth. But if the salt loses its salti-ness, how can it be made salty again? It is no longer good for anything, except to be thrown out and trampled by men.
>
> "You are the light of the world. A city on a hill cannot be hidden. Neither do people light a lamp and put it under a bowl. Instead they put it on its stand, and it gives light to everyone in the house. In the same way, let your light shine before men, that they may see your good deeds and praise your Father in heaven." (Matthew 5:13-16)

So, let your life preserve what will decay. Allow the light from your life to penetrate the darkness, to be that shining city on a hill. Aiming to have that kind of character and resulting action reminds me of what renowned author and broadcaster Malcolm Muggeridge said about Mother Teresa's impact:

> Accompanying Mother Teresa, as we did, to these different activities for the purpose of filming them — to the Home for the Dying, to the lepers and the unwanted children, I found I went through three phases. The first was the horror mixed with pity; the second, compassion, pure and simple; and the third, reaching far beyond compassion, something I had never experienced before — an awareness of these dying and derelict men and women, these lepers with stumps

instead of hands, these unwanted children, were not piti-able, repulsive or forlorn, but rather dear and delightful; as it might be, friends of long standing, brothers and sisters. How is it to be explained—the very heart and mystery of the Christian faith? To soothe those battered old heads, to grasp those poor stumps, to take in one's arms those chil-dren consigned to dust bins, because it is His head, as they are His stumps and His children, of whom He said whoso-ever received one such child in His name received Him.[6]

During his earthly ministry, Jesus embodied the kind of leader others wanted to follow. His greatest power wasn't his healing or miracles, but the love and humility that radiated from him. He possessed that kind of love that really influences others. Not every-one can work miracles or move people with great oratory, but every-one can love. In this way everyone who loves is well off; they're living the good life.

Spiritual greatness means living and teaching about God's king-dom. A disciple sees the world through God's eyes. Jesus said,

"Anyone who breaks one of the least of these command-ments and teaches others to do the same will be called least in the kingdom of heaven, but whoever practices and teaches these commands will be called great in the king-dom of heaven. For I tell you that unless your righteous-ness surpasses that of the Pharisees and the teachers of the law, you will certainly not enter the kingdom of heaven." (Matthew 5:19-20)

He pointed out that the Pharisees were experts on the law but they didn't understand it. They memorized it and figured out imaginative ways not to practice it. They abused it, and the kind of righteousness they possessed was useless. As a result, they'd be considered the least in the kingdom. In contrast, those who practice from their hearts the principles of the law as redefined by Jesus will be called great in the kingdom.

Faith means doing the will of the Father. Jesus was radical during his earthly ministry, and he remains so today because he challenges our dysfunctional understanding of faith. He said,

> "Not everyone who says to me, 'Lord, Lord,' will enter the kingdom of heaven, but only he who does the will of my Father who is in heaven. Many will say to me on that day, 'Lord, Lord, did we not prophesy in your name, and in your name drive out demons and perform many miracles?' Then I will tell them plainly, 'I never knew you. Away from me, you evildoers!'" (Matthew 7:21-23)

Over the centuries, Christians have meditated on these words, debated them, and sometimes simply ignored their confusing nature. This passage challenges our well-packaged theologies, including our teaching that faith is agreement with scriptural propositions but not necessarily with behavior.

As Jesus ended the Sermon on the Mount, he said that faith is like the man who built his house on the rock; when the storms came, the house stood (see verses 24-25). So the question becomes, how do we build our house on the rock? How do we position ourselves and prepare to live for him? These choices and the way we position our lives is called faith.

Jesus explained non-faith as when people build their lives on the wrong foundation. When trouble comes, the false foundation crumbles beneath the weight of life (see verses 26-27). Agreement isn't enough; faith becomes real only when we obey. Obedience is the only worthy goal of a Christian spirituality.

2. Transformed Character: Live the Way Jesus Lived

We can talk in many different ways about how Jesus lived. We might study his life and its various dimensions, including the mystery of Jesus as God-man and how much deity he did or didn't employ during his earthly life. Some have even contemplated the mystery that Jesus naturally aged—that he looked thirty-three when he was thirty-three—and what he would have looked like if he lived to age seventy-five, one hundred, or older. Would he have developed arthritis, an enlarged prostate, and clogged arteries? Would he have taken the senior discount at Denny's? We could scour the depths of theological texts to determine what Jesus knew and when he knew it. But our purpose in exploring the way Jesus lived is much more practical.

So let's focus on his character. Let's explore what Jesus' encounter with Satan in the wilderness revealed about his character. How did he remain true to the cause and, as a result, finish his mission and save the world?

First, we need to set the scene: "Then Jesus was led by the Spirit into the desert to be tempted by the devil. After fasting forty days and forty nights, he was hungry" (Matthew 4:1-2). From these verses, we know the elements of the encounter between Jesus and Satan: a willing servant, the leading of the Spirit, the determination and creativity of the Enemy, Jesus' loneliness, and the natural hardship caused by the convergence of temptation and hunger. With the scene set, let's look at what each temptation Jesus faced tells us about his character.

Temptation 1: Will the spiritual appetite exceed the physical appetite? Jesus was hungry and in need. Time + hardship + deprivation = vulnerability, at least for most of us. Yet Jesus shows us how character fights back:

> The tempter came to him and said, "If you are the Son of God, tell these stones to become bread." Jesus answered, "It

is written: 'Man does not live on bread alone, but on every word that comes from the mouth of God.'" (verses 3-4)

Satan struck at an opportune time and challenged Jesus at his most vulnerable place—the needs of the body. The fact that Jesus could have turned the stones into bread probably made this situation even more tempting. Frankly Jesus' temptations were many times more intense than ours.

Jesus answers, based on God's Word and wisdom, "Man does not live on bread alone." He didn't say that people don't need food or that we don't have human needs. Remember, Jesus had been fasting and praying for forty days and forty nights, so we have to consider how that prepared him to meet his archenemy.

Certainly time alone in the wilderness gave Jesus opportunity to clear his mind and quiet his soul. And he interacted with God; after all, scorpions and vultures have a limited vocabulary. Add prayer, a discipline of engagement, and meditation (mulling God's truth on life and mission over and over again). While Jesus denied himself physical sustenance, his spiritual nourishment intake was a sumptuous feast.

Jesus was facing the cross—a mission that required his all, the ultimate sacrifice. He knew all along that he could back out, so he chose spiritual weapons rather than the weapons of the world. He fought Satan by drawing spiritual energy from his Father. He attacked Satan by withdrawing from doing, planning, and figuring things out. He fought the battle from the inside out. Jesus demonstrated again and again that being alone with his Father was the site of the real battle, the place where things really happened.

Jesus was telling Lucifer, "I live by every word that comes from the mouth of God." Something supernatural forms in us when we take in God's truth; it settles deep within us and grounds us, giving our spirit a place to stand.

How prepared are we to live like Jesus? Will we practice the same priorities and invest in the same resources in order to be prepared?

Temptation 2: Will character moderate the needs of ego? Satan's next temptation cleverly appealed to Jesus' ability:

> Then the devil took him to the holy city and had him stand on the highest point of the temple. "If you are the Son of God," he said, "throw yourself down. For it is written: 'He will command his angels concerning you, and they will lift you up in their hands, so that you will not strike your foot against a stone.'"(Matthew 4:5-6)

In essence, Satan was saying to Jesus, "Come on, show me what you've got! You can fly!" Satan wanted Jesus to join the world of religious competition, to climb the ladder of success, to get his identity needs met by seeking fame and recognition from peers. But Jesus answered him, "It is also written: 'Do not put the Lord your God to the test.'" In other words, Jesus said, "Don't be frivolous with me."

Only Jesus could die for the world based on who he was and what he alone could do. He was committed to being both unnecessary and irrelevant to the world's value system.

That should be our compass and calling. Instead of falling for the tempter's means and methods as our primary mode of ministry, we should value the development of character. By trusting the slower process of discipleship, we'll experience a much bigger payoff: the development of Christ's character in us and the changing of the world.

Temptation 3: Does the satisfied soul desire to worship or control? This time Satan tempted Jesus by promising a shortcut: Avoid the pain; have it all now; don't go through the process.

> Again, the devil took him to a very high mountain and showed him all the kingdoms of the world and their splendor.

"All this I will give you," he said, "if you will bow down and worship me."

Jesus said to him, "Away from me, Satan! For it is written: 'Worship the Lord your God, and serve him only.'" (Matthew 4:8-10)

Why die for these people? Why suffer the rejection and pain? Why assume their sin? Jesus doesn't fall for it. He experiences the taste of victory, and this story tells us what victory looks like. The victory is that when we resist the Devil, he must flee. It's so sweet! Yet we resist daily, because the battle with Satan continues: "When the devil had finished all this tempting, he left him until an opportune time" (Luke 4:13). These words of C. S. Lewis seem appropriate:

> I would much rather say that every time you make a choice you are turning the central part of you, the part of you that chooses, into something a little different from what it was before. And taking your life as a whole, with all your innumerable choices, all your life long you are slowly turning this central thing either into a Heaven creature or into a hellish creature: either into a creature that is in harmony with God, and with other creatures, and with itself, or else into one that is in a state of war and hatred with God, and with its fellow creatures, and with itself. To be the one kind of creature is Heaven: that is, it is joy, and peace, and knowledge, and power. To be the other means madness, horror, idiocy, rage, impotence, and eternal loneliness. Each of us at each moment is progressing to the one state or the other.[7]

3. Transformed Relationships: Love as Jesus Loved

When did you first know that God loved you? I don't mean intellectually agreeing to the statement that Jesus died for your sins and gave himself for you. I mean, when did you first experience God's love?

I first experienced God's love in July 1968 in a small village outside Nairobi, Kenya. I was a twenty-one-year-old college student known more for his jump shot than his ministry skills. Yet there I stood, with fellow students Starr and Debbie, in a field, singing Swahili songs to ourselves while we waited for a local pastor to gather villagers to hear our story.

When he arrived with about sixty-five people, he asked, "Who is going to preach?" Starr and Debbie pointed at me. I'd been a follower of Jesus for six whole months. I'd picked up a few pointers from others, so I preached my first sermon on Jesus' words, "You must be born again." To my shock and surprise, all sixty-five people wanted to give their lives to Jesus. Regardless of their reasons or that the dynamics of the tribal community meant the decision would include all or none, in that moment I was overwhelmed—stunned that God loved me enough to actually use me.

Today, thanks to some creative writers, we know about "love languages." God spoke my love language that day. It was the knowledge that he found me useful. And I've never recovered. The force of God's love that day transformed me.

When Jesus uttered his first new command—one that was more than an amplification of the law—he told his followers to love one another as he loved them: "A new command I give you: Love one another. As I have loved you, so you must love one another. By this all men will know that you are my disciples, if you love one another" (John 13:34-35). Let's take apart these verses to explore what it means to be transformed in a way that allows us to love as Jesus loved.

"A new command I give you." This command raises the stakes of love. It means more than "Do unto others as you would have them

do unto you." It means more than turning the other cheek, forgiving someone who hurt you, or blessing those who curse you. Jesus asks us to do the impossible: to love other people until they "get it."

A number of years ago my wife, Jane, and I attended a seminar that had the goal of revealing to participants what they actually believe and how they actually behave. Through a series of behavioral exercises administered over four grueling days, indeed I learned.

One exercise in particular stung me. After two days of getting to know the fifty-four participants, we were asked to evaluate one another. The facilitator instructed us to go to each person and call him or her by name. If we could not remember a name, we were to say, "I am sorry, but I do not care enough about you to know your name."

While some people knew every name or most of the names, I knew maybe one out of four. Of course, I didn't know beforehand that I had something to gain by knowing their names, so the real Bill chose not to make the effort. The exercise concluded with each of us telling the other person whether he impressed us as a "giver" or a "taker," based on our interactions of the first two days.

After the exercise, the facilitator seated us in chairs placed in a U pattern, with the person perceived as the most giving in seat 1, and the least giving in seat 54. I found myself in seat 50. At first I laughed it all off as a contrived environment. But then I asked a fellow participant why he thought I was a taker. His answer shook me: "When we did the exercise imagining who we would trust to deliver a message to our family after our death, it didn't seem that you cared about me enough for me to entrust you with my last words to my family."

This man saw me as detached (I was), as holding back (I was), and as somewhat arrogant (and I was). At that moment I realized I didn't love others as Christ loved others. Christ loved others until they knew that he loved them — until they actually experienced his love. And it became painfully clear that I needed to change.

Jesus reveals a new standard in his new commandment. He commands us to love others until it shatters defenses, brings down strongholds, tears apart barriers, and even slips through the firewalls of culture. This is the revolution that Jesus calls his disciples to, and it requires sacrificial living.

"As I have loved you, so you must love one another." As Jesus spoke these words, he addressed those closest to him who had gathered around the table in the Upper Room. We know how many of them had experienced his love. Jesus accepted the despised tax collector, Matthew, and even went to his home and interacted with his friends. The beloved disciple, John, the teenager, held a special place in Jesus' heart, and Jesus made special provision for his care (see John 21:20-24). Jesus went beyond the norm to accommodate Thomas, who had missed his appearance and who remained skeptical (see John 20:24-28). Jesus restored Peter, an impetuous and spirited man full of chutzpah, who had some great moments, such as when he said, "You are the Christ, the Son of the living God" (Matthew 16:16), and cavernous lows, such as the three-fold denial of Christ. Still Jesus brought him back to fellowship and ministry in a touching encounter by the sea (see John 21:7-19).

Because Jesus loves his disciples, both then and now, he also calls them to love much. He calls us to embrace our limitations and to let God be strong in loving through us.

"By this all men will know that you are my disciples." Because our commitment needs to be to love others until they get it, this would be the appropriate time for me to ascend to literary heights to move people to action. But I'm not an amazing writer. Just as well, because this commitment calls for more than emotional splendor. It requires a motivation from spiritual depths.

Instead let me issue a practical challenge. Think of someone who would benefit from your love. Who in your life is difficult? Who makes you grind your teeth? Whose messages do you want to put on the bottom of the pile? Or who, at all costs, do you avoid meeting? Picture the person right now. Now imagine a commitment on your part to love that person until she experiences your love. Move from general to specific, from theory to practice, from the fleeting wish to the actual grit and grime of loving.

4. Transformed Habits: Train as Jesus Trained

I'm not referring to how Jesus trained others but to how he trained himself. One of the mysteries of Jesus as God and man is that he was fully human. So the principles of learning and training applied to him.

We know that Jesus grew and that he learned. When he was twelve, his family took him to Passover. When they left, he stayed behind without permission, and his distraught parents found him three days later dialoguing with the teachers. He had great ability to understand and he had wisdom. Although he was a *wunderkind*, a high flier, a giant intellect, he returned home in submission to his parents.

So even though Jesus was perfect, he had to grow and learn. Luke wrote that Jesus increased in wisdom and stature (see Luke 2:41-52). He also learned through the things he suffered (see Hebrews 5:8). Life itself provides the fuel for our transformation, and the same was true of Jesus. His transformation took him from boy to man, from teacher to savior, from leader to Lord. Through his life, he demonstrated that he was worthy to be our sacrifice: "And having been perfected, He became the author of eternal salvation to all who obey Him" (Hebrews 5:9, NKJV).

Disciples decide to arrange their life around the practices of Jesus. We choose to follow him in his pattern of life — a life of humility, obedience, sacrifice, and submission. Regeneration takes place when we choose to follow him. A regenerated person is one who is justified, who receives legal standing with God. In that context, we enter the lifelong process called discipleship, where we're positioned to be spiritually formed by the direct act of the Holy Spirit.

Training, not trying: I think we should outlaw "trying." Trying occurs when disciples try to reach a goal without the proper tools. Training, however, means that we commit to rearrange our lives around the practices of Jesus. We don't *try* to practice spiritual disciplines: fasting, silence, solitude, chastity, sacrifice, study, and so forth. Instead, because Jesus practiced them, we *train* in spiritual disciplines. We've answered the call to follow him and to learn from him, so we want to live our life the way Jesus lived his. And over time, through a patient process, we allow the positive effects of discipline to change us.

Indirect effect: Just as weight training builds muscle mass, so spiritual exercise builds character. One sage noted that spiritual disciplines are to transformation what calisthenics are to sport. These disciplines have an indirect but positive effect. Spiritual disciplines are tools that prepare us to do what needs to be done, when it needs to be done, and as it needs to be done.

Use as needed: We don't need to use spiritual disciplines all the time. We should use them to strengthen ourselves spiritually when needed. Jesus practiced the disciplines in a healthy and balanced way. We don't see him have any angst about them. He simply did what met the need of the moment. Some were staples in his spiritual diet, while he only used others on special occasions.

Look at Jesus and what he practiced:

- silence (Matthew 4:1-11)
- solitude (Mark 1:35)
- fasting (Matthew 4:1-11)
- frugality (Luke 9:58)
- prayer (Luke 6:12)
- secrecy (Matthew 6:1-7; Mark 4:1)

- submission (John 5:18-37)
- humility (Philippians 2:5-8)
- obedience (Luke 22:41-42)
- sacrifice (Hebrews 10:9-10)
- study (Luke 2:41-52)
- fellowship (Luke 22:14)
- confession (Mark 8:31; 14:36)
- worship (John 4:21-24)

5. Transformed Service: Minister as Jesus Ministered

To minister means to serve. Jesus demonstrated his attitude toward his own mission when he said, "For even the Son of Man did not come to be served, but to serve, and to give his life as a ransom for many" (Mark 10:45).[8] This attitude has largely eluded contemporary leaders, because you can't give yourself as a sacrifice and at the same time manage your image.

In his personal memoirs Ulysses S. Grant told the story of a leader of a unit preparing for the Mexican War:

> At Camp Salubrity, and when we went to New Orleans Barracks, the 4th infantry was commanded by Colonel Josiah H. Vose, then an old gentleman who had not commanded on drill for a number of years. He was not a man to discover infirmity in the presence of danger. It now appeared that war was imminent, and he felt that it was his duty to brush up his tactics. Accordingly, when we got settled down at our new post, he took command of the regiment at a battalion drill. Only two or three evolutions had been gone through when he dismissed the battalion, and, turning to go to his own quarters, dropped dead. He had not been complaining of ill health, but no doubt died of heart disease. He was a

most estimable man, of exemplary habits, and by no means the author of his own disease.[9]

Here was a man who led without putting his own welfare and safety first. How common is this quality? Let's admit that it's rare enough that when someone exhibits this quality, we call it heroic. We bestow medals on police officers, soldiers, firefighters, and others who risk life and limb to pull people out of a burning home or pluck a drowning child from a lake.

However, I'm talking about more than one heroic moment in someone's life. I don't want to diminish acts of heroism, but I think Jesus modeled and taught a much more profound heroism — a heroism of character and purpose that produces a steady stream of sacrificial actions.

Can you imagine a life so lost in benefiting others that your personal needs and wants don't play a big role in your thoughts? Love, after all, means action directed toward the benefits of others. It's unnatural to achieve this state; most of us are self-conscious instead. For example, I often have trouble getting into worship at public gatherings because I can focus only on what I'm doing and what I look like to those around me.

The act of loving others sacrificially is unnatural. Most of us also avoid moving ahead into anything that looks like failure or that might include suffering. This was never more evident than when Jesus told his followers that he was about to be killed, that it would be painful on many levels, and that everyone would be embarrassed.

> Again he took the Twelve aside and told them what was going to happen to him. "We are going up to Jerusalem," he said, "and the Son of Man will be betrayed to the chief priests and teachers of the law. They will condemn him to

death and will hand him over to the Gentiles, who will mock him and spit on him, flog him and kill him." (Mark 10:32-34)

Imagine hearing these words today. We might think they sound pessimistic or that they lack the kind of faith we think we need—faith that wins the day or avoids trouble and shame. But Jesus led with weakness, failure, and rejection. He moved straight into everything that the human spirit naturally abhors. An attitude of willingness is the rite of passage to ministering as Jesus ministered, to following in his footsteps, to giving ourselves for others. As an associate of Mother Teresa once commented, "She is free to be nothing; therefore, God can use her for anything."

Ministry minus me: Some people just don't get it. They want to be Christian without being Christlike. They want a scholarship—a full ride—through life. But even scholarship recipients know they must produce. We can't receive rewards we don't deserve or positions we don't earn. An old friend once asked me a penetrating question about my motivation: "Bill, do you want to serve or just exercise your gifts?" Ouch! Maybe some comfort comes from seeing that even those closest to Jesus struggled with selfish motivations:

Then James and John, the sons of Zebedee, came to him. "Teacher," they said, "we want you to do for us whatever we ask."

"What do you want me to do for you?" he asked.

They replied, "Let one of us sit at your right and the other at your left in your glory." (Mark 10:35-37)

What were these guys thinking? Didn't they hear what Jesus had just said? They were thinking about themselves—about grabbing onto a winner's coattail. Jesus spoke, the sound waves passed over their eardrums, and the words were recorded in their brains. Yet James and John didn't get how following Jesus and their lives connected. Instead they thought, *What can we get?* James and John were quick; they did a bit of spiritual calculus, and suddenly the prospect of thrones, power, wealth, and grinding the Romans into dust came to mind. Like many ambitious disciples, they didn't understand the characteristics of leadership and how people change. They were consumed by their self-interest.

"Can you drink the cup?" Jesus' answer to James and John was both comforting and a wonderful way to say no. I can't help but apply his words to my prayers and requests, to gauge how I easily rationalize requests that will help my personal advancement.

> "You don't know what you are asking," Jesus said. "Can you drink the cup I drink or be baptized with the baptism I am baptized with?"
>
> "We can," they answered. (verses 38-39)

The thundering sons of Zebedee wanted recognition and reward so much that they immediately overcommitted themselves. "Bring it on! We can take it! We can drink it!" The taste of power was on their lips, and they wanted the position of honor.

Like James and John, most of us must face our pride in order to serve as Jesus served. Our pride often emerges from our competitive nature. C. S. Lewis wrote,

> Pride gets no pleasure out of having something, only out of having more of it than the next man . . . not of being rich, or clever, or good looking, but of being richer, more clever, and better looking. It is comparison that makes one proud. The sexual impulse may drive two men into competition if they both want the same girl. But that is only an accident;

they might as likely have wanted two different girls. But a proud man will take your girl from you, not because he wants her, but just to prove to himself that he is a better man than you.

Pride and competition are basic elements in Satan's strategy. With James and John, their lust overcame their good sense. They wanted honor without sacrifice, awards they didn't earn. These desires revealed their character flaws.

Then and now, Jesus calls his disciples to "drink this cup" if we want to be like him. But what's in the cup? It's *doulos*—becoming a slave for Christ. This means giving up my right to run my own life. For many, including Jesus, this resulted in betrayal, mockery, physical suffering, sacrificial living, and an ugly death. Jesus wants us to take the cup, turn it upside down, and drink it down to the dregs!

Servanthood, not competition: The rest of Jesus' disciples expressed their anger toward James and John.

When the ten heard about this, they became indignant with James and John. Jesus called them together and said, "You know that those who are regarded as rulers of the Gentiles lord it over them, and their high officials exercise authority over them. Not so with you. Instead, whoever wants to become great among you must be your servant, and whoever wants to be first must be slave of all. For even the Son of Man did not come to be served, but to serve, and to give his life as a ransom for many." (Mark 10:41-45)

To be indignant means "to be aroused, express displeasure." The remaining disciples weren't indignant because they saw something wrong with the requests of James and John. They were outraged that James and John tried to get an edge.

When we express our anger, we're often working from the same pathology as those we disdain. For example, several years before I moved to my city, a pastor there issued a challenge to his church. He said that if a thousand people attended a special service, he'd eat lunch on the roof. When the goal was met, he hauled a card table up to the roof and ate his lunch. When I heard this story, I told my neighbor, a pastor, about it. I was mocking and making fun of an idiot who would use such cheap commercial means to get people to church. Well, you guessed it: He laughed and said, "That was me!" Actually, he had what I wanted and had gone to extremes to get it. My problem was that I was just as driven, and I was also in judgment of my brother.

Jesus said his kingdom is not of this world. He ministered with a different kind of power — a power that crushes empires and brings down walls of division. If you want to be great, don't request an esteemed position. Instead go to the end of the line and serve. Jesus existed for others. Likewise his disciples should exist for others, and our ministry should be for others too.

6. Transformed Influence: Lead the Way Jesus Led

If we want to discover how Jesus led, we need to realize that it's similar in nature to understanding how Jesus lived. Primarily his leadership was a way of thinking. Jesus had a worldview; he revealed it in how he lived, in how he invested his time and effort. He conducted his life in a much more radical way than his culture thought important and desirable.

"Your attitude should be the same as that of Christ Jesus" (Philippians 2:5). The word translated as *attitude* is *phronos* in the Greek; it means "mindset or worldview." So how would we describe Jesus' worldview? What qualities shaped his character?

Humility: This was Jesus' core character trait, the foundation of his influence on others. We can better understand the quality of humility when we contrast it with an opposite. Before he presented the example of Christ's attitude, Paul warned against the destructive nature of selfishness: "Do nothing out of selfish ambition or vain conceit, but in humility consider others better than yourselves" (Philippians 2:3).

Selfish ambition means to long for something you want for personal gain. Vain conceit means you have a sense of pride with no basis for the belief. If conceit is wrong, then vain conceit is worse! Selfish ambition and vain conceit lie deep within us and in our environment. Satan has filled the pool with these negative qualities, and we're swimming in it.

In Jesus, we see his humility in his role as a servant. Although in his nature he was God, he became, in his nature, a servant. He had the ability to choose something else, but he chose humility. Jesus teaches us that humility releases power and enhances our gifts.

Submission: Jesus was able to submit to his mission because of his humility. When we look at his temptation in the wilderness and the other times he withdrew to pray, we can see that he based his choices on his close relationship with the Father. Jesus' eloquent and mystical dissertation on his relationship to his Father in John 5:16-23 reveals such a trusting connection that Jesus was willing to place his life in the Father's hands, while setting aside his own thoughts and plans.

Submission is a love word before it's an authority word. Submission represents what a servant does. As disciples, what will we do to make ourselves nothing? Jesus willingly took on humanity; we need to willingly take on Christlikeness.

Jesus appeared to be a man, but he was more than a man. He volunteered to sacrifice himself as a gift to the whole world. He left behind all that he considered unworthy: a life of fame, earthly power, and being hailed as God in the streets of Jerusalem. A writer might give up a Pulitzer, an actor the Oscar, an athlete the Olympic gold medal, a soldier the Congressional Medal of Honor—all sacrifices to be sure. But none of these compare with giving up the role of God for the part of a carpenter and a "failed" messiah.

Obedience: Jesus was obedient to death. He saw his mission through to the cross. Jesus submitted to death because that was his calling.

God calls every disciple to be obedient to death as well. What must die in us to follow in his footsteps? For me, it's almost always my agenda. Disciples must die a daily death that takes place hour after hour, day after day, week after week, month after month, until we draw our last breath.

Faith is only real in obedience. Jesus provided the greatest example in his agony at Gethsemane. He saw God's plan through because of his humility and submission, which manifested in obedient sacrifice.

Suffering: The Cross—the Passion of the Christ—was at the same time both the most horrendous and the most loving act of human history. The only perfect man died instead of all the other people who deserved it. Scripture reminds us that we'll suffer as well: "Everyone who wants to live a godly life in Christ Jesus will be persecuted" (2 Timothy 3:12). "In this world you will have trouble" (John 16:33). "To this you were called, because Christ suffered for you, leaving you an example, that you should follow in his steps" (1 Peter 2:21).

Notice that we don't somehow supplement Christ's suffering. Instead we join him in suffering in our obedience.

Exaltation: Eventually, and always, exaltation occurs as a result of humility, submission, obedience, and suffering. For Christ, this happened after death, with his resurrection, ascension, and arrival at the right hand of his Father:

> THEREFORE GOD EXALTED HIM TO THE HIGHEST PLACE
>
> AND GAVE HIM THE NAME THAT IS ABOVE EVERY NAME,
>
> THAT AT THE NAME OF JESUS EVERY KNEE SHOULD BOW,
>
> IN HEAVEN AND ON EARTH AND UNDER THE EARTH,
>
> AND EVERY TONGUE CONFESS THAT JESUS CHRIST IS LORD,
>
> TO THE GLORY OF GOD THE FATHER.
>
> (PHILIPPIANS 2:9-11)

Most of us who live in humility, submission, obedience, and suffering will also be exalted after death. Human exaltation differs from Jesus' exaltation in that no one will kneel, confess, or call any of us Lord. Our exaltation is more of a godly influence than a recognition or distinction of who we are. Even now God gives his influence to those who need it to benefit those who don't have it. When used for the benefit of others, influence is a wonderful trust.

Every faithful follower of Jesus can look forward to exaltation in the presence of a waiting God. In the meantime, we can make disciples and be disciples by seeking to follow and become like Jesus. We can live in ways that allow God to transform us into Christlike servants for the benefit of his kingdom.

SUGGESTED RESOURCES

Following Jesus: Biblical Reflections on Discipleship by N. T. Wright (Eerdmans, 1995). A New Testament scholar takes a fresh look at the life of Jesus.

Celebration of Discipline: The Path to Spiritual Growth by Richard J. Foster (HarperSanFrancisco, 1998). Updated twenty years after its first release, this treatment offers excellent and easy-to-understand descriptions of the practices of Jesus.

CHAPTER 5

THE DISCIPLE-MAKING ENVIRONMENT: WHAT MAKES THINGS GROW

IN THIS CHAPTER
- HOW ENVIRONMENT AFFECTS GROWTH
- NECESSARY INGREDIENTS FOR A HEALTHY ENVIRONMENT
  TRUST
  GRACE
  HUMILITY
  SUBMISSION
  AFFIRMATION

"What the world needs now is love sweet love." That's how the song goes anyway—an easy fix for all the world's problems! Think of all the other pitches employing love as a sales and marketing tool. If you like pastries, Pillsbury will tell you that "Nothin' says lovin' like somethin' from the oven." Maybe your kids like hot dogs and beg you to buy Armour brand, because theirs are "the dogs kids love to bite." If you like to travel, try Delta Airlines, because "They love to fly, and it shows." Or maybe you like everything about fast food, so as you eat your Big Mac at McDonald's, you boldly sing out, "I'm lovin' it!" In the amorphous world of song and sales, we understand love as warm glances, smiles, tears, handholding, and—apparently quite often—food.

Just about everyone agrees that love is life's most powerful force. However, few people really understand love or have any idea how to create an environment of love. For our discussion of disciples and disciple-making, I want to define love in its boldest form: an action designed for the benefit of another. I hope to share some practical ways to love others that will create an environment for spiritual growth.

HOW ENVIRONMENT AFFECTS GROWTH

Can disciples grow in any environment? Dietrich Bonhoeffer grew in prison and even inspired fellow prisoners and guards with his strength. Millions more have benefited from his *Letters and Papers from Prison.* Aleksandr Solzhenitsyn wrote, "Thank you, prison camp," for how his imprisonment contributed to his spiritual growth. Victor Frankel became world renowned for his work in *Man's Search for Meaning*, which described how he survived Nazi persecution. He spoke of how no one can take away another's power of choice — the inner control to choose to be content and at peace.

Humans have demonstrated the ability to survive, even to thrive, in the most inhospitable environments and horrendous conditions. So we know that people can also grow spiritually in spite of toxic families and churches. But I don't want to explore how Christians grow in spite of their environment. Instead let's look at the best environment for spiritual formation.

Too Close and Too Demanding: The Parable of the Turtle

Almost everyone has heard the story about the little boy who tried to get a turtle to come out of its shell. He took a stick and poked the turtle to get its attention. As the boy continued to prod the frightened reptile, he couldn't understand why his friend didn't want to come out and play. His older sister came along, took the traumatized victim, and held it in her hands for a few minutes. Slowly the turtle's head and legs emerged.

A lot of Christians feel like the turtle being poked with the stick. Even when we feel motivated to grow, if we get poked, we retreat to the safety of our shells. When we try to get into groups and say yes to offers to invest in spiritual development, we still stay in our shell. Sometimes we don't want God to get that close. Other times we think that to grow or to train to be godly will be too demanding. Or we fear failure. And perhaps most often, we look around to other people in the groups and ask, "Can I trust me with you?" I'm sad to say that in the majority of Christian environments the answer has been no. So back into the shell we go!

The question "Can I trust me with you?" reveals our yearning for acceptance and for a safe place to be real. The goal isn't being "real" in a rude way, telling people off or spitting out inappropriate information. Instead we want places to be real in an honest sense. We want to be honest about our dreams, disappointments, and differences. Why is this such a big deal that we come out of our shell? Because when we stay in our shell, religious activity — including well-intentioned, well-planned, and well-led programs — can and often does fail.

NECESSARY INGREDIENTS FOR A HEALTHY ENVIRONMENT

So how do we bring people out of their shells? Poking them with a stick certainly doesn't work. In order to flourish, people need trust, grace, humility, submission, and affirmation in their environment.

Trust

The shell-shocked people who ask, "Can I trust me with you?" reveal the most important requirement for spiritual development: finding at least one person in your life you can trust. Let me make an important distinction. Notice I didn't say, at least one person you *do* trust, but one you *can* trust. *Can* means you've thought through the reasons for trusting the other person.

Trust is based on integrity; you can trust a person who has proven reliable and honest. However, this doesn't mean that person always agrees with your ideas or supports your behavior. But you can trust her to listen without judging or condemning you. When you find someone you can trust, then you can be vulnerable. Having one trustworthy person provides you with a safe haven of open and honest acceptance. You can allow yourself to come under that person's influence.

Trust is key, because we only take in the truth we trust. And that trust has to do with the messenger as much as the message. When you trust someone to the point you become vulnerable, you're giving that person permission to speak into your life. This is where transformational traction takes place. You are starting to make progress.

So choose carefully, because the other person's character will help shape yours. Look for someone whose actions reflect his words. Someone whose character you admire. Someone with a reputation for confidentiality. If you can't find such a person, pray! Pray fervently; God will be faithful to give you such a person. Above all, don't give up. Keep searching and praying.

Relationships of trust provide the foundation for transformational discipleship. Only in trusting relationships can we honestly deal with barriers to obedience and overwhelming sins that hold us back from spiritual growth. Certainly it requires courage to say to God, "Lord, I'm not afraid of you using [person's name] to make changes in my life."

The result of this vulnerability will reflect what Jesus described:

When a student is fully taught, he "will be like his teacher" (Luke 6:40).

Grace

Another element needed for us to flourish as disciples is grace. Grace means treating others better than they deserve to be treated. It means looking past faults to give others our praise and support. Most of us have trouble offering grace on our own, but when we tap into God as our resource, we can draw on the grace that he pours out on every person.

God treats us all much better than we deserve to be treated. When we work to create an environment of grace, we produce a culture of acceptance in which people see the value and good in others. We definitely don't ignore sins, faults, or problems. In fact, we can handle those issues better in an environment of grace. When we offer people a place where they feel safe, affirmed, and more able to risk, they'll be more open to change.

When I mentioned this topic to a friend, he objected to the idea that we should overlook people's natural weaknesses and focus on their strengths. He claimed that this would allow people to be sloppy; if we can't hold people accountable, they'll create a huge mess. But I think the opposite is true. When people feel safe and affirmed, they open up to others' input into their lives. Think about your own experiences. When someone who loves you speaks into your life and affirms what you do well, you almost always welcome it. The people who love you and whom you trust have incredible power and influence over you. When we can answer the question, "Can I trust me with you?" with a resounding, "Yes!" because of grace, discipleship will work as we make ourselves available for transformation.

Humility

Humility, Christ's primary character trait, is ground zero for personal transformation. Without humility, Christ wouldn't have submitted himself to the Father or made the sacrifice of his own life for the whole world.

One reason even the very best discipleship plans don't result in transformation is that they don't start with humility. Humility forms the environment and relationships that make transformation possible.

We can define humility in several ways. St. Benedict created a ladder of humility with twelve rungs.[1] To humble means to "make oneself low, to level a mountain, to bow down, or to be a person of the earth."[2] Frankly, most of us have an innate understanding of humility; we know it when we see it. In addition to Jesus' powerful example, Peter wrote that God opposes the proud: "Humble yourselves, therefore, under God's mighty hand, that he may lift you up in due time" (1 Peter 5:6).

Just as humility is Jesus' primary character trait, it should be the foundation we build on as we seek to follow him and be formed into his image. Think of it this way: without humility, there's no submission; without submission, relationships of trust can't exist; without relationships of trust, we won't make ourselves vulnerable; without vulnerability, no one can influence us; and without influence, we won't change.[3]

Submission

Jesus' humility allowed him to divest himself of the rights and privileges of deity, and he submitted himself to the will and agenda of his Father.

Submission is a love word before it is an authority word.[4] You submit to others because you desire to enter into a relationship that benefits you and those around you. Submission doesn't involve someone "keeping you in line," but allows someone to help you keep your commitments to God. Submission means saying, "I choose to let others love me."[5] Without submission three negative things happen:

1. Your needs won't be met.
2. You can't practice humility, the character trait that allows you to submit.
3. You shut out others from loving you.

When you do submit to others and invite them to join you on the journey, your needs will be met, you will practice humility, and others will be able to love you. This makes you a growing disciple who then influences others with Christlike character.

Nothing could be more radical or countercultural than Christians who submit to other people's needs. This is a key place where churches and ministries today should invest their energy. Living this way would send our paltry efforts to be relevant through new worship forms, hip looks, and trendy language to the ash heap of irrelevancy. Certainly efforts to renew and redefine worship and to connect with cultural trends have their place, but they pale in the face of what will happen when the people of God submit to each other and live for each other.

Affirmation

We all need affirmation. Without it, some ugly things happen in our lives. Affirmation confirms our identities.[6] We hear that others appreciate our strengths and contributions. We risk coming out of our shells.

When others don't affirm us, we begin to affirm ourselves. If no one pays attention to us, we start doing things to get others to notice us. Obvious examples include the blowhard at a party or the teenager who acts up at school. Even if we don't go to that extent, most of us find ourselves in times when we turn to affirming ourselves. Imagine sitting in a meeting at work for hours, and no one notices you. When you finally speak up, your thoughts are dismissed. How does that feel? Do you get anxious and look for opportunities to score points to bolster your sinking feelings of insignificance? This scenario is sad for at least two reasons. First, if you knew that the group fully accepted and respected you, you could relax and be yourself. Second, the fact that we all relate to this scenario reveals our pathological dependence on others for our identity.

Let's paint a different scene. What if the meeting started with an exercise of affirmation to reinforce your gifts and communicate how others feel about your contribution? This would create a safe environment where you could relax and give genuine input not coming from a crisis of unmet need.

Here's a good example of affirmation: How would you like serving as pastor of the church at Ephesus after the apostle Paul? Following a hard-working and gifted person is tough enough, but an apostle as well! His successor, Timothy, was younger, known to have a nervous tummy, shy, and easily intimidated (see 1 Timothy 4:11-16; 2 Timothy 1:7-8; 2:1; 4:1-4). Surely he heard lots of opinions about how he compared to Paul and how he should conduct his work as pastor. Paul, a highly passionate man who loved and hated with great force, sensed Timothy's needs and began his second letter to him with these powerful affirmations.

- I thank God for you.
- I pray for you night and day.
- I think about you all the time.
- I remember your tears.
- I long to see you.
- I am filled with joy when I am around you.
  (See 2 Timothy 1:3-4.)

Affirmation is powerful. It creates an environment that gives people permission to drop their defenses and allows deep change to take place.

I've never known affirmation to arouse sin, and the belief that it does reveals a twisted theology. When I receive praise, I want to do better. When a brother or sister in the faith affirms me, I don't become conceited. Instead I feel humbled that God thinks so much of me that he sends one of his children to affirm me. The messenger is almost as good as a dove descending and a voice from heaven saying, "This is my beloved child, in whom I am well pleased." For that reason, I want to make an even greater effort.

Affirmation becomes a way of life in an environment of grace. It reminds people that God values them. This is more than theology; it's a truth they experience. Affirmation allows people to be broken before God and to deal with unconfessed sin, shame, and the other inner-life issues that destroy our good effort at discipleship.

Summary

Trust, grace, humility, submission, affirmation — these foundational and essential elements create community. Suspicion, criticism, pride, self-will, and competition — these caustic and damaging qualities destroy community. Every community includes all of these, so each member must decide the following: Will I endeavor to live as a person of trust, grace, humility, submission, and affirmation? Will I be an example of these traits of Christ to others so we can create the kind of community in which disciples can grow? Will I help my fellow disciples to be able to answer yes to the question, "Can I trust me with you?"

SUGGESTED RESOURCES

Beyond Your Best: Develop Your Relationships, Fulfill Your Destiny by Bill Thrall and Bruce McNicol (Jossey-Bass, 2003). A summary of the better-known *The Ascent of a Leader* by the same authors, this book addresses interpersonal relationships, environments of grace, relationships of trust, and the power of affirmation.

TrueFaced: Trust God and Others with Who You Really Are by Bill Thrall, Bruce McNicol, and John Lynch (NavPress, 2004). A vivid story of grace told by moving from one room to the next in a house. One of the best studies on grace available, it contains unique insights.

The Safest Place on Earth by Larry Crabb (W Publishing Group, 1999).

Log onto www.leadershipcatalyst.org for information on training by Leadership Catalyst: "Creating a High Trust Culture." Leadership Catalyst's seminars and workshops provide practical ways to cultivate the characteristics discussed in this chapter.

THE STAGES OF DISCIPLESHIP

M any people love the turning of the leaves in the fall. Parents sometimes describe their child's misbehavior as "just going through a phase." Preparing to move to a nursing home is often a very difficult stage. Seasons, phases, and stages are part of our everyday language. We tend to define and understand life through them.

Just as we all progressed through grades of school and go through stages of a career, we also pass through stages of spiritual challenges as we mature. A friend once remarked to me, "About the time you get a handle on lust, hair stops growing on your head and starts coming out your ears!"

While some people resist the idea that we can measure something as mystical as spiritual progress, clear examples of spiritual stages can be found in Scripture:

- Recent converts shouldn't be considered for leadership (see 1 Timothy 3:6).
- New believers should long like newborn babies for the

pure spiritual milk of the Word (see 1 Peter 2:1-3).
- Disciples shouldn't be caught in a perpetual spiritual babyhood (see Hebrews 5:13).
- Mature followers of Jesus are distinguished from those who, like infants, are tossed to and fro by the winds of doctrine (see Ephesians 4:14).

The apostle Paul graphically stated the problem of spiritual immaturity in his first letter to the Corinthian church:

> Brothers, I could not address you as spiritual but as worldly —mere infants in Christ. I gave you milk, not solid food, for you were not yet ready for it. Indeed, you are still not ready. You are still worldly. For since there is jealousy and quarreling among you, are you not worldly? Are you not acting like mere men? For when one says, "I follow Paul," and another, "I follow Apollos," are you not mere men? (1 Corinthians 3:1-4)

All of these passages and many others make it clear that all Christians should mature spiritually—evidenced by love for one another, the fruit of the Spirit, and faithful service in the work of the kingdom.

MATURITY:
A COMMUNITY PROJECT

Paul defined mature Christians as those who "reach unity in the faith and in the knowledge of the Son of God and become mature, attaining to the whole measure of the fullness of Christ" (Ephesians 4:13).

Two thoughts strike me about this definition of maturity. First, such an attainment in this life seems impossible. Second, Paul wrote these words to a community of fellow disciples rather than an individual.

Unity in faith and unity in knowledge means sharing a common understanding of what we believe and how we should live together. The "whole measure of the fullness of Christ" refers to the responsibility of the community of Christians to manifest and represent Christ on earth. The mysterious organism called the church exists to show Christ to the world as one.

I want to express this clearly, but in a way that I fear will be misunderstood: As Christians, we become the corporate Christ. As Bonhoeffer so eloquently put it, Christ exists on earth through his body. Hear me clearly: This doesn't extinguish the doctrine of omnipresence or the ways Christ directly intervenes in our daily life. It simply means that God gave the body a lot of responsibility. A few verses later, Paul wrote, "From him the whole body, joined and held together by every supporting ligament, grows and builds itself up in love, as each part does its work" (Ephesians 4:16).

We each have roles within the body individually, but we can build ourselves up in love only when we have others to love. With the basic understanding that maturing—increasing in Christlike character—is a community project, we can look at the stages of how we mature, based on how Jesus led his disciples to live and grow.

PHASES, STAGES, AND STEPS OF SPIRITUAL DEVELOPMENT

Ever since Plato, Socrates, and Aristotle trained their apprentices, leaders have wanted to help learners make progress. Part of that means helping the student or learner know where she stands and how she's doing. I've found three models that illustrate the core of how Jesus taught: Robert Coleman's eight steps of training; Rick Warren's diamond of discipleship; and the idea of spiritual growth being both sequential and segmented.

Eight Steps for Training Disciples

Robert Coleman's eloquent and succinct *The Master Plan of Evangelism* essentially took apart Jesus' life and put it back together again, identifying eight steps Jesus used to make and to equip disciples. Let's look at a summary of those steps.

1. *Selection — people were his method.* Jesus believed that people should reach other people. He could have used an exclusive barrage of miracles, or he could have brought everything to conclusion while on earth. Instead he chose common men and women like us to reach the world. This demonstrates not only his love for us, but also his confidence in us.

2. *Association — he stayed with them.* With the first disciples, the essence of Jesus' training meant just letting his disciples follow him. He drew them close to himself, becoming his own school and curriculum.

3. *Consecration — he required obedience.* Jesus expected his disciples to obey him. He didn't require them to be smart, but he wanted them to be loyal — to the extent that obeying him became the distinguishing mark they were known by. "Disciples" meant they were the Master's "learners" or "pupils." Later Jesus' disciples became known as "Christians" (Acts 11:26), a fitting description of obedient followers who took on the character of their leader.

4. *Impartation — he gave himself away.* Jesus gave his disciples

everything: what the Father had given him (John 15:5); his peace (John 16:33); his joy (John 15:11); the keys to his kingdom (Matthew 16:19); and his own glory (John 17:22,24). He withheld nothing, not even his life.

5. *Demonstration — he showed them how to live.* Jesus showed the disciples how to pray, study, and relate to others. More than twenty times the Gospels recount Jesus' practice of prayer. He taught the disciples about the use of Scripture by extensively using words from the Old Testament. As the disciples saw Jesus interact with Nicodemus, the woman at the well, the rich young ruler, and many others, Jesus showed them how to talk to and how to treat others.

6. *Delegation — he assigned them work.* From day one, Jesus prepared his disciples to take over the mission. He gradually turned over responsibility, sending out the seventy (Matthew 10:1-42) and giving extensive instructions to the Twelve (Luke 10:1-20). He told the disciples to follow his methods, to expect hardships, and to go out in pairs. Following his resurrection, he clearly gave the disciples the responsibility to take the gospel to the entire world (Matthew 28:18-20; Acts 1:8).

7. *Supervision — he kept checking on them.* When Jesus gave the disciples work to do, he followed up. He listened to their reports and blessed them. When he was with the disciples, he spent time helping them understand the reason for a previous action or preparing them for a new experience. He used questions, illustrations, warnings, and admonitions to teach the disciples what they needed to know to reach the world.

8. *Reproduction — he expected them to reproduce.* Jesus told the disciples to pray for workers (Matthew 9:36-38),

and he called them to teach everyone to obey his teaching (Matthew 28:20). He required the costly elements of leadership development and reproduction, and expected the disciples to reproduce by finding other disciples who would also follow Jesus.[1]

The Diamond of Discipleship

Rick Warren's popular book *The Purpose-Driven Life* uses the simple illustration of a baseball diamond to capture the idea that spiritual progress is a journey. Thousands of churches have adopted and adapted this "Life Development Process."[2] It looks like this:

- First base or class 101: Committed to membership — the process of knowing Christ
- Second base or class 201: Committed to maturity — the process of growing in Christ
- Third base or class 301: Committed to ministry — the process of serving Christ
- Home plate or class 401: Committed to missions — the process of sharing Christ

Warren sees spiritual growth as a process that occurs over time in the context of community. The diamond gives church leaders practical handles, providing easy-to-understand concepts they can use to rally leaders and the whole congregation. When combined with the *Forty Days of Purpose* program, discipleship becomes concrete.

However, like most popular programs, this tool can create a dependence on even more packaged programs. I'm being critical here in a detached, diagnostic way. I wouldn't discourage anyone from using such tools, because they can be tremendously helpful for getting churches going in the right direction, but I'd caution churches not to become dependent on prepackaged programs. Think of them as booster shots or launching points, because they don't deal with the mystery and subtleties of Christian spiritual formation. That can only occur when spiritual people seek God together and find their own way. Disciples must eventually struggle in prayer to know what God wants them to do next.

Sequential and Segmented

Both Coleman's eight steps and Warren's baseball diamond demonstrate that spiritual growth is a process. When we think more deeply about the process, we realize that it's basically both sequential and segmented. It is sequential in that disciples can graduate from one phase to the next. They can grow in responsibility, and they don't face any limits regarding opportunities to grow. Segmented means each phase possesses its own characteristics.

JESUS' MODEL FOR
DEVELOPING FOLLOWERS

In his classic 1871 book, *The Training of the Twelve*, A. B. Bruce showed how Jesus gradually took his disciples through a process that infused them with the qualities that made them trustworthy to be carriers of the gospel. Bruce said, "The twelve arrived at their final intimate relation to Jesus only by degrees, three stages in the history of their fellowship with him being distinguishable."[3] Those three stages were "come and see," "come and follow me," and "come and be with me."

I've taken Bruce's three phases and added a fourth to show how the disciples finished their training and moved on to carry out their mission.[4] I don't intend for the four phases of how Jesus trained his followers to be a systematic theology or for them to redefine the purpose of the Gospels. Instead these observations come from asking the question, "Did Jesus use a specific design or process for developing his most faithful followers?"

Jesus marked these four phases with his own words. We might want to think of them as four key invitations.

1. "Come and see" occurred during a four- or five-month period when Jesus introduced a group of disciples to the nature of himself and ministry.
2. "Come and follow me" was a ten-month period when the five, plus others, temporarily left their professions to travel with Jesus.
3. "Come and be with me" lasted nearly twenty months. During that time, Jesus concentrated on the Twelve he called to be with him so they could go out and preach.
4. "Remain in me" describes the most dramatic change the disciples underwent. Jesus was leaving and they would begin relating to him through the Holy Spirit and through the church. This phase began in the Upper Room and continues into the present.

Let's look more closely at each phase.

Come and See

Text: John 1:35–4:46

Time: Four to five months

Participants: Andrew, Nathaniel, Peter, Philip, John, James, and others

Characteristics: During this information-gathering and investigation phase, the disciples made only a light commitment. They learned about the person of Jesus and the nature of his ministry and mission. Jesus wanted the disciples to know God himself, so he began here.

Introduction to himself: The most revolutionary relationship of all is the one God created us to enjoy with him. That's what Philip, Andrew, Peter, and Nathanael experienced during their first forty-eight hours with Jesus (see John 1:35-51).

God prepared these men's hearts to meet Jesus. When Jesus passed by them, he simply invited them to "come and see" something. God had orchestrated it all, using John the Baptist to prepare Andrew and Philip to be ready to follow. Jesus was the kind of person they wanted to follow. He was real, and he instilled in these men the passion they needed to recruit their families to follow him too.

This is the natural way the kingdom of God grows. Once Christ is alive in you, you serve as a spiritual guide to those willing to "come and see." The first step is inviting people to "come," which means giving time and space to those seeking God. What they should "see" is the reality of God in your life. Then you simply pray, recognize how God is working, and introduce seekers to the reality of Christ. You don't need to use formal presentations or spectacular experiences, just ordinary and local means of life.

Introduction to ministry: Ministry means serving others in the name of Christ. The disciples had the wonderful experience of learning how to serve others from Jesus himself. Through their experiences together, Jesus taught the disciples that ministry wasn't about them—it was about those being served. In John's gospel, we see Jesus serving people at the wedding at Cana of Galilee (see John 2:1-10); storming through the temple and encountering the Pharisees (see 2:12-22); interviewing Nicodemus (see 3:1-21); and having a conversation with a Samaritan woman (see 4:1-26).

When Jesus turned water into wine at the wedding at Cana, he demonstrated his willingness to help people in practical and mundane ways. However, clearing the temple provided high drama that gets at the heart of God's plan to redeem the world. God hates the misuse of his sacrificial system for personal gain. Jesus' verbal confrontation with the religious leaders was a clash of worldviews. The Pharisees simply wanted to preserve a system that benefited them, but Jesus was committed to the mission of rescuing a world from doom.

While the conflict in the temple was public, Jesus' interview with Nicodemus could not have been more clandestine—a secret meeting at night with Nicodemus slipping into and then out of the presence of Jesus. Jesus gave Nicodemus the message he would have told the other Pharisees if they'd been open to his teaching.

Finally, the conversation with the Samaritan woman showed how Jesus took a personal interest in the lowest of society—a person his disciples would have avoided or even ridiculed, if they'd had the opportunity.

All of these stories tell us something critically important about how God's kingdom works. One of the most striking aspects of this short period is the variety of ways one person can affect others.

Local and ordinary ministry: The way we minister says a lot about our character. What we choose to do and make a habit becomes our character. Then our character affects people around us. Jesus ministered from his character. He chose a life of humility, submission, sacrifice, and service. When ordinary people act in faith, God acts through them.

In fact, the most pressing need in most local congregations is that we own the truth that all of us are ministers. It seems that most Christians believe they're consumers. They see their faith and life in the community of their congregation as a way to receive benefits from Christ, a way to get some sort of "get into heaven" card that salvation provides. This leads to acceptance of a non-discipleship Christianity. Just as consumer Christianity rejects the idea that everyone must be a disciple, it also rejects the need for everyone to be a minister.

Let's state that another way: Jesus modeled that ministry is all about others; consumer Christianity is about us acquiring what we want.

For personal spiritual transformation, we need to reform back to the kind of ministry Jesus modeled. If we don't, we must ask if we're prepared to face the fact that the church might not ever reform. Eugene Peterson put it bluntly when asked if the church can reform:

> Hasn't happened. I'm for always reforming, but to think that we can get a church that's reformed is just silliness. . . . We have a goal. We have a mission. We're going to save the world. We're going to evangelize everybody, and we're going to do all this good stuff and fill our churches. This is wonderful. All the goals are right. But this is slow, slow work; this is soul work, this bringing people into a life of obedience and love and joy before God. And we get impatient and start taking shortcuts and use any means available. We talk about benefits. We manipulate people. We bully them. We use language that is just incredibly impersonal — bullying language, manipulative language.[5]

The church will always have problems, and people will always have problems with the church. Yet it's the only place for us to be. Peterson urges us to realize that the way we do ministry is just as important as the end result. We need to follow Jesus and build the kingdom his way.

Mission: Ministry means serving others. Mission also includes serving others, but relates directly to the instructions of Jesus, who carries out a mission for his Father. A call to mission frames the reasons for ministry, that is, where the ministry will go and what its ultimate meaning will be. Put most simply, mission gives ministry a sense of purpose.

Jesus introduced mission near the end of the "come and see" period. After he spoke with the Samaritan woman, she returned to her village to tell people of her experience with Jesus. Meanwhile the disciples return from buying food at the local market.

> His disciples urged him, "Rabbi, eat something."
>
> But he said to them, "I have food to eat that you know nothing about."
>
> Then his disciples said to each other, "Could someone have brought him food?"
>
> "My food," said Jesus, "is to do the will of him who sent me and to finish his work. Do you not say, 'Four months more and then the harvest'? I tell you, open your eyes and look at the fields! They are ripe for harvest." (John 4:31-35)

Can you see Jesus' genius? When he said, "Come and see," the disciples didn't realize how it would change their lives. And now Jesus gives a grand challenge—an embryonic Great Commission—and begins to show how their lives will change. Their "food" will become doing God's will and finishing his work. Jesus opened up the supernatural life by exposing them to himself and then to the nature of ministry. Then he told them to act—to enter into the work.

Jesus charged his disciples to act. But before they entered into the work of the mission, he told them to return home and think about it while he went off on his own. What followed was a two-month interim between the "come and see" phase and Jesus' next invitation, "Come and follow me."[6] During this time, Peter, Andrew, James and John, Nathanael, Philip, and others returned to their professions. The fishermen, in particular, had plenty of downtime waiting for fish to bite when they could reflect on the life-changing experience of being with Jesus. They had spent time with him, experienced him, observed the nature of ministry, and heard the challenge of mission. When he next invited them to "come and follow," they would be ready.

This phase of how Jesus developed his disciples shows the importance of preparing people for ministry and mission. We often wonder why people don't respond to a call to mission. Perhaps we need to examine if we've prepared them to say yes. Creating a thirst in people for more requires time and effort. In this first stage, disciples get a taste of Christ, what he does, and what he'll do with us. Think of ways you can create space and time to allow people to explore the person of Jesus with you and others in your faith community.

Come and Follow Me

Text: Matthew 4:19 and Mark 1:16-18
Time: 10 to 11 months
Participants: 70 to 120 consistent followers
Characteristics: Through Jesus' teaching and example, he desired
to establish followers in the priorities of the absolutes of
Scripture, the importance of prayer, the need for community,
and the work of outreach.

The invitation: When it was time to take his disciples to the next level of commitment, Jesus extended a second invitation to four fishermen—Andrew, Peter, James, and John: "Follow me . . . and I will make you fishers of men" (Matthew 4:19). He started a revolution with these simple, profound, and wise words. They provide us all of God's wisdom on how to get others to take action. Immediately the men dropped their nets and followed.

Invitation without alienation: Jesus invited these men to follow him, but he didn't demand anything, tell them off, or demean them. Even if they'd said, "No!" it's unlikely Jesus would have scolded them.

In Luke 9:57-62, three men declined Jesus' invitation to follow him. Based on Jesus' response to the first man, it seems he required some assurance that Jesus would provide lodging and meals. The second man wanted to go bury his father, a way of saying, "I can't do it now, but maybe later, when the timing is right." The third man had every intention of following, but first wanted to say good-bye to his family. Jesus recognized these as good excuses, but still just excuses for not saying yes.

We can presume that Jesus didn't brood over people who said no to him. And certainly he invested himself fully in those who said yes. People who followed Jesus couldn't be consumed with concerns of eating, sleeping, lodging, or geographic stability. They'd understand that the main agenda was proclaiming the kingdom of God. And they wouldn't look back, but choose to go forward together with no regrets.

A successful invitation: Jesus gave the disciples an invitation rather than a demand, and he didn't alienate those who eliminated themselves. You can't make a case for being left out if you choose to opt out of an opportunity. This is the genius of Jesus' method. Think of how many churches and ministries have split when the leader oversold the opportunity and then demeaned those who didn't want to participate as unspiritual or unwise. Jesus' way shows us how to motivate appropriately and how to appeal to others to commit to following Jesus.

"Follow me" was personal. Joining a program has such a different feel from "Join me and we'll work and live together." The latter offers relationship, closeness of fellowship, and friendship. The power of friendship is a primary motivation for participating in ministry.

When you ask people about their dearest friends, you'll often hear stories of how they've gone through challenges together. Some of the best stories about deep relationships come from people who went through war together, who achieved an impossible athletic goal together, who built something together, or who went through something horrific together. People create a special bond when they launch out into the abyss as a team to attempt the impossible.

One of most compelling aspects of Jesus' invitation was that the disciples could continue to be with him. And when we allow the person of Jesus to be formed within us, we provide the reason for others to follow us. Following Jesus is personal, which is why God designed discipleship as one person helping another person to follow Jesus together.

"I will make you" imparts responsibility. You can't teach someone to swim by throwing him into the water and commanding him to swim. And you can't train someone spiritually by simply holding a class where she takes a lot of notes and fills in a lot of blanks.

Jesus provided live, in color, on-the-job training. When he said, "I will make you . . ." he promised the disciples that he wouldn't ask them to do things that he hadn't trained them to do. They observed Jesus for months before he gave them specific mission work. When he did send them out, it was two by two, and review and reflection followed (see Matthew 10:1-42; Luke 10:1-24). Jesus' teaching method was "do it" and then "teach it"; often the disciples would watch him do something, and then he explained his actions or words to them. We can see this when he prayed, cast out demons, and walked on the water, as well as when he told many of his parables.[7]

"Fishers of men" gave vision. People need big reasons to give a big effort. Jesus cleverly devised his invitation for these fishermen to help them see their role. They would now employ their skills to do the same things Jesus was doing to change the nation they lived in.

Self-image—the picture you have in your mind of yourself—drives your behavior. If I think of myself as a good golfer, I'll practice and play golf to keep improving that self-image. If I think of myself as a brilliant scientist, I'll devote most of my time to theory and experimentation. If I think of myself as an ambassador for Christ, I'll make sure my daily work involves serving his kingdom.

Jesus took the disciples' self-image as fishermen and enlarged it into world-changing revolutionaries. Interestingly, in addition to giving the disciples a vision, this caused their chests and heads to swell, creating many debates, disappointments, and displays of arrogance.

You have an image of yourself and your vision for life. By reading these pages, you show that you see yourself as a partner with the original disciples. You come from a long line of regular people who gave the world reasons to be repulsed by the church, but who also displayed the glory of God to millions. Just as the Great Commission was done to us, it's time to thank God for those who chose to love us and make it possible for us to desire to reach others.

Come and Be with Me

Text: Mark 3:13-14

Time: 20 months

Participants: Primarily the twelve disciples

Characteristics: During this transitional phase, Jesus prepared the Twelve to take responsibility for world mission.

The historical Twelve: While Scripture names twelve of Jesus' closest disciples, hundreds of people followed Jesus at one time or another. Thousands came to hear him teach and longed for his healing touch. Jesus knew that he needed to prepare others to take a special place in advancing the message of the gospel. To do this, he once again used his regular life as a teaching laboratory. Look at what he taught the Twelve.

Compassion drives mission. Jesus took on needs as he and the disciples confronted them.

> Jesus went through all the towns and villages, teaching in their synagogues, preaching the good news of the kingdom and healing every disease and sickness. When he saw the crowds, he had compassion on them, because they were harassed and helpless, like sheep without a shepherd. Then he said to his

disciples, "The harvest is plentiful but the workers are few. Ask the Lord of the harvest, therefore, to send out workers into his harvest field." (Matthew 9:35-38)

This episode, often seen as the source of all mission, shows the heart of God rising from the dusty roads of Palestine amid vast unmet need. Whose heart doesn't break when confronted with images of human suffering? Jesus not only saw the disease and physical suffering, he also saw suffering souls. But he didn't throw up his hands and simply lament the need for more shepherds to care for these directionless souls.

What do you really see when you observe someone's suffering? The lost and broken of the world are in third-world cities, but they're everywhere else too. Sometimes they're hungry and covered with the smell of their disease. Yet others are bloated with plenty and covered with fine leather and fur. Our heart breaks for people, regardless of their location or economic condition. We lament, but then we leave the work to someone else. We see the problem as too large for one person to address.

Would you be surprised to know that Jesus reached the same conclusion? When he saw people "without," desperate for help, he said, "The harvest is plentiful but the workers are few." In saying this, Jesus wasn't surrendering. Instead of throwing up his hands in defeat and asking, "What can we do about it?" he urged his disciples, "Ask the Lord of the harvest . . . to send out workers into his harvest field." Multiplication is God's work, and if his workers desire more workers, God calls them to pray and he'll send more.

He went out and prayed all night. Jesus didn't begin a recruitment drive for more workers. Instead he spent the night in prayer. Soon he selected the men we call the Twelve: "Jesus went up on a mountain-side and called to him those he wanted" (Mark 3:13). Notice that he didn't call people who applied or people who really wanted to be his disciples or individuals that other people thought he should select. In addition, he spent time in serious prayer and reflection before he selected them. Even though Jesus was God, he needed to pray. He required a connection with his Father and the Holy Spirit.

We all need to take time to listen for the voice of God. This means sorting out options, clearing our minds, and examining our motives. It means involving others, such as calling for group prayer and discussion.

Compassion leads to multiplication. Preparing others to work for God builds on their God-given compassion. We might wonder how to harness the great compassion that flows through the spiritual veins of humankind. Jesus' answer was to develop and train willing workers.

This kind of compassion led an Albanian nun to start a mission to the dying in Calcutta. Mother Teresa recruited others to help in seemingly hopeless situations, and her compassion led to the establishment of many other such works around the world. The same kind of compassion can produce workers to help the homeless, Bible study leaders, evangelists, and others.

Jesus chose the disciples for two purposes. The first was relationship. Although humankind lost God's direct presence when Adam sinned, God has progressively drawn us back to him ever since. Being in Jesus' presence is worth whatever it takes. The disciples were eager to be "with him" in a special way, yet they also knew they had work to do. The Christian experience involves more than a contemplative relationship with God. While retreat has its place—for instance, as a quiet respite to prepare for or temporary relief from the mission work—the joy of serving God comes from a sense of accomplishment and the experience of working alongside others you respect.

Second, Jesus chose the disciples to send them out to preach. Their transformation led to their mission: "He appointed twelve . . . that he might send them out to preach and to have authority to drive out demons" (Mark 3:14-15); "He called his twelve disciples to him and gave them authority to drive out evil spirits and to heal every disease and sickness" (Matthew 10:1).

Jesus calls us as his disciples for the same purposes. He wants us to have a relationship with him and with others we work alongside. And he wants to transform us in a way that leads to our mission. We might preach by proclaiming the gospel as a pastor or evangelist, or we might "preach" by simply living among the lost and broken of society and making a difference in the regular and ordinary.

I like the way theologian and rabbi Abraham Joshua Heschel put it:

> The world needs more than the secret holiness of individual inwardness. It needs more than sacred sentiments and good intentions. God asks for the heart because he needs the lives. It is by lives that the world will be redeemed, by lives that beat in concordance with God, by deeds that outbeat the finite charity of the human heart. Man's power of action is less vague than his power of intention. And an action has intrinsic meaning; its value to the world is independent of what it means to the person performing it. The giving of good to the helpless child is meaningful regardless of whether or not the moral intention is present. God asks for the heart, and we must spell our answer in terms of deeds.[8]

When we answer God's call to "Come and be with me," we'll naturally connect the "being with God" to "going out to preach." This is the way it works—for our good and God's glory.

Remain in Me

Text: John 15:5,7
Time: A few hours in the Upper Room, and then a lifetime
Participants: The faithful Eleven and the entire church

Characteristics: Learning to live with and be empowered by the Holy Spirit.

Jesus led the disciples through an introductory phase, "Come and see"; an establishment phase, "Come and follow me"; a preparation for leadership phase, "Come and be with me"; and now he takes them through the most drastic change of all, "Remain in me."

Exit Jesus, enter the Holy Spirit.

The disciples learned that Jesus would indeed leave and give them the responsibility to carry on the mission he began. They would learn a new and different way to relate to God — the way all future followers would also relate to God. All disciples since Christ's ascension have lived in the "remain in me" phase. In practical terms, in this phase well-prepared disciples graduate from the earlier phases and take on their own work. However, no one outgrows the need for support and encouragement. The original disciples continued to live in community and help each other keep their commitments to God. Remarkably, based on biblical and historical accounts, they all remained faithful to the end.

Jesus transformed the disciples' lives by leaving them physically. When Jesus told the disciples that he would be leaving, they were shocked and sad. He said,

> "Now I am going to him who sent me, yet none of you asks me, 'Where are you going?' Because I have said these things, you are filled with grief. But I tell you the truth: It is for your good that I am going away. Unless I go away, the Counselor will not come to you; but if I go, I will send him to you." (John 16:5-7)

Jesus tried to tell his shell-shocked disciples that everything would get better. Imagine giving up your life to spend several years working alongside Jesus, and then he announces, "I'm leaving"! Resisting change is human nature, and this entailed much more than most changes.

Jesus knew that his disciples didn't welcome this change, but he also knew he'd prepared them for three years. He even knew that within a few hours they'd all scatter in fear and that Peter would deny him three times. In other words, he was prepared to let them stumble, fall, and *fail*. Yet Jesus knew that much of his character had already been formed in them. They might zigzag all over the spiritual terrain, but they'd find their footing and carry his work forward. In fact, as he promised, the disciples exceeded his works (see John 14:12-14).

Most of us resist when changes and challenges occur. We fear that things won't be better. Yet if we're well-prepared and faithfully coached, we can be certain of a fruitful future when we're willing to sacrifice the comfort of the familiar and plunge forward into the unknown.

Jesus transformed the disciples' lives by leaving them the Holy Spirit. Of course, the disciples didn't know that the Holy Spirit would ensure the success of their calling. They would need to relate to Jesus in a different way, a transition that would affect how they moved forward with his mission:

1. In leadership: moving from Christ leading the apostles to elders leading a congregation
2. In guidance: moving from Christ's personal presence to the Holy Spirit's presence, the ministry of God's Word, prayer, and the wisdom of others
3. In training: moving from Christ's preparation of leaders to a community of leaders engaged in developing apprentices
4. In outreach: moving from individual evangelism to evangelistic teamwork
5. In pastoral care: moving from Christ alone meeting

people's needs to Christ meeting needs through gifts of
the body

The disciples could make such drastic changes because the Holy
Spirit would do his work. He would serve as counselor, friend, teacher,
guide, parent, and a reminder of all that Jesus had taught them.

Jesus transformed the disciples' lives by leaving them with responsibility. Paul summarized it well:

All this is from God, who reconciled us to himself through
Christ and gave us the ministry of reconciliation: that God
was reconciling the world to himself in Christ, not counting
men's sins against them. And he has committed to us the
message of reconciliation. We are therefore Christ's ambassadors, as though God were making his appeal through us.
We implore you on Christ's behalf: Be reconciled to God.
(2 Corinthians 5:18-20)

When Jesus physically left the world, he created the need for his
followers to step up to the task of fulfilling the mission he began.
As Paul put it, the rescue mission now belongs to us. Jesus reassures
us, "Remain in me." We are God's strategy, so we must tell others.
The words of a spicy Quaker, Elton Trueblood, come to mind: "The
Church or something like it must be cherished, criticized, nourished
and reformed. The Church of Jesus Christ, with all its blemishes, its
divisions and its failures, remains our best hope of spiritual vitality.
However poor it is, life without it is worse."[9]

But Trueblood didn't stop there. He reached for the grander
vision:

One of the truly shocking passages of the gospel is that in
which Jesus indicates that there is absolutely no substitute

for the tiny, loving, caring, reconciling society. If this fails, he suggests, all is failure; there is no other way. He told the little bedraggled fellowship that they were actually the salt of the earth and that if this salt should fail there would be no adequate preservative at all. He was staking all on one throw. . . . One of the most powerful ways of turning people's loyalty to Christ is by loving others with the great love of God. . . . If there should emerge in our day such a fellowship, wholly without artificiality and free from the dead hand of the past, it would be an exciting event of momentous importance. A society of genuine loving friends, set free from the self-seeking struggle for personal prestige and from all unreality, would be something unutterably priceless and powerful. A wise person would travel any distance to join it.[10]

The four stages Jesus used to train his disciples show us the value of knowing how to lead others with wisdom and skill. He carefully nurtured and challenged his followers. Then he released them to carry on his work. What a frightening and amazing privilege!

Suggested Resources

Jesus Christ, Disciplemaker by Bill Hull (20th anniv. ed., Baker, 2004). Offers an in-depth look at the four phases of Christ's training methods presented in this chapter. The thesis of the book is that Jesus intentionally trained his followers in an organic relationship over a period of three-plus years.

The Master Plan of Evangelism by Robert Coleman (Revell, 2006). The most succinct and on-target work regarding how Jesus related to his followers.

The Training of the Twelve by A. B. Bruce (Kregel, 2000; first published 1871). Probably the most comprehensive work on Jesus' relationship to his followers, this book is primarily an exposition of biblical passages. Rich in texture, but be warned: it contains more than five hundred pages of very small print.

The Purpose-Driven Life by Rick Warren (Zondervan, 2002).

Conformed to His Image by Ken Boa (Zondervan, 2001). Connects the Myers-Briggs Inventory to twelve kinds of spirituality, providing an important tool for thinking through personality and spirituality.

The Making of a Leader by J. Robert Clinton (NavPress, 1988). This work on the individual and seasons of life provides valuable help when coaching or guiding others. It provides a perspective grand in its sweep yet practical in its insight.

CHAPTER 7

CHRISTIAN SPIRITUAL TRANSFORMATION

When I was growing up, I had a friend named Bobby Logan. Bobby was my alter ego, existing only in my mind. Yet he dominated my life. Bobby could hit like Mickey Mantle, jump like Bill Russell, and pass a football like Johnny Unitas. He always came through in the clutch, scoring a winning touchdown or dropping a thirty-footer at the buzzer.

Bobby was great at all sports, but his best sport was basketball. As I spent hundreds of hours practicing and doing drills, Bobby was always there. Together we pulled off some miraculous feats, winning game after game on last-second shots. We beat the Celtics in the NBA finals, whipped the Russians for the Gold Medal in the Olympics, and stomped John Wooden's UCLA Bruins in the NCAA championship game. No one had the quickness, vertical leap, shooting eye, or competitive fire to match Bobby.

Although Bobby inspired me, as I developed my own persona and success he faded into the background. The only thing Bobby did was sports. He didn't go to school or have parents. He didn't have a girlfriend or live in a house. He had no faults, but he had no virtues either. Like Peter Pan, Bobby never grew up. He went on to enter into another little dreamer's thoughts.

Now my dreams are spiritual. Bobby wasn't real, but Jesus is. I want to be like Jesus. I could never be as good as Bobby, and I can't become perfect like Jesus, but I can take on Jesus' character, making his thoughts, feelings, and values mine. And just as those hours and hours of practice transformed my athletic life, the time I spend practicing spiritual disciplines can transform my inner person. I want to move beyond simply agreeing that being like Jesus is a good thing and invest in the process.

We call this process spiritual transformation. The word *transformation* comes from *trans* (Greek, *meta*), meaning to move something from one place to another; and *formation (morphe),* meaning to change (see Romans 12:2; Galatians 4:19). In spiritual transformation, we *move* from the person we are and continue to *change* by degree into the image of Christ (see 2 Corinthians 3:16-18).

THE TRANSFORMATIONAL TRIANGLE

The following diagram, the Transformational Triangle, attempts to illustrate in a simple way the elements we need for spiritual transformation.[1] Let's look briefly at each of these elements.

Community
The center of the triangle represents community: living together in common conditions with common devotion. The early church in Acts 2 exemplified community by:

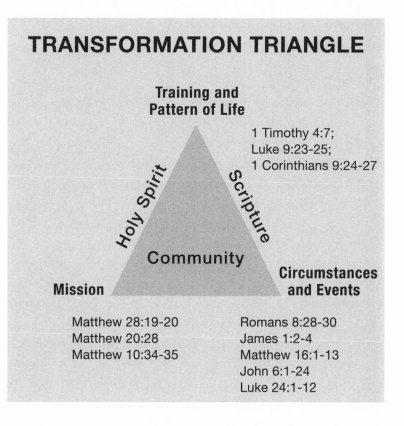

- devoting themselves to the apostles' teaching
- sharing common beliefs
- being together and having everything in common
- meeting together every day
- eating together with glad and sincere hearts

Community describes the relationships we form to help us live out our beliefs. God never intended us to follow Christ and engage in the disciplines of this life alone. God knows—and oh, so do we—that we do better when others help us. In community, others hold us accountable for our heart's intentions, they test our words and sentiments, and they rescue us from a life of waste and self-indulgence.

The Holy Spirit and Scripture

As disciples, we choose to live under the authority of Scripture and to submit to the will of the Holy Spirit. Further, we gain the most benefit from the Holy Spirit's work and God's communication to us through his Word in the context of community. As individuals, we don't have the power we need to live the Christian life or grasp the whole of Scripture.

Training and Pattern of Life

"Training and Pattern of Life" refers to choosing the life of following Jesus—positioning ourselves to be disciples. Fed up with our addictions and sins, we repent and choose the life God has created for us. As disciples, we start by saying, "I will deny myself and take up my cross"; "I will discipline myself for the purpose of godliness"; "I will run the race set before me" (see Luke 9:23-25; 1 Timothy 4:7; 1 Corinthians 9:24-27). We make a conscious decision to live by the Rule.[2] Jesus provided the example for this pattern of life: a life of submission, sacrifice, and obedience, built on a foundation of humility.[3]

This part of the process both marks the starting line and represents the essence of discipleship. We make following Jesus our life's goal and intention. Faith is following and following is faith. The first action requires creating time and space to train. We don't try to become like Jesus; instead we make a commitment to train to become the kind of person who naturally does what Jesus would do. The intention of our heart and the action of training provide proof that the Holy Spirit has given us new life, as well as the grace and resources to go on the journey (see 2 Corinthians 5:17; Ephesians 2:10; Philippians 2:13).

Events and Circumstances

We all travel through life experiencing events and circumstances that shape us. How we interpret them determines how God forms and transforms our inner person. Ideally we'll look at life's events and circumstances in light of Scripture, with insight from the Holy Spirit, and in the context of community. God never meant for us to face the trials of life alone. In community, God brings his resources together for the benefit of his people.

In Scripture, we see many of the events and circumstances that shaped Jesus' first disciples. He formed their thinking and built their faith on the Mount of Transfiguration, at the feeding of the five thousand, during the clearing of the temple, when he walked on water, and so forth. Negative experiences—such as encounters with the Pharisees, the threats on Jesus' life, his arrest, and their abandonment of Jesus in a time of crisis—also shaped the disciples. They loved Jesus, but they also failed him. We all fail and continue this tradition of the human condition.[4]

Yet, just as he did with the first disciples, God takes our failures and suffering and uses them to help us grow (see Romans 8:28-30; James 1:2-4). As the old saying goes, "Pressure produces." The events and circumstances of life squeeze out what's inside us, revealing our spirits. Yet in God's hands, these trying times can re-create our spirit.

When we face either uplifting or destructive experiences outside of community, we often misinterpret them. This misinterpretation leads to a malformation of our spirits, and we become filled with either pride or bitterness. But when we position ourselves properly —following Jesus in submission and obedience—any experience can result in positive transformation.

Mission

Mission refers to God's mystery that you only find yourself when you lose yourself in serving others. Earlier I referred to this as taking up our cross.[5] Disciples carry the cross on their shoulders as the symbol of Jesus' sacrifice and suffering. In addition, our own sacrifice and suffering can be very real. Perhaps the greatest sacrifice is giving up the right to run our own lives, putting to death the dream of creating our agenda and of being in control. Taking up our mission requires slaying our impulse to lead Jesus instead of follow him, to put our desires first and get around to God's desires later, or not at all.

When Jesus told his disciples that he must die, Peter took him aside and rebuked him. Peter couldn't understand how Jesus' life would make sense if he was arrested and killed just as he was gaining popularity. Jesus, however, rebuked Peter in the presence of the other disciples, saying, "You do not have in mind the things of God, but the things of men" (Mark 8:33). Jesus then turned to the crowd following him and presented the mysterious challenge of mission:

> "If anyone would come after me, he must deny himself and take up his cross and follow me. For whoever wants to save his life will lose it, but whoever loses his life for me and for the gospel will save it. What good is it for a man to gain the whole world, yet forfeit his soul? Or what can a man give in exchange for his soul?" (Mark 8:34-37)

The only way we find our life is by giving it away. That's why Paul called us "living sacrifices" (Romans 12:1). Without this mission impulse, we fall into the trap of endlessly waiting for a "call from God" before we go to the world and make disciples. We've already been called! If Jesus personally visited every hesitant disciple and reissued his order to make disciples, we'd be under no more obligation than we already are.

The Whole Triangle

So let's put together how God transforms us. We position ourselves by choosing to live a certain pattern of life and to be trained. We choose to place ourselves in community. We willingly live under the authority of Scripture and submit to the will of the Holy Spirit. We interpret events and circumstances in light of Scripture, with insight from the Holy Spirit, and in the context of community. And we find fulfillment as we serve others—living life to the full (see John 10:10; Ephesians 2:10).

THE ROLE OF SPIRITUAL DISCIPLINES IN TRANSFORMATION

The spiritual habits, or disciplines, have a rich history. Depending on the source, writers have identified twelve to twenty disciplines.[6] A fairly comprehensive list includes Bible reading, meditation, Scripture memorization, prayer, worship, evangelism, service, stewardship, fasting, silence, solitude, journaling, submission, and frugality.

Most evangelical Christians focus on just seven of the disciplines: Bible reading, Scripture memorization, prayer, worship, evangelism, service, and stewardship.[7] This limiting of the disciplines doesn't help the disciple develop habits of the heart. Pastors often exhort their congregations to practice these disciplines and might offer a class or small group for some basic training. Yet the actual practice of the disciplines ends up falling to individuals to make it on their own.

Who's to blame for this separation of discipleship from community? Most of us are self-protective. We put up barriers to letting others get involved deeply in our lives. We also want transformation without change and character development without pain.

However, as discussed in chapter 5, we need to learn and take on the characteristics of submission, humility, and vulnerability before we can expect spiritual transformation. We must submit ourselves to God, show humility in our relationships with others, and practice vulnerability by willingly opening ourselves to the influence of others.

Why Practice Spiritual Disciplines?

Most of us think of discipline as negative. We discipline our kids when they misbehave. Soldiers face disciplinary action when they don't follow the orders of their commanders. A boss might put an employee through a probationary period as a disciplinary measure for not meeting certain goals.

But practicing spiritual disciplines has much more of a preemptive and positive quality. As author and philosophy professor Dallas Willard notes, "The practice of the spiritual disciplines [is] essential to the deliverance of human beings from the concrete power of sin."[8] The relationship between discipline and disciple is also important. Pastor John Ortberg notes, "Disciplined people can do the right thing at the right time in the right way for the right reason."[9]

Spiritual disciplines develop habits of the heart: The practice of spiritual disciplines develops habits of the heart that make a disciple more capable of answering the call of God. When Jesus asked Peter, James, and John to wait and pray nearby while he went to wrestle with his Father about the difficulty ahead, three times these disciples went to sleep. Then Jesus spoke those most penetrating words: "The spirit is willing, but the body is weak" (Matthew 26:41). This episode answers why we need to practice the disciplines. Jesus told the disciples that by participating in a certain action — in this case, staying awake and being in prayer — they could reach a quality of spiritual strength otherwise impossible. In other words, practicing the spiritual disciplines doesn't accentuate our strengths, it addresses our weaknesses.

Think about the contrast in the first disciples after the Holy Spirit's power came upon them. In the garden, they couldn't stay awake and pray for even a few minutes. Later they sustained the discipline of prayer for ten days (see Acts 1–2). Notice that being empowered by the Holy Spirit is essential; in fact, the Spirit of the disciplines *is* the Holy Spirit.[10] But it's just the starting point. Too many Spirit-filled followers are undisciplined, untrained, under-used, and ineffective.

Being filled and empowered with the Spirit speaks to the intention of our hearts. It gives us the desire to be trained. But desire doesn't do the training.

Spiritual disciplines are tools. Just as the desire to be trained doesn't equal being trained, the disciplines have no value in and of themselves. It's self-indulgent to produce spiritual depth just for depth's sake. That goal would only birth pride — the king of sins. It reminds me of bodybuilding, in which people dedicate themselves to an impressive physical program of exercise and diet. Some even enter bodybuilding competitions, where they prance about on a stage and display their well-oiled and sculptured bodies. But sometimes I wonder, What can one of these bodies do that a normal body can't? Probably very little.

Similarly, there are disciples who exercise and create impressive spiritual muscles simply for display — Look at how long I pray. Notice how much I fast? God speaks to me all the time. I give a great deal. Look at my big fat journal! — are a stench in God's nostrils. Of course, most people wouldn't be so blatant, but the same attitude comes out in subtle ways. My point is, there's no virtue in spiritual exercise without a reason. We find the correct reason in the Great Commission: losing ourselves in "the mission" (see Luke 9:23-25).

In other words, the aim and substance of following Jesus shouldn't be about prayer, Bible study, or meditation. These tools simply serve the greater purpose of knowing God. They help us develop intimacy with God and fitness for serving.

We might think of spiritual disciplines more like calisthenics.[11] Calisthenics — push-ups, jumping jacks, leg lifts, sit-ups, and pull-ups — help condition our bodies so we can better use our natural athletic gifts. In a similar way, spiritual disciplines condition our spiritual lives so we can better use our God-given spiritual gifts.

Our churches are full of gifted people who want to serve. But they're not in spiritual shape, which leaves them unprepared to serve *well*. We need to get past the stereotypical image of spiritual exercise for exercise's sake and realize that these disciplines prepare and condition us to serve to our fullest potential.

Spiritual disciplines work indirectly. Again, spiritual exercise works much like physical exercise. I've exercised most of my life—in fact, I'm addicted to it. It's an integral part of my well-being. Exercise sets into motion a series of positive events inside the body: The heart rate rises. Blood flow increases as veins and arteries open wider. Oxygen flows throughout the body. The heart gets stronger. Muscles maintain or increase their strength. Exercise allows me to continue playing basketball, to walk long distances, to lift my luggage into overhead compartments, to play with my grandson, and to carry things for my wife.

Spiritual exercise also sets into motion a series of positive events that strengthen and transform our character. Scripture describes how transformation happens:

- "By the renewing of your mind" (Romans 12:2)
- By "being transformed into his likeness . . . from the Lord, who is the Spirit" (2 Corinthians 3:18)
- By "being renewed day by day" (2 Corinthians 4:16)
- By being "conformed to the likeness of his Son" (Romans 8:29)
- By "Christ . . . formed in you" (Galatians 4:19)

How do reading, memorizing, meditating on Scripture, and the other disciplines transform our mind and then change our behavior? I don't know—it's a mystery! But they transform our mind and train us for everything God wants us to accomplish for him. The apostle Paul described the results as being "thoroughly equipped for every good work" (2 Timothy 3:17; see also 1 Timothy 4:7; Hebrews 5:14; 12:11; 2 Peter 2:14).

God uses the desire to grow spiritually within our heart, the work of the Holy Spirit, and the habits developed by spiritual disciplines to form within us the character and qualities of Christ. It's a supernatural work of the Holy Spirit in combination with our wills.

With this understanding, let's look at three principles that should govern our practice of spiritual disciplines.

Principle 1: Training Leads to Godliness

At the moment of spiritual birth, the Spirit of God plants himself in us and provides the source of our motivation. The Holy Spirit "factory installs" in us a desire to be like Jesus. Whether we like it or not and whether we admit it or not, this places within us a perpetual hunger for holiness.[12] We can rely on the apostle Paul to put it in direct terms: "Train yourself to be godly" (1 Timothy 4:7).

Sounds like work, doesn't it? How can you practice fifteen-plus disciplines all at once? The answer is, You can't and you shouldn't. Eugene Peterson likens the disciplines to a set of garden tools. He sees the soil of a garden as the human soul, the rain and sunshine as the staple disciplines such as prayer and interaction with the Scriptures. Just as the gardener keeps other tools in his shed to use when needed for tilling, weeding, planting, and other tasks, the disciple pulls out fasting, solitude, worship, journaling, and other disciplines for when she needs them.

For example, sometimes we need to use the tools of extended times of prayer and fasting. Not long ago, my wife spent a day of intense prayer, solitude, listening, and fasting, something she needed just to intensely nourish her soul. In other words, we don't need to be intimidated by the number of disciplines available any more than we need to be afraid of the hundreds of TV channels at our fingertips.

The road to godliness is a road of discipline. The word *train* comes from the Greek *gumnazo*, from which we derive *gymnastics* or *gymnasium*.[13] This word drips with sweat and feels like burning muscles. It also seems antithetical to the contemporary evangelical image of Christian growth.

We easily go to extremes, both in our thinking and in our doing. One of those extremes is the belief that grace is opposed to effort. Some Christians resist the practice of spiritual disciplines because they equate effort with earning some sort of "grace points" with God. Some of this resistance comes from a reaction to the malpractice of spiritual disciplines by monastic movements.[14] Many evangelicals also have an almost inherent resistance to the Catholic teaching and liberal theology that has been the home of the spiritual disciplines for the past few hundred years.

Even though many Christians cast it aside, the disciplining of our natural impulses is central in the teaching of Scripture. The spiritual disciplines are an absolutely necessary part of believing in and following Christ. Somehow the self-denial Jesus described as basic to faith in and following him has incorrectly disappeared from the salvation equation.

An interesting recent development involves the emergence of a very healthy return to spirituality. This includes a correct practice of the disciplines. Look at what this appropriate perspective of the spiritual disciplines *doesn't* include: implying that salvation is somehow earned or maintained; thinking that God will lavish more love or praise on an individual's spiritual efforts; thinking the disciplines must dominate life to the point that their practice actually obstructs or replaces intimacy with God; and most importantly, permitting the disciplines to become the mission rather than the Great Commission.

God opposes earning but urges effort. God doesn't want us to try to earn salvation through the practice of any set of disciplines. But that doesn't mean he opposes all effort. In fact, some of the great passages in the New Testament extol effort:

- 1 Corinthians 9:24-27: running to get the prize
- 2 Corinthians 11:23-29: working hard, facing dangers, laboring, toiling, and losing sleep
- Galatians 4:19: suffering pain as severe as childbirth
- Philippians 3:12-14: pressing on and straining
- Colossians 1:29: laboring and struggling with all energy
- 2 Timothy 2:1-7: being strong, enduring, competing like an athlete, working as hard as a farmer

Like the old saying goes, "You can't steer a parked car." God honors and urges us to put forth effort when it comes to spiritual training and growth.

Don't go it alone. Because discipline doesn't come naturally to most of us, we should seldom work out alone. We should seek a community of people who help care for our souls.[15]

We need encouragement when it comes to discipline. One TV report recently noted that 70 percent of Americans don't exercise. Of the 30 percent who do exercise, only 10 percent exercise alone. The remaining 90 percent who exercise do so because of accountability or encouragement from a friend. When it comes to spiritual exercise, it's absolutely essential to attach ourselves to at least one other person. I can't think of anyone I know who made significant spiritual breakthroughs without the help of friends. Many people have said, "I'm going to go deep with God," but unless they submit to the help of others, they're not likely to grow, apart from suffering. The help of others is part of the road of discipline that makes transformation into godliness possible.

Principle 2: Practice Creates the Trained State

I've practiced a lot of things in my life. When I kept practicing, it usually paid off. For example, I was in training to play basketball and piano, but after a year of lessons and realizing that being six-foot-six benefited me more on the court than at the keyboard, I quit the piano. I've also practiced preaching and writing just as a physician practices medicine. One of the most important reasons we practice is so that we'll do things the same way every time. Whether it's dribbling a basketball, playing a musical instrument, or painting a beautiful watercolor, we practice so that the skill and knowledge become second nature.

Let's briefly unpack the way that one of my favorite passages explains the relationship between practice and spiritual training:

> We have much to say about this, but it is hard to explain because you are slow to learn. In fact, though by this time you ought to be teachers, you need someone to teach you the elementary truths of God's word all over again. You need milk, not solid food! Anyone who lives on milk, being still an infant, is not acquainted with the teaching about righteousness. But solid food is for the mature, who by constant use have trained themselves to distinguish good from evil. (Hebrews 5:11-14)

The undiscipled disciples: The writer describes undiscipled disciples with the phrase "by this time you ought to be teachers." These verses show that undiscipled disciples aren't new, yet we've accepted undiscipled discipleship as a normal condition. It's the common cold of the church: we haven't found a cure, so we accept it as a fact of life.

Perhaps some portion of people attending evangelical churches really aren't Christians. Perhaps they call themselves Christians, but they're unwilling to become Christlike. They engage themselves in church activity but have not repented of their sin or committed to follow Jesus. I think it is clear that Jesus defined belief as following him.

Another group of people have truly repented and try to follow Jesus in good faith. But somehow they've reduced what it means to follow Jesus to church attendance, financial giving, and serving on a board or committee. This hasn't been a conscious choice; it happens by custom and church culture. No one challenges this second group to choose "the life." No one helps them focus on intentional discipleship that leads to internal spiritual transformation.

Together these two groups make up the undiscipled disciples. Again, the result is that the body of Christ pays a huge price — the high cost of non-discipleship. We might call non-discipleship Christianity the elephant in the room. We deny that the elephant is there. We throw a huge tablecloth over it and call it a coffee table. But the cost of ignoring non-discipleship Christianity is staggering: We forfeit both a predominantly vibrant church and the fulfillment of the Great Commission.

We feed the elephant and he stays strong and dominant. What does he eat? His favorite dish is that everyone's commitment level is "acceptable." This entrée comes with a side dish of meeting the demands of the immature and passive-aggressive underachievers. For dessert, the elephant gobbles up occupied church leaders forced to arbitrate conflict among people vying for power.

Non-discipleship Christianity doesn't expect people to take the kingdom of God to work and make disciples. Who has time and energy for that? Instead these non-disciples spend the majority of their time and effort keeping the elephant well fed. But this results in less joy, weakened passion, and paltry fruitfulness. The cost is so high because non-discipleship Christianity leaves wasted lives. Life-changing experiences remain on the shelf. Pastors spend most of their time and energy trying to satisfy the prevailing desires of the congregation.

I know how hard it is to stay on course and be pure in philosophy and strategy, but the acceptance of non-discipleship Christianity is a leadership problem. The solution will come when leaders model what they believe their followers should do. This will take a group of tightly knit leaders who are willing to take a lot of criticism in order to starve the elephant and feed their souls.

The Enemy's strategy involves keeping us away from the habits of the heart that will develop Christ's character in his people. Remember, as I noted in chapter 4, the mission of the Great Commission is more about depth than strategy. Taking on the mission requires a revolution of character transformation.[16]

"By this time you ought to be teachers." In essence, the writer to the Hebrews was saying to his spiritually immature readers, "You have some really bad habits." Instead of serving as proponents for the kingdom of God, they had stagnated and lost their passion. Their spiritual formation was actually a malformation of passivity and a retreat from making disciples themselves. Remember, reproduction is a clear expectation of discipleship.

Some people feel uncomfortable with bold reminders that we're practicing a Christianity that Scripture never describes as appropriate. To speak about it is considered rude or in bad form. However, I believe it's vital. Because it occurs so often in Scripture, I'm also certain that it's biblical to speak up.

"Solid food is for the mature, who by constant use have trained themselves." Maturity results from constant use. This means repetition or practice, and that requires discipline. Real change takes time as new and good habits slowly take the place of old and bad habits. In the midst of this time, we can wage horrific battles within. In *The Screwtape Letters,* C. S. Lewis described the lack of perseverance of many Christians: "There is no need to despair; hundreds of these adult converts have been reclaimed after a brief sojourn in the enemy's camp and are now with us. All the habits of the patient, both mental and bodily, are still in our favour."[17]

If we don't actually acquire a new habit, any change we experience is only temporary. Think about how most of us operate this way. Something inspiring moves us (a good and needed step). God then moves us to action through our minds and emotions. But with the inspirational moment as our base rather than the true changing of our habits, we easily slip back to the same habits as before. Sadly this once again delays the advance of God's kingdom.

Remember, we practice these disciplines so the skill and knowledge become second nature.

Principle 3: Perseverance Makes Transformation a Reality

Most of us realize that if we practice something for long enough, we create a new habit. Have you noticed that many gifted people don't live up to their full potential? They won't train. They won't keep up their efforts long enough for their gift to become a powerful force. The power of habit comes when we take a difficult and awkward task and make it natural and easy.

I've mentioned that I spent my teen years devoted to playing basketball. I had some natural talent, but I wasn't the most talented. I wasn't blessed with great jumping ability, which meant that bigger and quicker players could block my shot. So I decided to learn the hook shot. My goal wasn't simply to learn the hook shot, but to master it with both hands. First I practiced it with my right hand. Within a few weeks, I'd mastered the right-hand hook. Mastering the left-hand hook took months.

While I was comfortable and confident in my backyard, the real test came in the heat of competition. Guarded by bigger and quicker opponents, I first shot with my right hand. The shot went in. Next I faked my opponent and hooked with the left, and it also went in! Now players guarding me didn't know if I'd drive to the basket, pull up and knock down a jump shot, use a fade-away jumper, or go down low and hook either right or left. When I made that first lefty hook on a surprised defender, all the days and weeks of practice were worth it. I didn't have to think about what I was doing; it just came naturally in the moment.

That's what the spiritual disciplines can do for us. When we memorize Scripture, for example, we can recall a verse and choose not to sin when faced with a tough battle. We don't have to think about it; it just comes naturally in the moment. That means the discipline has served us so we can better serve God.

Don't give up. We can change only when we stick with spiritual discipline. The apostle Paul wrote, "Let us not become weary in doing good, for at the proper time we will reap a harvest if we do not give up" (Galatians 6:9).

I wasn't as talented as other athletes, but I went further because I practiced longer and harder. I played basketball every day, year 'round, from the time I was fourteen until I was twenty-one. My mother made me take Christmases off. I played in backyards, alleys, schoolyards, gymnasiums. In the winter, I played in converted haylofts that housed basketball courts. My goal was simple: My mother made thirty-nine dollars a week, and unless I got a basketball scholarship to a university, I'd have to enlist in the Army.

I actually made this commitment when I was fired from my newspaper route. The paper manager came to my home to confront me about an unpaid bill and customer complaints. It was all true; I'd spent the money I'd collected and I'd missed customers. The craggy old guy challenged me, "What are you going to do with your life? You're a disaster!"

I looked him straight in the eye and said, "I'm going to college on a basketball scholarship."

He screwed up his face, threw up his hands, said "That's a laugh!" and walked out the door.

I was fourteen years old, and at that moment I dedicated myself to practice the disciplines of basketball. Four years later, I walked onto the college campus and my bill was already paid.

I stayed focused on my goal because it was clear and concrete. However, spiritual goals can be ethereal, hard to grasp, and even harder to keep in our grasp. The antidote for weariness is keeping the vision in mind, staying at the disciplines that you deeply believe will one day pay off. You'll face days when prayer seems like drudgery, when silence leads to unplanned naps, and when listening for God's voice results in mental rabbit trails. But Paul tells us that we'll reap a great harvest if we don't give up. During these times, hang your hope on the belief that your efforts will pay off.

Training isn't just trying. When it comes to spiritual transformation, we can certainly see the importance of training:

- Paul spoke of training ourselves to be godly (see 1 Timothy 4:7).
- The writer to Hebrews emphasized that constant use and practice leads to being trained (see Hebrews 5:14).
- Paul wrote that the Scriptures provide the primary means for training in righteousness, which equips us to do "every good work" (see 2 Timothy 3:16-17).

Becoming godly is very different from trying to be godly. Trying to be godly doesn't work—training does. I could challenge my church members to run seven miles. First I would deliver an inspirational message to fire them up, and they'd be brimming over with a desire to run the seven miles. We would then gather in front of the church and run together in order to encourage one another. But almost no one would be able to run the seven miles. Many would make courageous efforts to extend themselves to reach the goal, but the first-aid station and recovery tent would be filled with the injured and the sick. A few people would make it, and their success wouldn't depend on age or strength. Those who finished would be the ones who already ran as a way of life.

Let's change just one part of the scene. If the entire church started *training* to run seven miles, within a few months most of them would at least be able to speed-walk the distance.

Trying to be godly without training to become godly would be just as injurious to the spirit as trying to run seven miles without training would be to the body. Simply put, we must practice the spiritual disciplines that form pathways to the heart of God and transform us into godly people. Training—not trying—is the key.

Training changes our perspective. The distinction between trying and training is revolutionary. We often resist effort and discipline because it seems like an external effort to gain an internal change. But we can change that perspective. Don't think of training as straining to make something happen. Instead just do what God prescribes, and leave what happens up to him.

CONCLUSION

The key to inner transformation is to make the spiritual disciplines habits. Being trained is a product of practice. These habits mystically change the composition of our souls. Prayer, solitude, and fasting can break the chains of lust or sexual perversion. The discipline of worship can release us from constant preoccupation with ourselves. Keeping a prayer journal can replace depression and bitterness with joy and forgiveness. The practice of the disciplines involves submission of the body,[18] submission of the will, and the consistent submission of life's appetites to the lordship of Christ.

Spiritual disciplines aren't about information, but about the formation of our spirits and the attitudes and actions that rise from exercising these disciplines. We practice them until they become second nature, until we enjoy God's presence more than TV or an evening with friends.

Throughout history, followers of Jesus have practiced spiritual disciplines. They're simply an extension of the practices Jesus and his earliest followers carried out. As with calisthenics, the effect of these habits is indirect. While practicing these activities falls within our power, God does something mystical with them: he enables us to accomplish what we can't do with direct effort.

SUGGESTED RESOURCES

The Message of Galatians: Only One Way and *The Message of Romans: God's Good News for the World* by John R. W. Stott (InterVarsity, 1988 and 2001, respectively). Look for Stott's excellent treatment on Galatians 2:20 and related texts in Romans dealing with the flesh, the new person, and transformation.

Renovation of the Heart by Dallas Willard (NavPress, 2002). One of the great thinkers of our time provides a complete treatment of transformation.

Celebration of Discipline by Richard Foster (HarperSanFrancisco, 1998). A classic approach to the traditional disciplines that champions reading the works of ancient Christianity.

Spiritual Disciplines for the Christian Life by Donald S. Whitney (NavPress, 1994). Whitney ably mainstreams spiritual disciplines into evangelical life.

The Spirit of the Disciplines by Dallas Willard (HarperSanFrancisco, 1991). This is my favorite. It's balanced and presents the case in penetrating statements that are hard to ignore or gloss over.

PERSONAL APPROACHES TO DISCIPLE-MAKING

I had seven basketball coaches from ages thirteen to twenty-seven. Each one contributed to my life, but my high school coach had the most impact. He gave me responsibility and great encouragement. Mostly he just believed in me, and he let other people know he believed in me. He helped me decide what college to attend and stayed interested in me through my college career. I felt so affirmed by him that I would have done almost anything he asked.

A coach and an athlete provide a good illustration of the importance of a personal approach to disciple-making. We can be and make disciples in a lot of different ways, including everything from sermons on Sundays to softball on Saturdays, but let's look at the core dimensions of discipleship. In this chapter, we'll look at those personal, or one-to-one, ways of being and making disciples.[1] In chapter 9, we'll look at how small groups facilitate discipleship. And in chapter 10, we'll explore the role of congregation and community in discipleship.

The Personal Dimension

Perhaps the first thing we think of when it comes to discipleship is one-on-one interaction. Organizations like The Navigators established this image in the evangelical mind. Until the 1950s, the evangelical and mainstream church did most of their spiritual development in groups, such as in Sunday school classes, worship services, retreats, and special conferences. If an individual received special attention, it occurred primarily through counseling or casual friendships. While leaders, teachers, pastors, and faithful disciples of all kinds have invested in one-on-one discipling relationships for fifty years, postmodern minds now consider this formal approach to spiritual formation passé.

By formal, I mean segmented and sequential. As discussed earlier, *segmented* means a planned training time for people at certain stages of spiritual maturity, while *sequential* means graduating from one level of development to another. Although people who'd describe themselves as postmodern continue to experience gravity, aging, and the changes of seasons, they're generally not friendly to structure in the spiritual realm. The emergent generation thinks in terms of relationships rather than formal teaching arrangements.

The only thing permanent is change, and in the twenty-first century, change seems to come at us faster than we can imagine. Of course, God is unchanging, and so is our need for personal human attention. So let's look at how this personal dimension connects to discipleship in three basic ways: coaching, mentoring, and spiritual direction.

Coaching: Skills and Task

In the 1980s and 1990s, many writers and trainers discovered a new "philosophical planet": A good leader often serves as a coach.

This perspective became popular among secular consultants, and in due time spilled over into Christian circles. Of course, anyone who has played sports at any level already has experienced this to some degree. But for the record, the first time I ever read someone compare a pastor to a coach was in a work by Elton Trueblood:

> Some are now coming to believe that the least inadequate or distorting term for a spiritual leader in a congregation is "coach." The word has overtones which modern man comprehends very well, indeed. Furthermore, the image of the coach is one which can be universally honored by young and old alike. . . . The glory of the coach is that of being the discoverer, the developer, and the trainer of the powers of other men. This is exactly what we mean when we use the biblical terminology about the equipping ministry. . . . Since the equipping minister must not be above the heart of the battle, he is, ideally, not only the coach, but a "playing coach," sometimes carrying the ball himself and sometimes seeing to it that another carries it.[2]

A Coaching Primer

Think about what coaches do. Most coaches begin as players of a game, and at a natural transition point, they begin to play less and coach more. In sports, a time comes when a coach no longer can play the game at the level she once played at.

In other realms of life, being a player-coach can be a lifelong experience. In these areas, the player-coach employs mental and emotional skills rather than physical skills. Because of his experience, manner of teaching, and care for the player, the coach becomes a credible voice. Perhaps the most important connection between a player and a coach is emotional; they experience the mutual benefit of relationship. The connection grows strong with success, which leads to celebration and trust.

Robert Clinton, an associate professor at Fuller Seminary, and Paul Stanley, international vice president of The Navigators, define coaching this way: "Coaching is a process of imparting encouragement and skills to succeed in a task through relationship."[3] These authors also list several characteristics of coaching.

Coaching involves a relational process in which the coach, who knows how to do something well, imparts skills to a follower, who wants to learn those skills. Often organizations and corporations assign coaches to young executives to teach them a new job or help them navigate through the tumultuous waters of leadership.

Ideally coaching takes place on the job and in person. However, coaching increasingly takes place over the telephone or on the Internet. Because this electronic method is much less relational, the coaching is usually very specific to a skill or task. In fact, that's what distinguishes coaching from mentoring or spiritual direction: coaching focuses on skills, is specific, and has a starting and ending point.

I've had younger leaders ask me to coach them in writing, in developing disciple-making infrastructures, in leading a church through change, and in spiritual direction. I enjoy these relationships and also enjoy contributing in areas where I'm strong. But no one has asked me to help with organizational theory, financial management, counseling, or other areas where I'm less equipped.

The Coach's Function

Why would a disciple need a coach? Clinton and Stanley list the following as the main functions of coaches:

- to impart skills
- to impart confidence
- to motivate people in order to bring out the best

- to model the importance of learning the basics of a skill
- to point people to other resources
- to observe people in action
- to evaluate people's experience and give them feedback[4]

If you have the right skills to match a person's needs (or if you're seeking a coach and you find someone with the right skills to match your needs), it makes sense to move ahead into a coaching relationship.

The Ten Commandments of Coaching

The coach and the individual being coached need to agree on some basic principles to guide their relationship. Again, I turn to Clinton and Stanley, and adapt their Ten Commandments of Coaching:

1. Establish the mentoring relationship.
2. Jointly agree on the purpose of the relationship.
3. Determine how often you'll interact.
4. Determine how you'll handle accountability.
5. Set up ways to communicate during your meetings and between meetings.
6. Clarify the level of confidentiality you'll maintain.
7. Set the starting and ending points of the coaching relationship.
8. Determine how and how often you'll evaluate the relationship.
9. Clarify and modify expectations to fit how the relationship will occur in real life.
10. Bring closure to the mentoring relationship when you reach the agreed-upon ending point.[5]

Coaching can be an effective approach for a one-to-one discipleship relationship. In many ways, the apostle Paul served as Timothy's coach. He encouraged and trusted Timothy to

- command, teach, set an example, preach, and teach (1 Timothy 4:11-13)
- flee from the love of money; pursue righteousness, godliness, faith, love, endurance, and gentleness; fight for the faith (6:10-12)
- use God-given gifts; speak and live with power, love, and self-discipline (2 Timothy 1:6-7)
- be strong, pass on the teaching, endure hardship (2:1-3)

Paul certainly worked to impart his own skills—as well as his attitude about life and his commitment to the gospel—to his younger student. He served as a coach to develop Timothy's own skills and to equip him to lead.

MENTORING:
BECOMING A PERSON

At first glance, coaching and mentoring seem to be two words that describe the same process. Yet the difference is meaningful. While coaching focuses on skills and equipping, mentoring helps others make sense of their lives. More specifically, spiritual mentoring helps an individual gain awareness of his personhood as he lives under God. A godly mentor can help us emerge from the limits of self-fulfillment and narcissism to discover the joy of living for others. James Houston, professor of spiritual theology at Regent College, writes,

> Becoming a Christian is a demolition of one's identity from the ruins of self-enclosure as being individualistic—literally "in-human"—whereas to be human is to be a social

being. Instead, one becomes more "open," not only to other people, but also to become radically reconstituted as a "person-in-Christ."[6]

I find these words riveting because they nail down some important thoughts about the battle between self-centeredness and Christlikeness. We all battle to break free from the clinging and clawing hands of self. As an anonymous writer put it, "Without God, not even people are interesting." We become interesting when we begin to live out God's dream for us—when we become a person for others.

What characterizes mentoring? I like the story of a true historical relationship between the French royal tutor Francois Fenelon and the Duke of Burgundy, eldest grandson of King Louis XIV and heir to the French throne. Fenelon's assignment was mentoring the young duke.

> From age six to fourteen years old . . . Fenelon has a tough and dangerous task to perform. The duke was an *enfant terrible*. Saint-Simon observed, "He was so impetuous as to desire to break the clocks when they struck the hour summoning him to do something he did not like, and fell into the most extraordinary fury against the rain when it interfered with his desire. Opposition threw him into a passion." In other words, he was a child autocrat like his grandfather, another Ulyssean figure. Yet by the time Fenelon had completed his mentoring duties eight years later, the duke had become gentle, patient, wise beyond his fourteen years, and Fenelon's friend for life.[7]

This example illuminates the essence of the role of a mentor. A mentor influences a self-absorbed person, whose self-fulfillment lies at the center of all things, to live as a balanced social being under the authority of God. A mentor helps the individual she mentors become indifferent to fame and influence, and independent from the temptation to rewrite even God's story to be about self.

While coaching requires the coach to be competent in specific skills, mentoring focuses on the mentor's character. At its heart, mentoring involves the transformation of a person's soul. This radical change means the mentor has the same effect on a person and in the same way that Jesus did. Mentoring leads the mentoree to be free from self-reliance and a self-sufficient spirit.[8]

Mentoring is closer to the core meaning of discipleship, because discipleship is about one person following another and becoming like that person. Let's dig a little deeper into what mentoring accomplishes in the process of discipleship.

Mentored to Be a New Person in Christ

Mentors help their friends avoid what philosopher and theologian Søren Kierkegaard called the "sickness unto death." *Sickness* is the right word for people missing God's purpose for their life. Kierkegaard referred to it as being confronted with God's grace and then turning away from it. In fact, this is the tragedy of non-discipleship Christianity: people who profess conversion but don't act in faith.

Only God can create personhood. Only he can help disciples discover how they fit into the total scheme of things. When we look into the starry night and ponder how small and insignificant we are, only God can rescue us from despairing thoughts and raise our value with his specific purpose. God uses mentors to help disciples realize how important we are "in Christ." Again Houston provides direction for the mentored life, citing five insights that spiritual mentorees need to be aware of:

1. Christ's disciples don't choose him; he calls them.
2. Jesus' call is inclusive, for all of us are sinners.

3. Discipleship means a radical reorientation of our existence. It means giving up everything to "follow Jesus."
4. We share in the ministry of Jesus to heal the sick, to give to the poor, and to live in light of God's kingdom.
5. Above all, we express to others Christ's love, just as he does for us.[9]

Mentored by God's Word

Kierkegaard provides mentors and disciples guidance on how to relate to the Scriptures. To really appreciate Kierkegaard, we need to remember that he was a pest and irritant to the Danish church. He called them to practice what they preached and then to preach what they practiced.

Although Kierkegaard often leaned toward complexity, he approached how disciples should engage God's Word in a simple and practical way. Transformational faith begins, he thought, with a truly alive and vibrant relationship of the disciple to the Scriptures. The following guidelines have so much life in them because he wanted the Scriptures to live. If we take this kind of attitude and approach, transformation most certainly occurs.

- Be "alone with God's Word." Don't allow commentaries to get in the way of the text itself.
- Create silence for God's Word. Otherwise you can forget that it is God's Word or not hear it above the "noises" of your own cultural dispositions.
- Regard Scripture as the mirror you look into and respond as you see yourself as a sinner.
- Read Scripture contritely, humbly, and open to God's message.
- Read it responsively, with the intention to act on it and "do the truth."

- Allow the biblical narrative to draw you into its storytelling.
- Appropriate personally the message of God's Word for yourself.
- Read Scripture hopefully, believing "all things" are possible for God.[10]

Kierkegaard's guidelines remind me of Karl Barth's well-known statement: "I have read many books, but the Bible reads me." In a way, we submit to God's Word. We see it as much more than a textbook. Even more remote should be the view that we study the Scriptures to inform others — to blast them with volumes of holy facts about God. Instead it is a book that God speaks through right now. Being discipled through God's Word involves first seeing it as God's living truth that we must hear and do.

I love words. I love study. I love the richness and depth of Scripture. But I also know the emptiness of knowledge without transformation. It's not our goal to simply master the facts of the Bible. That knowledge would probably lead to pride, a danger the apostle Paul warned against: "Knowledge puffs up" (1 Corinthians 8:1). God has a way of letting the air out of us when we get puffed up with knowledge about Scripture.

Mentored for Worship in Community

In the context of mentoring, I define worship as a corporate gathering of believers who thank and praise God and also expect to hear from him. Worship offers a form of self-denial: In worship I remove myself from the center of things. Perhaps no greater challenge exists for most of us than to make a worship experience about God rather than about us. We seem to have a propensity to think of worship as meeting our needs. But that's not worship — it's idolatry.

As two women left a worship service, one complained, "I didn't really care for that."

Her friend had a spunky reply: "Good, because we weren't worshiping you."

The only thing that matters about our worship is that God cares for it. While we might have different personal tastes in terms of worship style, the truth is that an appetite for communal worship must possess a growing selflessness. Houston describes why the corporate nature of worship is so vital:

> There is another element in Christian worship: it is communality. Worship is what befits all the people of God, who together acclaim, "Our Father." Individualism has no place at the Lord's table. It is a characteristic our Lord condemned in the disciples at the Last Supper. Likewise, the apostle Paul chided the Corinthians for their so-called "love feasts," based on their carnal way of life. Their self-indulgent, self-centered, self-referential focus was in utter contrast to the self-giving love and humility of Christ himself. Likewise, he rebuked the Galatians for being conceited, competitive, and envious of each other. Clearly, such situations inhibited any possible communality, not to mention eliminating gratitude to the Savior and Lord.[11]

Worship becomes a key part of discipleship because, in worship, we break ourselves of the habit of interpreting all events in God's story as centered in ourselves. We learn to think of ourselves as participants, as supporting cast, as servants who focus on the drama's main character: the triune God we serve.

Many disciples automatically understand that worship isn't just a commodity to be consumed. They "go to church" though they might be arrested, imprisoned, tortured, or lose their job. Even worse, their family could be punished for their crime. Although these stories seem far away and almost mythical to many of us, they take place daily around the world. These believers understand the cost of worship in community. For them, worshiping alone isn't enough. They must be with others because the otherness of worship makes it Christian. They understand the interdependent nature of Christian faith and how they absolutely need community.

I feel most saddened by how most of us Americans treat worship, as if it were a product we consume. Someone once asked Eugene Peterson, "What's the single most important act of the Christian that could do the most good for the church in America?" After a thoughtful pause, Peterson answered, "Go to the church nearest your home, shut up, and like it."[12]

When we see worship as a product to consume, we practice a form of idolatry. We turn worship into a self-conscious exercise in self-indulgence. How many times have we stood in worship wondering, "Should I raise my hands? What will people think?" And how many times have we had other thoughts related to feelings: Do I feel warm? Am I moved emotionally? Why don't we sing more songs I know? Why do we need to stand for so long? Why is the music too loud, too fast, too slow, too old?

Can the American church stop shopping and start serving?

Yes. This is where a mentor comes in to help a friend be free of such cultural shackles. A mentor somehow reminds a disciple that worship is about otherness—a God who is other and other followers of Jesus who want to understand how he contributes to their lives. Worship is a selfless act. That's why it becomes the apex of discipleship. James Houston said, "We are discipled above all to live selflessly."[13]

I'm not aware of any six- or eight-step list to become a selfless worshipper, and I'll resist the temptation to create one. Let's recap what mentoring or discipling a person entails:

- First, mentoring means helping another person enter into the true meaning of personhood, that is, live out God's dream for her in society.

- Second, mentoring means moving into an existential, right-now relationship to God's Word. We read God's Word, we let it "read" us, and then we do what it tells us.
- Third, mentoring means living in community and participating selflessly in its most profound act: worshiping God together. In worship, we can display our utter dependence and God's absolute competence; only then can worship become God-centered and not self-worship.

SPIRITUAL DIRECTION: SPECIFIC SOUL CARE

Do we have room in our thinking for yet another approach — spiritual direction? Spiritual direction, an ancient and the most Catholic of the discipleship methods, was born during the monastic movement of the fourth century. In a single sentence, Dallas Willard encapsulates its history: "Spiritual direction was understood by Jesus, taught by Paul, obeyed by the early church, followed with excesses in the medieval church, narrowed by the Reformers, recaptured by the Puritans, and virtually lost in the modern church."[14]

I see the primary distinctive of spiritual direction as one person helping another person work out his spiritual walk in very specific applications unique to that person. Bruce Demarest, a professor at Denver Seminary, defines spiritual direction this way: "Spiritual direction refers to the structured ministry in which a gifted and experienced Christian, called a spiritual director, helps another believer grow in relationship with and obedience to Christ."[15]

Many people leave a church service with unanswered questions that require time and experience to answer. Houston notes, "The emotional education of our inner lives does not have much priority in today's church."[16] Demarest writes,

Soul-care searches out hindrances to prayer, obstacles to intimacy with Christ, and responsiveness to the Spirit's leading. Spiritual helpers allow the life of Christ in them to flow into other Christians to bless, empower, and release the good seed of faith and love. Some discipleship programs strive to form the Christian from the outside in. Soul care, on the other hand, seeks to form the life from the inside out.[17]

Characteristics of a Spiritual Director

Demarest succinctly captures the qualities a spiritual director should possess. He or she must be

- a person of vital Christian faith
- a possessor of needed knowledge in theology and the spiritual classics
- an individual who is seasoned in ministry
- a person of loving concern
- a person who possesses discernment
- someone who has experienced some suffering and failure[18]

Distinctives of Spiritual Direction

All three areas of personal interaction for discipleship—spiritual direction, mentoring, and coaching—touch each other like food on a plate. One of the main differences is the origin of the leader's resource material. A spiritual director has chosen to read the ancient masters and drink from the deep well of the monastic tradition. She has likely also made a commitment to learn from that tradition how to practice spiritual disciplines. The church today possesses a two-thousand-year-old treasury of devotional and spiritual writings that spiritual directors willingly tap into.

C. S. Lewis loved the classics and was a fan of old books. For him, choosing between an old and a new book was no contest. "The new book is still on trial," he wrote. "It has to be tested against a great body of Christian thought down through the ages."[19] Here are some of the masters and a primary set of writings by each one:

- Athanasius, Eastern Father (died in 373): *On the Incarnation*
- Saint Augustine, Western Father (died in 430): *Confessions*
- Julian of Norwich, Catholic (died in 1413): *Revelations of Divine Love*
- Thomas à Kempis, Catholic (died in 1471): *The Imitation of Christ*
- Lancelot Andrews, Anglican (died in 1626): *Private Devotions*
- François Fenelon, Catholic (died in 1715): *Christian Perfection*

Choosing a Spiritual Director

With spiritual direction, what you choose to read is important, as is choosing the person who'll give you direction. You'll likely choose a person who also has a background in the traditions of spiritual direction, spiritual formation, and the classic writers. Often evangelical Christians can't find someone like this. Many have found a solution by entering monasteries for a brief period to learn the benefits of disciplines such as contemplative prayer, fasting, reflection, silence, and solitude. Very few mainstream evangelicals saturate themselves in Saint Benedict's ladder of humility or Teresa of Avila's *Interior Castle*.

Spiritual direction is typically less directive than coaching or mentoring. By design, it helps a person find his own pathway that will help free him from the sins and habits that so easily entangle.

CONCLUSION

As an analogy from the twentieth century, coaching has very modern roots. It involves developing skills and equipping leaders for a task. Mentoring springs from an ancient foundation, and has been more popular among Protestants. It means helping people become disciples who serve others through their relationship to society, to the Word of God, and to worship. Spiritual direction is ancient and Catholic—born during the monastic movement of the fourth century. Spiritual directors serve as guides, helping people in their walks with God.

All three of these one-on-one approaches hold appropriate places in the disciple-making toolbox. Who the disciple is and how that individual learns will often determine which approach works best.

SUGGESTED RESOURCES

COACHING

Connecting: The Mentoring Relationships You Need to Succeed in Life by Paul D. Stanley and J. Robert Clinton (NavPress, 1992).

MENTORING

The Mentored Life: From Individualism to Personhood by James M. Houston (NavPress, 2002).

Let Your Life Speak: Listening for the Voice of Vocation by Parker J. Palmer (Jossey-Bass, 1999).

THE MASTERS

SPIRITUAL DIRECTION

Satisfy Your Soul: Restoring the Heart of Christian Spirituality by Bruce Demarest (NavPress, 1999).

Listening to God: Spiritual Formation in Congregations by John Ackerman (The Alban Institute, 2001).

In the Name of Jesus: Reflections on Christian Leadership by Henri Nouwen (Crossroad, 1993).

The following books provide a sampling of many of the masters listed in this chapter: *Devotional Classics: Selected Readings for Individuals and Groups* by Richard J. Foster (HarperSanFrancisco, 1998); *A Guide to Prayer for Ministers and Other Servants* by Reuben Job and Norman Shawchuck (Upper Room, 1983).

THE ROLE OF SMALL GROUPS IN DISCIPLESHIP

I have a friend who stays away from small groups in churches because he feels that he's been burned. He and his wife have been in groups they loved and groups they hated. Amazingly, once this love-hate situation occurred with the same core group of people.

The small group started with one older couple leading. These leaders unselfishly and tirelessly loved and ministered to the group members. They did a lot of things right: mostly making sure they focused on the members' spiritual growth. My friend loved this group.

But when those leaders retired and moved away, another couple from the group stepped in to lead. At first, things seemed okay. But instead of focusing on the members' spiritual growth, these leaders majored on the mechanics of the group: how meetings ran, who brought the coffee, whether or not assignments got done, what kind of outreach the group would do. My friend hated it then.

The reality is that both leaders did some things right and some things wrong. Imagine a small-group setting where the leaders focused on group members' spiritual lives and at the same time used the structure of the group to further enhance the way group members grew. In this chapter, I'd like to be preemptive and look at how small groups function best and how they fill a vital role in discipleship.

By the way, in this chapter I often address the role of small-group leaders. But that doesn't mean you should skip to the next chapter if you're not a leader. Instead, as you read, think through what kind of group member you are or would like to be. How do you support your small group leader? What would it take for you to step up your commitment to the next level and consider leading a small group?

Starting groups is easier than maintaining them. How you start a group determines whether you can maintain it. Healthy groups don't even find their stride at six meetings. Perhaps they become pretty effective at around six months, or their twenty-fifth meeting. Of course, the popular trend to make groups forty days long makes maintenance a moot issue. Almost anyone can keep something going for forty days, but making it work longer takes some skill. People will usually find the expedient more attractive than the difficult.

To be fair, much good has come from the forty-day approach. It whets the spiritual appetite of many docile believers, and I support anything that gets spiritual glands salivating. To be just as fair, I'm disappointed by the lack of ongoing ministry after forty-day groups. Though the advertising for these programs gives the impression that they cause long-term change, I'd guess that is the exception rather than the norm.

Until this fashionable cycle ends, talking about long-term groups will have limited appeal. My hope is that the forty-day mania will end up being the very catalyst of more extensive small-group discipleship.

If you plan to start groups that last just forty days once a year, you don't need to read on. Skip this chapter. If you're still with me, let's consider some basic principles for getting long-term small groups started.

PRINCIPLES FOR STARTING GROUPS

If church leaders want effective platoons of determined believers working together to reach their networks for Christ, small groups are the way. If they want a system that finds and equips other leaders, small groups are the way. If they want to provide the best forum for creating the community necessary for accountability, small groups are the way.

Establish a Beachhead

If you're the leader of a small-group ministry—a pastor, staff member, or lay person charged with the task—how do you get started? First establish a beachhead—a pilot small group composed of potential small-group leaders. You'll lead this group in the way you want them to lead others. The key is choosing the right potential leaders and knowing what kind of group you want to start.

However you select your group, focus on choosing people with willing hearts, teachable spirits, and a desire to identify with your church's (or other ministry group's) philosophy of ministry. Look for people who have the time, interest, and gifts to lead.

Orientation

Next invite the potential leaders to your home or a comfortable setting to hear what you're planning. Explain why you've invited them. Let them know why you think they are the best choices.

Then present the vision you have for small groups, and talk about the value of leading and influencing others. Challenge this group to pray about being involved in launching and leading groups that will eventually multiply and help hundreds or thousands. Assure these potential leaders that you'll spend the next several months together, and when that time is over, they'll be prepared to lead others.

The Prototype

Again, the group you've gathered serves as a prototype group where the apprentice leaders will learn skills essential to small-group success. In this group, you'll model everything from directing a Bible discussion to leading prayer, from drawing out needs to building community. The pilot-group members will also learn hands-on as they take turns leading the group. They'll also team together in evangelistic outreaches.

As a group, you'll hold each other accountable for various projects, and you'll help each other during difficult assignments. These shared experiences raise the chance of the group's success; there's no substitute for learning through participation.

Customize the Group

Restaurants often invite customers to "build a breakfast," customizing their meals with various items from the breakfast menu. Try this in your small-group setting as well. Rather than locking into a set of materials or a program before you select group participants, customize it to fit the interests and needs of the group.

TYPES OF SMALL GROUPS

Your pilot group will be most successful if you develop a set of principles that guide it. The type of group you want to create will determine the principles your group agrees on. You might choose from the following types or create a hybrid from two or more. Any of these types of groups can work, as long as you build a group that meets the primary objective of keeping people growing into the image of Christ.

The preamble to building any group must be *knowing the objective*. And the primary objective of every group must include mission. Most groups implode because they make their mission too small. A group that reaches only into itself becomes self-indulgent and insulated. Small groups should also have secondary objectives, such as training people to witness, studying the Bible, understanding biblical teaching on finance, supporting those in crisis, or reaching out to the poor.

Covenant Groups

These open groups are low in commitment and last from six to twelve weeks. They provide a way to introduce people to the small-group experience. Group members don't need to complete assignments, and anyone can come regardless of when they start, even until the last couple of weeks.

Support Groups

These groups focus on addressing specific issues that hinder people's spiritual growth. Because they require some intimacy, they often operate as closed groups (see "Open and Closed Groups" below). But some of these groups do find a way to stay open to anyone who needs the kind of support the group offers.

Basic Accountability Groups

These groups usually require about a yearlong commitment. They help members establish good habits in the practice of the spiritual disciplines. Generally, everyone agrees to the basics of the group commitment in these closed groups.

Ongoing Accountability Groups

These closed groups agree to work together year after year, a year at a time. The members have completed a year in a basic accountability group. The key to keeping these groups healthy is sending out members who start other groups. Otherwise they tend to collapse under the weight of their own unused knowledge.[1]

Open and Closed Groups

Eventually you'll face the question of whether your small group should be open or closed. In open groups, anyone can come at any time. These intentionally try to reach new members. Closed groups, on the other hand, don't accept new people after the mission is stated and the members are securely in place.

Several years ago, the Fuller Church Growth Institute conducted a study on the effectiveness of open and closed groups. The study divided a large number of pastors into two groups. All pastors in group A consolidated their adult Sunday school classes, and group B kept multiple classes in place. After a certain length of time, attendance in the consolidated groups declined, while the number of each separated group multiplied.

Years earlier, Richard Myers of the Church Federation of Greater Indianapolis established this principle, which was documented in the American Baptist filmstrip, *Let's Face It*. Myers' Law can be stated like this: "The church grows both in number and in meaningfulness to its members as the number of face-to-face groups increase."[2] In other words, churches don't grow by getting more people into the same class or small group; they grow by adding more classes or small groups.

We see two important lessons here: First, a church will grow *numerically* as it increases the number of its outreach or open groups, because a proactive and intentional open group will naturally reach outsiders. Second, a church or ministry will grow *spiritually* as it increases the number of its closed groups.

Open groups, such as those modeled by megachurches, provide unlimited possibilities for growth. Growth experts who advocate open groups do so because open groups accomplish outreach and numerical growth better than closed groups. I agree that churches should have some open small groups in order to attract and assimilate people who are seeking. But I see open groups as playing a supporting role to the closed. The long-range goal of Christians gathering in small groups should be discipleship rather than evangelism. In fact, evangelism will result from proper discipleship. The lack of passion for the Great Commission comes from a lack of character—a lack of spiritual depth—rather than a lack of strategic vehicles for reaching others.

The closed group works best to develop disciples spiritually, primarily for two reasons:

1. *An open group can't provide the necessary structure and accountability.* Open groups often lead to large numbers of untrained and undisciplined people who think they are trained. In a closed group, the members commit to specifics such as time frame, skill development, and outreach. Everyone shares the learning experience at the same time. They learn to entrust themselves to one another.

2. *Closed groups provide an atmosphere for practicing spiritual disciplines.* A strong small-group structure is crucial in the early stages of developing spiritual disciplines, which are a vital part of learning to connect with God. One reason so many people bear so little fruit stems from their lack of experience in sustained, disciplined living. They're not free to engage God because the appetites of the flesh still reign in their daily life.

People who graduate from a closed group can more effectively lead either open or closed groups, because those steeped in the disciplines can teach those who are less experienced. Open groups, which are populated by Christians at various places in their spiritual pilgrimage, need a highly skilled leader who can monitor and lead them.

When churches offer only open groups, with people at various spiritual levels gathering in the same groups, mediocrity will result. It's like throwing everyone in the shallow end of the swimming pool; everyone thinks that staying there is normal. A few might venture into the deep end. Some might learn the backstroke or the breaststroke. Some might even start diving off the edge of the pool or from a diving board. But most will stay in the shallow end, where swimming is easy and comfortable.

Offering just one type of open group, where everyone stays in the shallow end, eventually leads to self-directed spirituality—spirituality defined as "meeting my own needs." Self-directed spiritual development is a lousy idea; it skirts the real issue in maturity: submitting to others in the body of Christ.

Instead we need groups that step up commitment as time goes on. Groups need to challenge their members to do things that are uncomfortable, because that leads them to the spiritual maturity they desire.

Basic Principles for Every Group

Once you've established a clear objective and determined to establish groups that will foster spiritual growth, work to incorporate the following basic principles into the life of your groups.

Be Intentional

Small-group leaders need to avoid the trap of promising more than they can deliver. Rather than telling group members that they'll become biblical examples of mature disciples by joining a group, let them know that if they keep their commitments and give themselves to the process, they'll experience a depth of relationship with Christ that will spur them on for the rest of their lives. Assure them that they'll learn a process that will sustain them if they continue it after leaving the group.

Provide Structure

While a group's statement of purpose provides a basic foundation, a covenant that group members agree to will provide solid structure. A covenant speaks about specific expectations, such as attendance, participation, and arriving on time. I believe that one of the basic tenets of successful spiritual progress is showing up on time. It displays an attitude of readiness and respect for others in the group. Character results from the accumulation of habits, and developing good habits takes place through repeated action. A solid structure helps group members develop good habits and reach their goals.

Strive for Intimacy

A group has just a few weeks to transform itself from being based on a structural foundation to being based on love and support. The group's covenant works only to the extent that people establish relationships and bond to one another. Love and support provide the strongest form of accountability. Intimacy creates a safety that permits people to lower their defenses and be authentic. Only then can people deal with their obstacles, such as the sins that keep defeating them.

The most important moment in spiritual warfare is when I make others aware of my most closely-held wounds and sins. In this environment, what the apostle Paul admonished can take place: "Warn those who are idle, encourage the timid, help the weak, be patient with everyone" (1 Thessalonians 5:14).

Insist on Outreach

Every small group needs a mission outside itself. Christ was a man for others, and disciples should be people for others. If a group's world doesn't extend outside itself, the resulting selfish attitude can actually be destructive to the group members' faith. This kind of group will be self-absorbed and will eventually implode. Without outreach, Bible study becomes academic, prayer turns stale, and fellowship becomes superficial.

Outreach provides a catalyst for spiritual development. Groups should include it in their covenant and, more importantly, in the group's soul. Jesus taught that reaching out to others is essential to meeting our own needs. If we want to find our purpose, we must deny self. This biblical truth is fundamental to discipleship. We say no to self in order to say yes to God. The same holds true for small groups; the only difference is that we say yes corporately.

Commit to Reproduce

Through a carefully managed apprenticeship system, groups can expand quickly and with integrity. Healthy Christians reproduce, healthy churches and ministries reproduce, and healthy small groups reproduce. This principle of reproduction can permeate an entire small-group network.

However, groups won't reproduce if the expectation to do so is absent. Members of the group need a vision for reproducing and they need the will for it. If the desire to reproduce isn't in a small group's DNA, they'll delay reproduction and even resent it. An easy way to place the expectation to reproduce within a group is to designate a start and end date for the group's existence. Time frames that fit the group's mission will benefit everyone. Some groups can fulfill their mission in six weeks, some in six months, and others in two years.

Healthy small groups combine every element necessary for growing healthy and reproducing disciples. They offer spiritual nurture and support, ministry skill development, accountability, training in outreach, long-term relationships, and worship. They develop leadership skills and provide the best people-gathering instrument the church possesses. Small groups within a church provide the emotional nerve center of the congregation. Most members call their small group "home." The small group provides the best forum for creating community and the optimum environment for making disciples.

PERSONAL PREPARATION FOR STARTING GROUPS

Before you embark on starting small groups, the primal urge must be pulsating in your soul. Only the Holy Spirit can implant this urge in you. You really must want to do this, because you'll be tested anytime you lead people on a journey. Even when they want to take the trip, you can be sure they'll challenge the process. Seek to hear God's voice and know that your faith community is ready spiritually.

You'll need a clock, a calendar, and a compass. The clock tells you what time it is right now. The calendar tells you how long it will take you to get to your destination. And the compass will guide you as you go.

It's imperative that you spend time in prayer and research to develop a plan before approaching others. By plan, I don't mean some impressive strategic plan that will eventually gather dust on all the recipient's bookshelves. Instead your plan might look something like this:

> I want to help people walk more meaningfully with God, to be fully invested in the life of discipleship. I think it will take two years using the curriculum I've chosen. I need five people to start on this journey with me. I have an objective, a process, and a time frame in mind. I'll ask potential participants to be a part of the process, and before they commit, they'll understand why, what, and how long.

More information than this usually is counterproductive and becomes fodder for disagreement.

As Steven Covey wrote years ago in *The Seven Habits of Highly Effective People*, "A leader begins with the end in mind." A leader can't pass the responsibility for this on to someone else; you can delegate the mechanics of small group life, but it's your task to communicate and maintain the vision. People will hear the passion in the leader's voice, see the determined look in the leader's eyes, and measure the effort in the leader's actions. The leader must make the small-group effort personal, and that means participation. The most powerful aspect of leading is modeling. Anything less and small groups won't become integral to the life of the congregation, because the leader doesn't embody the values.

VARIOUS START-UP METHODS

Earlier I mentioned that how you start groups determines whether you can maintain them. Similarly, the amount of time you spend starting a group should be directly proportional to how long you want the group to last.

Develop a Master Group

When you've selected individuals to "practice" the small-group experience as they grow into leaders, you can generally shorten the life of this master group to about one-fourth the time that the actual groups will last. In other words, if you ultimately create groups that will last for two years, expect the model group to meet for six months. If the eventual groups will last one year, make the model three months.

For longer groups, you need to provide enough time for people to get the idea. Long-term groups have a higher threshold for skill and philosophical understanding. Leaders need time to experience the various challenges they'll face in groups with longer commitments.

If you shorten the eventual group's life to twelve weeks or less, you can just model that length. In other words, if the group will last twelve weeks, then model it in the master group for twelve weeks. If the group will last just six weeks, model it for six weeks. If the groups will consist of intensive weekends, have your master group meet for a weekend.

Whether the groups you ultimately form are short-term or long-term, be sure your master group members have a chance to touch on all the important elements that will make the group work. You want to make sure they are ready and will duplicate or multiply what was intended in the first place.

Once the master-group members form their own groups, the next step is to meet regularly with the group leaders. Typically the longer the groups continue, the more sophisticated the organizational structure needs to be.[3]

Use the Quick-Start Approach

One way to launch groups is the popular quick-start approach. While this has some limitations, it does have brevity on its side. Generally this method begins with a weekend retreat or seminar during which potential leaders volunteer to lead groups. These leaders get an overview of the materials they'll use, and then they start the groups. The underlying philosophy of this approach says, "We have many people who are already capable of leading others. With a little help and good materials, they can do it."

Groups started this way can function well for short periods. However, sometimes the leaders lack depth and experience. This method carries a higher risk than the master-group approach, but if managed well, it can work. The master-group approach often moves more slowly, but it leads to more solid transformation. The quick-start works well in churches experiencing rapid growth, where the groups serve as assimilators. The established culture is one of quickness and change, so these groups don't have time to stagnate.

Inspire and Hand Out Materials

This is probably the least effective way to start small groups, but it has some merit. A lot of great materials on the market almost teach themselves. Many include a video training component. A pastor or ministry leader pulls together other interested leaders, lays out the small-group plan, and hands out materials to the leaders who desire to go forward with starting a group. The management of the groups is simple: the church arranges for people to sign up for groups and then appoints leaders.

COMMUNICATE THE REASON FOR SMALL-GROUP MINISTRY

When God plants himself in us and we hear the call to follow him, we find it easy to say yes. But when we hear the words *training*, *discipline*, *plan*, *schedule*, or *accountability*, enthusiasm can weaken. So how can you best communicate compelling reasons to give small groups a go? Start by raising the value so people will be prepared to pay the price.

I'm always amazed at what some people will pay for a car. Some take a practical approach and drive a sensible car. But others choose a distinctive auto with a much higher price tag. Why are some people willing to pay for the top of the line? Because someone sells them on the value of the product. The premium car will drive better, last longer, be more comfortable, or provide status.

I see many leaders behaving like bad salesmen. They talk about the cost of small-group discipleship without extolling the value of following Jesus. These leaders then accuse the people who won't commit of being selfish. The other thing bad salesmen do is lower the price until someone bites. When it comes to small groups, this cheapens what cost God everything.

A Sample Approach

In Matthew 28:18-20, Jesus clearly stated that we are to be disciples and make disciples. What is a disciple?

- A disciple interacts with God through the Word and prayer (see John 15:7).
- A disciple makes a significant impact on people around her (see verse 8).
- A disciple responds to God's calling in obedience (see verses 9-10).
- A disciple is internally contented and at peace (see verse 11).
- A disciples loves others as Christ loved (see verses 12-13).

Key thought: You can't make disciples without accountability, and accountability requires structure. Structure is the key to breakthroughs that affect attitudes and actions. So what kind of activities should disciples engage in? They should engage in activities that mirror the characteristics listed above. They should also

- participate in a group of fellow disciples who seek to connect with God through interacting with the Word of God and learning to be people of prayer
- seek to live among the lost and broken in their spheres of influence and to affect others through their character the way Jesus modeled for us
- answer God's loving sacrifice for them daily with a response of obedience to his call on their life
- exercise faith in such a way as to live in inner peace and the joy that comes from an obedient life
- love others without holding back and find ways for those around them to experience their love

Disciples develop these characteristics when they choose to submit to the spiritual authority of others in a faith community, such as in a small group.

Selecting Leaders

You can find reams of material on training leaders, but the selection of leaders is rarely discussed, even though it is more crucial. Even the best training won't make a non-leader into a leader. No amount of expertise can compensate for a person who isn't faithful or who doesn't have time do what he promised. The following qualities of leaders contain the condensed wisdom of many years and many people.

Character

While the need for character in leaders seems like a no-brainer, it's surprising how many churches ignore it. One of the first things that should strike you about Jesus, the early church, and Paul's instructions is that character is basic to leadership (see Mark 3:13-14; Acts 6:1-7; 1 Timothy 3:1-16; Titus 1). Regardless of someone's talent, if character isn't developed properly, the result is negative. Jesus taught us through his example that an individual's character determines her impact. He modeled the character qualities of humility, servanthood, obedience, sacrifice, and love. If you want to be the kind of leader that others follow, you must pass the simple spiritual test that you're teachable, humble, and making forward progress.

Suitability

Perhaps nothing is quite as sad as a person who's bad at what he loves. Millions of people prove this statement on golf courses around the world every day. In spiritual terms, nothing is worse than a godly non-leader who is asked to lead. Often criticism crushes that person's willing spirit.

People who lead should display an aptitude for leading. They don't need to be macro-leaders—those who can lead large movements through inspiration. However, they do need to demonstrate that they can lay out a plan, can run a simple program, and are open to being trained. And one of management guru Peter Drucker's famous questions to ask when choosing a leader is, "What's the assignment?" If a leadership role calls for toughness, then the leader should be tough. If it calls for diplomacy, then she needs to be relationally intelligent.

Availability

It seems obvious that a leader needs to be available. Yet often someone asks a talented person to take on a responsibility that he's perfect for—and willing to do. This must mean it's God's will, so congratulations all around! But then the person misses a meeting, falls behind on an assignment, and doesn't return phone calls. He apologizes and reaffirms his interest, but the behavior continues.

Sometimes this indicates a lack of faithfulness. But most of the time, the person wasn't really available in the first place. A realistic look at his schedule should have led him to say no. So the most mundane but important question to ask a potential leader is, "This will take ten hours a week. Do you have the time?"

Faithfulness

Faithfulness is the rite of passage into Christian leadership: "Now it is required that those who have been given a trust must prove faithful" (1 Corinthians 4:2), and "The things you have heard me say in the presence of many witnesses entrust to reliable men who will also be qualified to teach others" (2 Timothy 2:2).

The work of the harvest is impossible without faithfulness. Here's the simplest way to understand this: Faithful is the person who does what she agreed to do. She meets this requirement in both time and quality. Faithfulness comes from a person's inner desire to be faithful to God. The natural by-product of that heartfelt desire is obedience.

Training Leaders

The ongoing support of leaders provides insurance against the collapse of a small group's integrity. Once a group loses its integrity because its leaders have been neglected by those who lead them, only a flabby self-indulgence survives.

Not long ago I visited with a friend who'd been a member of the same small group for five years. When I asked what he liked about his group, he responded that they loved to eat together, share their lives, and pray. Everyone in the group was capable of leading groups, but my friend told me they had no plans to reproduce, to do any planned outreach, to memorize any Scripture, to support any mission, or to do any training that would challenge them. This group had collapsed in on itself. It was following the recipe for spiritual rot, and it was only a matter of time before the group started to smell. The leader of group leaders had failed to provide encouragement and support.

How can you avoid a similar fate? If you are the leader of leaders, implement the following simple ideas.

Establish a Covenant Relationship

A covenant is a promise. From the very start of any organized group, the leader of small-group leaders must convey this attitude: "I'm your servant. I'll serve you by coaching you, loving you, and even confronting you and helping you do the things you don't want to do. You can count on me to train you and give you all I know and all I am for the sake of advancing God's kingdom."

Hold Regular Leader Meetings

If you're saying, "Duh," it means you already know the value of getting small-group leaders together. How often you hold leaders meetings depends on the other support you give. Meeting once a month should be enough if you bolster that meeting by giving every small-group leader a "touch" at least once a week, such as a quick e-mail or a phone call. Leaders meetings can include anywhere from ten people to hundreds, but be sure to hold them regularly.

Hold One-on-One Meetings

If all the group leaders meet monthly, one-on-one meetings can take place four times a year, or as needed. This helps each leader deal with personal issues that might hinder her and her leadership. It also provides a place where the leader can feel safe to talk about victories and defeats, family and personal issues, or her spiritual journey. Don't neglect this aspect, because everyone needs a safe place to get help. Yes, it takes work, and you'll have to deal with scheduling conflicts, but you might help a leader avoid an impending disaster.

Encourage Playtime

We often overlook playtime. One of the rewards for leaders should be getting some playtime with one another. This can take so many forms—from baseball to scrapbooking—I'll resist the temptation to create a list. You can organize this for all of the small-group leaders or by interest. When men can be boys together and women can be girls together, something happens that binds them together.

Provide Continuing Education

The process of leading creates a hunger to know more. Small-group leaders receive practical, on-the-job education that's not found in most textbooks. Yet a place for "book learning" exists. Continuing education can enhance the knowledge and enrich the soul of your leaders, so introduce them to the teachings of ancient writers, to various forms of scriptural meditation, to the dynamics of change, to how to minister to broken people. Addressing these relevant topics—perhaps by bringing in an expert to teach at a retreat or summer training—provides great encouragement. And don't think of this as an option; it's a part of the church's responsibility to build the knowledge and abilities of its leaders.

MANAGEMENT OF COMMITMENTS

Do you want to love people? Then help them keep their commitments to God. Are you willing to have well-intentioned, spiritually motivated believers become hostile and turn on you? Then help them keep their commitments to God. Helping people keep their commitments to God might be a leader's greatest challenge, so consider the following helpful hints.

Establish Accountability and Support

Accountability sounds harsh only outside loving relationships. Part of being disciples is helping each other realize God's dream for all of us. That means engaging in specific activities that require discipline. Discipline is a community trait as well as a personal one; community discipline builds personal discipline. You can help develop this kind of environment through scriptural teaching, the example of leaders, and a plan to make it work.

Set a Structure

As the leader, you can help set the structure of small groups with some simple tools.

Tool 1. Develop a covenant that establishes the goals and objectives of the group. A covenant can be written for almost any group. Help group members see that signing a covenant is important.

- It will help group members understand what they're committing to do.

- It will help them understand the time and level of commitment they are making.
- It will give them a way to measure their progress.
- It will give their leader permission to hold them accountable.

Some might suggest that requiring people to sign covenants for small-group life is passé, that it's out of touch with the postmodern mind. My answer is that human nature doesn't change. People need to take tangible action that says to others in their community, "I'm really committed to this." If this is of no value, then all oaths—whether in court or in weddings—have no meaning. Can people be committed without an official act? Sure. But when you're trying to develop a culture of commitment and the goal is spiritual transformation, covenants are a very useful tool. They put on paper what people are feeling in their hearts and minds.

Tool 2. Set up an orientation meeting where potential group members can discuss questions and concerns before the group starts. They should understand what the discipleship process can do for them. After the orientation, they should take a few days to make their decision, understanding that if they agree to join the group, they're committing to be held accountable to the covenant.

Tool 3. Keep the covenant that the group agrees to. Churches are notorious for lowering expectations and becoming laissez-faire with structure and responsibility. Stick with the accountability that group members agreed to.

Assure group members that leaders are committed to integrity through consistency. People generally respect leaders who are objective and fair; if they don't, different problems are present.

Work Out Problems

Once group members make a commitment, leaders have the God-given responsibility to help them manage it. Remember, the commitment is really a commitment to God. Leaders have a sacred trust to be good stewards and manage these commitments. The following are a few time-tested ways to make it all work.

Keep current in holding members accountable. Don't let the sun set on infractions of the covenant. If you let time pass, you'll have an out-of-control group system. If you ignore the weeds in the garden, they soon take it over. It's easy to let people miss meetings, skip their assignments, have a critical spirit about things they don't like and blame the leaders for their unhappiness. When these cracks appear in their commitments, take action early and often, because it will save you greater trauma later. Don't wait to see if things will get worse, because they almost always do.

Not only does this do great harm to the group member who is ignored when he doesn't keep the covenant, it also breaks down group morale. Naturally, when group members see another member break the covenant without consequences, they feel their commitment must not be that valuable. The group begins to think that the entire group process is a façade.

Many issues are easy when you deal with them immediately. Often you can simply provide early encouragement to those who are struggling. It's so much better to encourage early than to discipline late.

If you haven't kept current, ask forgiveness. When a leader fails herself and the group members by not keeping current on infractions, she must first ask for the group's forgiveness. This might seem strange, but neglect finds its birthplace in the heart of the leader. This humble-servant attitude likely will startle everyone, especially the person who has been waiting and wondering why no one has talked to him about his delinquency. When the leader begins with, "First I must ask your forgiveness; I have sinned against you by not helping you keep your commitment to God. Would you forgive me?" the group member will normally say, "Yes," and then add, "I need to ask for your forgiveness as well for my lack of commitment."

This can be a beautiful picture of redemption, grace, and forgiveness that serves as a launching pad for even closer relationships and stronger commitment.

Discern whether a person is unwilling or unable. A good rule of thumb says that if people are unwilling to keep their commitments, it's a spiritual issue. If they're unable to keep their commitments, it's a management issue.

There are two kinds of unwillingness. The first is a belligerent attitude that says, "I'm not going to do this. It's over, and I will hold my ground." Such unwillingness is easy to identify, and the sooner you act, the better for everyone, including the unwilling person. The second kind of unwillingness combines fear and honest disagreement. Usually groups can make room for negotiation within a particular framework, and leaders can seek a reasonable compromise with the unwilling group member.

The unable, on the other hand, are people who can't—or think they can't—continue to be a part of the group. Again, this is more of a management issue. For instance, a married couple facing troubled times thought that when they separated they would be unable to continue in the same small group. The group felt that if they would submit to counseling and work on their marriage, they could both continue. They consented, and many years later are doing well in their marriage.

Sometimes people move or have a dramatic work-related change. Illness disrupts the flow of life, and many other events occur over which there is no control. In these cases, groups should usually release people with a positive send-off and blessing. Remember that the point of managing the commitments of others is to help them grow spiritually and keep their commitments to God with integrity. The ministry infrastructure must reinforce the values of the community and the definition of what it means to be a disciple of Christ.

Do you really want to love people? Then help them keep their commitments to God.[4]

SUGGESTED RESOURCES

Enter "Christian small groups" in an Internet search engine and an entire world will open to you. (My search yielded more than nine million results.) You can choose the kind of materials that fit your needs best.

Or enter "Christian cell groups." Cell groups often focus more aggressively on outreach and multiplication than on small groups in general.

To be more specific, look online for Willow Creek Church resources, Serendipity, Renovaré, The Navigators' 2:7 Series, and Saddleback Community Church for a variety of short- and long-term small-group options.

Leading Strategic Change: Breaking Through the Brain Barrier by J. Stewart Black and Hal B. Gregersen (Prentice Hall, 2003). Introduces the basic thesis that corporate change occurs only through personal change. Also introduces the concept of brain maps and how modes of thinking are deeply grooved into the mind. Includes some very practical guidelines for making change work for you and for those with whom you live, work, and play.

Building High Commitment in a Low-Commitment World by Bill Hull (Revell, 1997). Addresses ways to build high commitment, and the enemies and myths of high commitment.

CHAPTER 10

CONGREGATIONS, PASTORS, AND DISCIPLESHIP

IN THIS CHAPTER

- HOW LOCAL CONGREGATIONS DIFFER FROM OTHER MINISTRIES
- DIFFERENT LEVELS OF SPIRITUAL MATURITY
- TRAINING AND ORGANIZING THE CONGREGATION
- ADVICE TO CHURCH LEADERS

A woman who visited our church recently spoke openly with me about why she'd come and why she'd left her previous church. She had stopped attending her church when she felt it was going in a direction she could not approve. That was eighteen years earlier!

I said, "I sure hope you didn't give up on Jesus along with the church."

"Oh, no!" she exclaimed, "I didn't quit Jesus. I watched Christian TV. Then I heard about this church and decided to try it."

She hasn't returned.

Most of us have a tendency to idealize the church. We fall in love with the idea of church, only to be bitterly disappointed by its reality. The truth is that we all should have problems with the church because it's filled with sin and sinners. People fail, they make mistakes, they don't live up to their commitments, and they hurt each other. The idea that the reality of a church will match the ideal of the church is a hope we won't realize on earth. We'll always find ourselves in one kind of crisis or another.

A lot of people complain about the institutional character of churches, but what else could the church be? Frederick Von Hugel said that the institution of the church is like the bark on a tree. There's no life in the bark; it's dead wood. But it protects the life of the tree within. The tree grows and grows, but if you take off the bark, the tree will die.[1] All the authority structures we put in place in our churches—yes, even the dreaded committees—can and do serve as protection for life within the church.

Some special issues and pressures create the environment in which disciples live. We've already covered the disciple-making environment, the nature of Christian spiritual transformation, personal approaches to discipleship, and starting and maintaining small groups. This chapter will explore the unique challenges found in ensuring that the local congregation also makes the process of discipleship its mission.

If you're not a pastor, I strongly encourage you to think about the other side of the equation when I address pastors and leaders directly. How do you help or hinder your church's or your pastor's effectiveness?

IS BIGGER BETTER?

How different should the goals of the church body be from those of its individual members? I've already discussed at length the inner qualities of a disciple, as well as the spiritual disciplines necessary to form these qualities. Remember my stories of how basketball practice, practice, and more practice fueled by dedication and determination, which led to my goal of a college scholarship? Congregations need goals as well. We must be careful what those goals are and what practices our desire to reach them produce.

Consider the goals of two churches:

- *Church A:* We plan to reach a thousand people for Christ in the next ten years. We'll develop a plan to reach them, but first we must raise ten million dollars to build a sanctuary to house the additional thousand.
- *Church B:* The only way we can show that we serve a big God is to do big things and attract people to our God. We're going to build the biggest sanctuary in this state!

I wish I could say that I made up these two churches. I didn't. They're real, and their goals are all too common. These goals say far more about the unmet needs of the church leaders than about the church itself. People who need God are repulsed by such bravado. And they're attracted to genuine love, humility, caring, and people who exhibit the fruit of the Holy Spirit.

Because we're largely products of a consumer culture, we're easily impressed by big churches. The church has become expert at producing consumer Christians who are nice people, but who aren't formed into the life of Christ.

I'm not knocking large churches. I've pastored a large church, and it was no more or less important or interesting than smaller ones. I'm just saying that with regard to what really matters, so what? The pastor of a large church might have more influence in the culture, but again, so what?

Of the 350,000 churches in America, just over 1,200 have attendance of 2,000 or more—less than 0.4 percent. So I don't think large churches should always be the model for how churches should function.

Quality over Quantity

I'd like to convince church leaders not to be easily seduced by numerical success. We can learn as much from a small church as we can from a large one. Character is just as important as competence. I don't have the space to tell you every thing I don't mean by what I have just said. But I will go out of my way to say this: yes, small churches exist that are competent, and large churches exist that have character. In fact, you can find both in abundance in either size.

When Jesus delivered the Great Commission, he revealed God's plan for his church as well as for individual disciples. He charged the church to go to the world, because the world has no reason to go to church. Whether God blesses you with large numbers or small, if you're making disciples, you're leading as Christ led and instructed. So set worthy goals, lead by example, and leave the results up to God.

How Local Congregations Differ from Other Ministries

How does local church ministry differ from specialized ministries such as colleges, seminaries, missions organizations, and other parachurch organizations?

Church Is Ordinary

Golfers use the term "grinding" to describe their commitment to keep playing even when they're not shooting well. Some even call it "the glory of the grind." Most church ministry is like a round of golf. You start the round with stars in your eyes, full of hope. You hit a few good shots and you feel great. You're like a golfer hitting it on the screws three hundred yards down the middle or sinking a thirty-footer for birdie. But then you hit a few freaky shots. You follow the birdie with a score so high a name doesn't even exist for it. In the same way, the daily and weekly grind of church life includes those days when everything goes right and you're filled with wonder and awe. But other days, everything goes wrong and you wish you were making lattes at Starbucks.

To be a good golfer or a good church worker, you must accept your mistakes and bad shots, put them behind you, and live in the moment. You need qualities like patience and perseverance to enjoy the highs and grind through the lows. The church will test us because most of it is very ordinary, slow work, often without immediate rewards.

Spiritual formation of the inner person into being like Christ takes place gradually and often unnoticeably. The effect is neither rapid nor magical. So disciples must learn to enjoy the journey — the entire experience — and keep it all in perspective.

Church Is a Product of the Consumer Culture

Consumer discipleship is an oxymoron. But I guess it acknowledges a certain mystery of spiritual life: Sometimes people choose to follow Jesus but can't seem to shake off the power of a culture of acquisition. Well-meaning people seem to get caught up in doing the right thing, but in the wrong way.

In general, Christians have a heart to serve Christ, but they behave in a way that says, "It's all about me." Sermons, worship services, children's programs, and the length of services have all been designed around the demands of church members. The culture tells us that the customer is always right, and at church the members are the customers. Further, when they work, they become volunteers. Volunteers work for free and shouldn't be expected to meet certain standards, right? And of course, you can't really fire them. Just thank your lucky stars they're willing!

This line of thinking is evidence of a Christian consumer culture. But the Bible calls us servants and followers of Christ.

We respond to his sacrificial act by giving our all. We take up our cross or mission, deny ourselves, and follow him. It should be our honor and privilege to serve. And when we serve, we should submit ourselves to spiritual authority through our spiritual leaders. We might live in a consumer culture, but as disciples, we're citizens of God's kingdom—a kingdom not of this world.

Worship isn't about us. Sermons aren't about us. The music isn't about us. We are *not* the central figures of this story; it is God's story. We're attached to God by prepositions: He is in us, with us, for us, and does things to us. We're not the subject or the verb; we're the object.

In this consumer environment, we're always walking a tightrope, trying to keep a balance between what people think they need and what they really need. The major challenge for pastors is leading disciples out of a consumer culture that says take care of self first and into the life of Christ that says put others first.

We need to teach disciples to go to church to serve, to contribute to others. And teach them that when they serve, their own needs will be met. This kingdom perspective buries personal tastes, slights, oversights, and the mistakes of others deep in the background.

DIFFERENT LEVELS OF SPIRITUAL MATURITY

Teaching disciples to set aside a consumer mentality would be easier if all Christians were at the same place in their spiritual lives. But of course, every single member of a church is at a different spiritual age. Let's look at a few stages in which most believers land.

The Seeker
A seeker is any person who seeks meaning and answers in a religious context. We usually think of a seeker as unchurched. All churches

should remove as many barriers as possible for seekers, yet there's no need to focus entirely on them.

There are commonsense ways to avoid embarrassing or confusing seekers, such as not pointing them out during church services and not practicing customs and methods they won't understand (unless those customs and methods are integral to the faith, such as the Eucharist or using biblical languages when teaching from the Bible).

Most seekers are looking for authentic spirituality, so they want to join in and learn the new culture. I'd advise against repackaging the gospel so that unchurched people find it more acceptable, because this can water down the teachings to the lowest common denominator. When this occurs, you end up with misinformed people who think they're Christians. Instead of striving for spiritual maturity, they'll become malformed, semi-obedient religious consumers—and they won't even know it.

The Starter

A starter is a new disciple who is eager, willing, and naïve in the ways of church. The most strategic move is to partner starters with healthy disciples who can walk with them through the first year. But the process shouldn't stop there. These mentor partnerships should be part of us for all our lives.

The Struggler

Strugglers have trouble working through difficulties. Because an entire classification of damaged or wounded strugglers now populates congregations, I want to dwell on this level a bit longer.

The numbers of strugglers is rising for three reasons:

1. There is a breakdown of a consensus on morality. As culture becomes less founded on a solid sense of right and wrong, pathology —behavior apart from the normal or accepted—increases and more people are damaged. As the breakdown of culture increases, the number of predators grows. And more predators translates into more victims.

2. As problems become more common, we talk about them more, which creates a therapeutic culture. While this culture has identified many problems and offered much help, it has also created a therapeutic industry that indiscriminately labels people as victims and mass markets attempted solutions. Certainly therapy and medications have helped many people, but sometimes the result is that victims don't deal with deeper issues, or they have permission to deal with them in harmful ways.

3. People who think of themselves as victims do not mature spiritually. Again, I'm not trying to minimize legitimate problems. Yet both those who have actually been victimized and those who are victims because of self-inflicted wounds can, in Christ, overcome their victimizations. Yes, they're in pain, but they could put their trauma behind them and walk in peace and power and joy. In both cases, the church needs to step in to bind up the wounds of those in need, while always pointing them forward to maturity with hope. The church serves as a spiritual trauma center, helping all those wounded and hurt to think of their pain as a normal part of maturing spiritually and helping them move beyond their difficulties by God's grace and through the love of his people.

We might call the inner and private world of human personality "below the line." This is the place where people stash their unresolved guilt, issues of shame, unnatural fears, estrangement from important people, and anger and bitterness, which all block spiritual growth. When we permit these pathologies to grow and establish a footing in us, they become barriers to obeying Christ. They take on the nature of "the sin that so easily entangles" (Hebrews 12:1).

The King James Version describes the sin that entangles as sin that "besets us." This sin dominates. We get stuck. We can't seem to get past it. It contorts us and we live with a false identity, covering up and hiding. Worse, this sin breeds a spirituality of legalism, where we substitute external behaviors for a truly transformed soul.

Some would recommend professional counseling to help people deal with these kinds of issues, thinking that they lie beyond the average person's ability to diagnose and cure. Indeed they do lie beyond the average person's ability, but they also lie beyond the most skilled therapist's abilities. The best chance people with besetting sins have to overcome their "below the line" issues is living in a safe and affirming community of disciples. In safety, people can open up to others who will care for them, understand their struggles, and encourage them forward. The actual healing work belongs to the Word of God and the Holy Spirit, who know exactly what will heal the soul.

I'm not trying to be simplistic here. Instead I want to be forthright and leave the profundity to the work of the Holy Spirit. Scripture calls the Holy Spirit our teacher (see John 14:26); he alone can carry the thoughts of God to the mind of man (see 1 Corinthians 2:10-16). Through weapons that are divine in nature, he can destroy strongholds of thought — the mental constructs that disable us (see 2 Corinthians 10:3-5), and he places in us a new mind or attitude that leads to real transformation (see Romans 12:2).

Counselor, author, and professor Larry Crabb put it well in the title of his book *The Safest Place on Earth*. He proposes that a loving community of disciples provides the best culture for dealing with our deepest needs. Remember the parable of the turtle in chapter 5? The most crucial question that a broken person can ask is, "Can I trust me with you?" If the answer is yes, healing can follow.

The Stagnant

The stagnant people are stuck spiritually as a result of neglect. They neglect the practice of spiritual disciplines and choose to live off yesterday's manna — the doctrines and experiences from the past. Stagnant people can be very dangerous to the church because they tend to be unteachable and complaining. Often they hold tight to the organization's traditions and relics. At times a test or dramatic change in their lives stirs them from their spiritual slumber.

While stagnant people certainly deserve to be loved and cared for, they also should be exhorted and disciplined when necessary. The biggest mistake a pastor or church worker can make is giving undue attention to stagnant people or allowing their complaining spirits to bring discouragement.

The Stable

The stable people are faithful and growing disciples. You can count on them to train, to give, to serve, to encourage, and to pray for others. Leaders should spend most of their time cultivating these people. They provide the key to reaching many of the stagnant. They willingly stand alongside the struggler. They help the seeker feel welcome. They happily give direction to the starter.

TRAINING AND ORGANIZING THE CONGREGATION

Most of us like order. Even in our postmodern era, as some people categorically reject truth and others tout a wandering spiritual life with no clear road signs, our minds are still wired to work best when we receive information that is organized and in sequence. Religious researcher George Barna has found that one of the greatest impediments to spiritual development was the choice of churches to teach in a random rather than systematic way.

> The problem is not that the content itself is weak, but that the content is not provided in a purposeful, systematic manner. As a result believers are exposed to good information without

context and thus lose that information because they have no way of making sense of it without the bigger picture of faith and life. Consequently, we rate sermons on the basis of their value to what we're experiencing at the moment and assess the usefulness of books and lessons in terms of how entertaining or erudite they are. Ultimately, believers become well versed in knowing characters, stories, ideas, and verses from the Bible, but they remain clueless as to their importance.[2]

In other words, without organization and sequence, people's minds resemble a huge pile of Christmas ornaments, but there's no tree to hang them on. They need an established framework or structure to help them think through the life of following Jesus.

This isn't true just when it comes to presenting information. It's also true of how people grow spiritually. Most churches use the model of "teach and then do." Yet much of Jesus' instruction employed the method of "do and then teach." Luke 4–8 presents a good balance of the two. Unfortunately, we've lost that balance in the church.

In fact, the church often tends to "teach and then *not* do." To have their spiritual hunger cultivated, people need to see the benefits of knowing God and experience him in action. This is why Scripture repeatedly reminds us of the importance of example and imitation (for example, see 1 Corinthians 4:16; 11:1; Philippians 4:9; 1 Thessalonians 1:6; 2 Timothy 2:2; 1 Peter 5:1-6). Otherwise exhortation falls on unprepared ears.

Start at the Beginning

When new people enter a congregation, never assume what level they're at spiritually. You can avoid these assumptions if you provide some kind of introduction to the church's beliefs, customs, and values, such as a class.

Every church has some kind of philosophy, and at some point

everyone should receive a formal presentation of that philosophy. If a church doesn't take this step, it will find even veteran members who don't agree on the church's basic purpose, mission, and methods. This staple of congregational life also provides a way to sort out where people are on their spiritual journey.

Realize That Some Will Always Be Spectators

Pastors must acknowledge that at any given time a number of people will remain uninvolved in congregational life apart from attending worship services. While you can recognize this reality, you can never preach or lead with a sense that it's okay. A number of complaints will inevitably arise from this group, and my seasoned advice remains the same: Don't allow the semi-obedient, passive-aggressive people of your congregation to dictate to you. Paying too much attention to these people will knock the entire train off the tracks, creating a tremendous diversion and a drain on church leadership.

Use a Development System

Whether your church develops people through mentoring, coaching, or spiritual direction (see chapter 8), small groups (see chapter 9), or Jesus' model of "come and follow me" (see chapter 6), make sure your development system brings eager people to the surface. Some of these people will be the future leaders of your congregation. The development system should allow you to evaluate new people, place them where they belong, and then prepare them to serve in ways that best suit their character and competence. The best training won't take place in a classroom, but as people minister to others.

Use Careful Management

No matter what systems you have in place for developing people, always keep in mind that weeks and months don't provide enough time for forming the person of Christ in an individual. The spiritual formation process is lifelong, and church systems must step up to meet this challenge. That means regularly, constantly, and repeatedly helping people find their place in healthy duos, triads, and small groups that stimulate them to move ahead and help them keep their commitments to God. Character also means helping people keep their commitments to others. Often that part of character development is lacking.

Keeping track of people—shorthanded as "managing"—is a loving act of leadership. Knowing how people are doing and what they're doing requires effort, but it pays big dividends. People feel loved and cared for; they know they're not alone. I've been involved in many good faith programs designed to nurture and train members. The primary lesson I've learned is this: What was managed succeeded; what was not managed well failed. People who are being "managed" will *feel* loved and cared for if their "managers" show genuine interest in them, which actually *is* love and care.

However, if people feel like projects or cogs in an impersonal wheel, no amount of even the best management will work. For example, you can have a database that can call up information on people at the click of a mouse, but unless someone regularly stays in contact with the people in the records through e-mails, notes, phone calls, and personal contact, the information is useless. This might seem so obvious that I shouldn't need to include it, but even leaders with warm hearts can be neglectful if they don't use the information in front of them.

Of course, simply speaking warm words of affirmation isn't enough. As always, you need to show people with your actions that your words are valid.

ADVICE TO CHURCH LEADERS

So far, we've explored how churches function, what levels of spiritual maturity exist in churches, and how to train and manage the people in churches. Let's turn to the life of church leaders.

Again, dozens of books examine the characteristics and qualities of spiritually healthy pastors. Yet this discussion of congregational life seems incomplete without at least addressing this topic briefly. So permit me to mention how the pastor/leader influences the spiritual life of the local church.[3]

Give Up the Gods

Giving up the gods is like detox. Their allure is so strong that you might need to go through a complete separation from them. This recovery period might be followed with a halfway house experience where you can practice the new life with a strong support system. So what gods must go?

Attendance: Many people who shaped my thinking have long departed to a better life. But they left behind wonderful ideas in their books. One such individual was Elton Trueblood. Consider what he said about our worship of church attendance:

> If Christianity is primarily a matter of attendance at a performance, it is not different in kind from a host of other experiences. Though membership may include attendance at performances of a certain character, such attendance is not the primary meaning of the Christian effort at all. The fact that this is not generally understood is one of the chief evidences of the spiritual erosion which distresses us.[4]

Trueblood believed that the emphasis on church attendance predates Christianity. The feasts of Israel focused on getting as many people as possible to the temple on special occasions. Trueblood noted that the focus of the church should be quite different: "The most important thing to God is the creation of centers of loving fellowships, which in turn infect the world. Whether the world can be redeemed in this way we don't know. But it is at least clear that there is no other way."[5]

Churches should focus on gathering together to inspire, encourage, comfort, train, and mobilize their members to penetrate their worlds. God's kingdom should increase naturally through families and other networks. Keep in mind that the focus should include the church gathered to connect to the world more than the church gathered for meetings. Our contemporary overemphasis on "worship service" is not just a misunderstanding of worship; it's also a tyranny that many people feel trapped within.

In our current religious culture, we've made attendance the most important measure of our success. We honor and extol the largest churches. Their pastors become an elite priesthood that others look to for guidance. But this belief system cripples us from focusing on what's required to fulfill the Great Commission.

Please understand that I don't believe large churches or their pastors are the problem. In fact, we should thank God for them and how they've helped us all. What I'm against is the belief that they are the standard we use for measuring success. When we do that, we reverse the inward and outward flow Scripture describes. The impulse to penetrate our world should be at least equal to the desire to gather for meetings. The early church met in homes, providing kingdom outposts close to those who needed the gospel.

Dallas Willard notes, "We must flatly say that one of the greatest contemporary barriers to meaningful spiritual formation into Christlikeness is overconfidence in the spiritual efficacy of 'regular church services.' They are vital, they are not enough, it is that simple."[6]

One way to give up the god of attendance is to replace it with a different goal. When our goal moves from wanting recognition from others to the transformation of others, we put the god of attendance in its place. If I'm committed to humility and submission, being irrelevant and unnecessary to the gods of my culture become easy.

As a leader, my commitment and reward involve enrolling members into the life and joyfully serving a role in their transformation. This allows every leader to make it, to succeed, and to live out God's dream for them through who they are. Attendance then takes its place as one possible fruit of the work, but it's never the proof of our talent or importance to God.

Increase: The need to increase and make things happen is at epidemic levels. The revolutionary American dream was freedom, liberty, and justice for all. Not long after that was secured, the American dream morphed into a materialistic one—for children to have it better than the previous generation, for each subsequent generation to be richer, smarter, and healthier.

Somewhere along the way, the American church bought into the American dream. Worse, we've stayed there so long we've become saturated in the dream's philosophy. We think that every year the church should grow and improve its programs.

The late teacher Christopher Lasch challenged this myth of progress:

> How does it happen that serious people continue to believe in progress, in the face of massive evidence that might have been expected to refute the idea of progress once and for all? . . . Insatiable desire, formerly condemned as a source of frustration, unhappiness, and spiritual inability, came to be seen as a powerful stimulus to economic development. Instead of disparaging the tendency to want more than we need, liberals . . . argued that needs varied from one society to another, that civilized men needed more than savages to make them comfortable.[7]

Our culture is drenched with competitive spirit. It started for me at age eight in Little League. I wanted to excel, and I based my popularity and self-worth on how I performed on the field. This followed me through my formative years and my athletic career. Then it went along for the ride into pastoral life. Like many young pastors, my goals were scripturally based but driven by a need to succeed. When our primary motivation is competitive, instead of compassion serving as the earmark of our lives, we get caught up in trying to increase our influence—our ministry cache.

Again, we can give up this god by adopting a new way of thinking. Priest, author, and teacher Henri Nouwen helps us:

> The way of the Christian leader is not the way of upward mobility in which our world has invested so much, but the way of downward mobility ending on the cross. Here we touch the most important quality of Christian leadership in the future. It is not a leadership of power and control; but a leadership of powerlessness and humility in which the suffering servant of God, Jesus Christ, is made manifest.[8]

When he saw Jesus, John the Baptist immediately said, "He must increase, but I must decrease" (John 3:30, NKJV). Think of the freedom that comes when we can lay aside the goals of title, prestige, power, influence, and an ever-increasing salary. Perhaps the toughest place to decrease is in the influence and power we hold over people around us. Any leadership based on increasing the leader is wrong.

God certainly does give increase and fruit. When we remove the competitive spirit from our souls, we can experience great increase in influence and prestige. But the litmus test is this: Is the influence Christ's or ours? When the increase belongs to Christ, you'll experience freedom because Christ has increased in you rather than because of you.

Competence: Part of the esprit de corps of popular leaders is based in having the right stuff. They seem to have an attitude that says, "We can relax now, because we've made the club. We're the elite who see things grow. We make things happen." I have no doubt about the talents of these leaders. However, depending on competence directly conflicts with the kingdom value of brokenness.[9]

A key to developing character is brokenness before God. Humility and submission produce an attitude of brokenness. Jesus modeled these very qualities as his core. The competitive world, however, sees brokenness as failure. When people speak of a person who changed careers and took less money or walked away from a more prestigious position, they might say they admire it. But you can tell by the look in their eyes that they're not speaking with conviction. When a leader admits that he feels burned out or that he didn't enjoy the pressure in the fast lane, the world's unspoken response often is, "Too bad they didn't have the right stuff."

The culture honors competence. But the myth of competence is thinking that we'll outgrow our weaknesses, sins, fears, and disappointments. The myth is that we'll reach a place of spiritual competence where we'll *get it together*. Those times never come. In fact, as we become more like Jesus, our dependence on God increases.

Brokenness means living in light of that reality. Don't godly people get over their brokenness? Apparently the apostle Paul didn't. He wrote about the thorn in the flesh:

> Concerning this thing I pleaded with the Lord three times that it might depart from me. And He said to me, "My grace is sufficient for you, for My strength is made perfect in weakness." Therefore most gladly I will rather boast in my infirmities, that the power of Christ may rest upon me. Therefore I take pleasure in infirmities, in reproaches, in needs, in persecutions, in distresses, for Christ's sake. For when I am weak, then I am strong. (2 Corinthians 12:8-10, NKJV)

The English words *weakness* and *infirmities* are translations of the same Greek word. The best translation seems to be *weakness*. Paul used his thorn in the flesh as a focus point and then extrapolated a larger meaning from it. He gladly boasted about his weakness, bringing it out in the open. He had no shame about his lack of competence or abilities. He led from his lack of abilities, saying, "I came to you in weakness and fear, and with much trembling." (1 Corinthians 2:3).[10]

Even Jesus honored his wounds. He carried the scars of crucifixion with him in his resurrected body. The disciples could see and touch them. Our wounds and weaknesses are real; our inabilities are exposed for others to see. When we lead with our weakness and our wounds, we gain a powerful way to touch others around us.

We don't lead as wounded victims, but as those who've found an answer in Christ, who heals us and enables us to live with and through our needs. In this state of humility, we can discover the real power for our lives, because God's power becomes mature, or perfect, in our weakness.

Giving up the gods of attendance, increase, and competence provides a start. We all serve other gods as well. But you get the point. Giving up these gods involves a new way of being, thinking, and doing. When we follow Jesus and imitate the way Jesus lived and taught, we become worthy of the name disciple.

Develop Your Inner Life

Nouwen believed that the following question lies at the heart of Christian leadership: Are the leaders of the future truly men and women of God, people with an ardent desire to dwell in God's presence, to listen to God's voice, to look at God's beauty, to touch God's incarnate Word, and to fully taste God's infinite goodness?[11]

Did you notice the qualities Nouwen mentioned?

- Dwell in God's presence.
- Listen to God's voice.
- Focus on his beauty.
- Taste his goodness.

These refer to a level of experience with God that's new to many of us. It begins when we spend personal time with God—but not in the form of the typical "quiet time." To be honest, my own quiet times were too often just me doing religious acts with very little experience of God. I find that when I'm rushed, I still fall back into the same superficiality.

Are you ready to face down your weakness, to uncover the stuff hidden in the darkness? For me, the process started with a word from God that came to me in a still whisper: "Bill, I'm going to break you. Don't run." I had romanticized the concept of brokenness, seeing it as an event rather than a process that becomes a state of being.

Give Yourself to the Principle of Discipleship

Yes, I was a self-disciplined, well-educated leader with an acceptable quiet time. But that wasn't sufficient to develop the qualities Nouwen listed. Instead I needed training to develop my inner life. How do leaders develop their inner life?

The command and the curriculum: God intends for his kingdom to grow through discipleship. Jesus gave both the command and the curriculum in the Great Commission: "[teach] them to obey everything I have commanded you" (Matthew 28:20). As I mentioned way back in chapter 1, Jesus commanded 212 things. That certainly provides a very rich curriculum!

The principle of God's plan of discipleship is the impact of one life on another—the character, skill, and perspective of one godly person influencing another willing person. The aim of the teaching is obedience, which should encourage those of us who believe that faith is action sustained by belief.

All of this means that as a leader, you can't be satisfied with just talking about what Jesus commanded. You must commit to living it out in community with others. The apostle John wrote, "For this is the love of God, that we keep his commandments. And his commandments are not burdensome" (1 John 5:3, RSV).

Remember, a disciple develops character in community with others. This book has covered the process of discipleship, and everything I've written applies to pastors and church leaders as much as it applies to any other disciples.

For example, you need accountability. Accountability happens in relationships of trust and in an environment of grace. Accountability without trusting relationships will feel militaristic and be short-lived. Therefore it won't get at many of the deeper reasons you're not growing. It will drive unresolved sin, guilt, and shame deeper into the hidden places of your soul. There they remain unhealed and eventually resurface in damaging ways. So start with someone you trust and who offers you grace to hold you accountable.

The method: The method is tried and true: "Entrust to reliable men who will also be qualified to teach others" (2 Timothy 2:2). This means that, as a leader, you choose to invest your best effort in developing faithful leaders who'll be able to reproduce. This might mean spending a good deal of your time meeting with a few people in order to create a larger impact later.

Neglecting this simple process for so many years has created our weakness as a church. Pastors and other leaders often don't have the patience and commitment to disciple individuals. It's just too tempting to build a larger congregation faster through preaching. A pastor's behavior reveals what he really cares about. Sadly many pastors care about success in numbers and being recognized for their skills. Leaders who want to follow Jesus must abandon this quest for "success." Of course, keep preaching and strategizing the best you can, but put your best effort in the training of faithful leaders. Staff meetings and an occasional leadership retreat don't cut it. You must make a sustained effort one-on-one or in groups of three or four to develop the best results. Consider Paul's advice to Timothy:

> Now you have observed my teaching, my conduct, my aim in life, my faith, my patience, my love, my steadfastness, my persecutions, my sufferings, what befell me at Antioch, at Iconium, and at Lystra, what persecutions I endured; yet from them all the Lord rescued me. . . . But as for you, continue in what you have learned and firmly believed, knowing from whom you learned it. (2 Timothy 3:10-11,14, RSV)

> What you have learned and received and heard and seen in me, do; and the God of peace will be with you. (Philippians 4:9, RSV)

These words scream *relationship* — working together, spending time with each other, knowing each other intimately. They speak of the influence of one person's character on another. As Nouwen said, "The greatest gift I have to offer is my own joy of living, my own inner peace, my own silence and solitude, my own sense of well-being."[12]

So take off the leadership garb for a moment and ask yourself, "Who am I influencing for Christ from my life, not from my position? If it wasn't my job to reach people for Christ, would I try? What evidence exists outside my professional efforts to prove it?"

If you want to give words power, you must be an example (see 1 Peter 5:1-6). Give yourself to being the kind of leader whose life affects those around you. Start small and think big. It's not splash and dash, but in time this process will work better than anything you've ever tried.

Give Yourself to Others

Give others what? Give them who Christ is in you, and teach them to follow him as you've learned to follow him. I have four recommendations:

1. Enroll yourself in the study and practice of the spiritual disciplines.
2. Enroll a select few in the process with you.
3. Teach it to everyone in your community.
4. Create a society of the willing.

Enroll yourself in the study and practice of the spiritual disciplines. Pastors usually choose theological education. My own was primarily evangelical, which means I had little exposure to spiritual formation literature. If this also describes you, I'd suggest a reading regiment in order to introduce yourself to this valuable resource.

For Concepts and Ideas:
- *The Cost of Discipleship* by Dietrich Bonhoeffer
- *The Company of the Committed* by Elton Trueblood
- *The Spirit of the Disciplines* by Dallas Willard
- *The Divine Conspiracy* by Dallas Willard
- *Celebration of Discipline* by Richard Foster
- *The Unnecessary Pastor* by Eugene Peterson and Marva Dawn
- *The Mentored Life* by James Houston
- *Working the Angles* by Eugene Peterson

For the Devotional Life:

- *Devotional Classics* by Richard Foster (introductory readings from the classic spiritual writers)
- *A Guide to Prayer for Ministers and Other Servants* by Reuben Job and Norman Shawchuck (structure based on the liturgical year, with many good readings from classic writers)

The Classics:

- *Imitation of Christ* by Thomas à Kempis
- *The Rule of St. Benedict*
- *The Confessions of St. Augustine*
- *Pensées* by Blaise Pascal
- *Introduction to the Devout Life* by Francis de Sales
- *Purity in Heart* by Søren Kierkegaard
- *The Spiritual Exercises of St. Ignatius*

Reading these books allows you to enter another world filled with mystery and heart devotion. These writers were great scholars with great minds and lives of discipline, yet their writing both comes from and speaks to the heart in a way foreign to us. As you read these books, you'll need to make allowance for beliefs and practices suitable only to the time when they were written. Reading and meditating on the classics will help you cultivate a heart for God.

Enroll a select few in the process with you. Every leader has the impulse to help others. Now that you've chosen this new way of following Jesus — his words, his works, his methods, and his character — you need others to walk with you. Find two others to provide you with the accountability and dynamic of three. (Two people can easily let things slide, and the lack of real progress becomes their secret. Three provide more accountability and transformational traction.) As we've discussed before, the goal is developing relationships of trust and allowing others to speak into your life.

After a few months to a year, you should see how this triad relationship has deepened your walk with God and with the two others. If you've gained something meaningful, prayerfully consider widening the group, with each of you choosing two others. Over two years, you could develop a core community of fifteen to twenty who have walked together. At that point, you have enough people in meaningful transformation for two things to result. First, the people involved will notice changes in their life. Second, their spouses, work associates, children, and friends will be commenting on the changes they've benefited from.

Teach it to everyone in your community. This means introducing and explaining the life. The need for the life. The call to the life. The habits of the life. You can introduce this through a sermon series or a retreat. Once you establish a core community through the expanding triads mentioned on page 274, you can safely broaden it without dilution. Because so many have experienced the benefits of those relationships, you'll easily captivate others.

Of course, in order to grow these relationships using the principle of discipleship, you need leaders who are already trained.[13]

Create a society of the willing. A segment of any spiritual group will hunger for more. In my case, 120 people agreed to meet with others to go deeper with God and to break through obedience barriers that had delayed their transformation. The higher we set the bar, the hungrier people became. What was supervised well flourished; what was supervised poorly failed. You can't make disciples without accountability and you can't have accountability with large numbers without structure.

The society will flourish if leaders model and manage it. This doesn't take a great deal of work. First, people need assessment, to establish where they are on their spiritual journeys. Next, based on assessment, they should be placed with others who have common interests or relationships. In fact, it's best if people choose their own partners to meet with. In addition, a curriculum is helpful, such as books to read, studies to complete—just some structure so people don't get lost in a directionless relationship.

Call or contact everyone once a month to see how they're doing and if they need help. If they have had a good experience, challenge them to add more people for the purpose of multiplication.

So there you have it. The challenge is immense, but the pressure is off. We enroll in this life with humility and in submission; we don't have to *make* anything happen. We simply must devote ourselves to live out the life Jesus lived. We give up the gods that distract us and have such a hold on our lives. We give ourselves to the development of the inner life, give our best effort to the discipleship principle, and then give ourselves to others. In the end there will be a new order of societies throughout this world of men and women who have chosen the life of following Christ. Those who have so chosen will be transformed and will transform those around them.

SUGGESTED RESOURCES

Appendix A, "Five Models of Effective Discipleship," on page 303 contains condensed excerpts from *Growing True Disciples* by George Barna (Waterbrook, 2001). Barna tells the stories of five churches he believes are doing an effective job of making disciples.

Appendix B, "Research for Evaluating Congregations," on page 309 gives a summary of the reasons evangelicals are doing poorly in developing their people.

Growing True Disciples by George Barna (Waterbrook, 2001). Provides a clear and concise look at the state of disciple-making in America.

The Master's Plan for Making Disciples by Win and Charles Arn (Revell, 1998). Has a church-growth feel to it and may be a bit too technocratic for some, but will appeal to those who desire high structure.

The Master Plan of Discipleship by Robert Coleman (Revell, 1998). Not the classic that *The Master Plan for Evangelism* is, but a good look at disciple-making from a respected leader.

The Disciple-Making Church by Bill Hull (Revell, 1998). Answers the question, "Did Jesus' disciples disciple others like he did them?" The answer is yes, but the reader will see that it was a lot more messy and disorganized than reported by many who think discipleship is about symmetry.

Working the Angles by Eugene Peterson (Eerdmans, 1990). A personal favorite filled with humor and biting insights. Peterson at his best.

SPIRITUAL GENERATIONS

My grandfather was fifteen minutes early for everything. It's just the way he was. I never needed training on how to be on time as an adult. My grandpa took care of that while I grew up, with his "spiritual formation" of me.

I also keep things simple. I have two belts: one casual, one for dress. I have two pairs of shoes: one casual, one for dress. It's how I was raised.

Discipleship is a lot like my training to be fifteen minutes early. My grandpa modeled a characteristic (being fifteen minutes early). I observed him modeling it consistently (he was fifteen minutes early to everything). I observed behaviors that led to the characteristic (keeping choices, like what belt or shoes to wear, simple). I realized that the characteristic was desirable (less stressful than running behind and being seen as an unreliable person). And I eventually made the characteristic my own (practiced it until it became part of my nature).

Perhaps the most common word associated with discipleship is *reproduction*. Knowingly or not, my grandfather reproduced a behavior in me. Just as Jesus trained his followers, we must do the same. The training of disciples makes fulfillment of the Great Commission possible, so if we neglect this process, the mission to the world will languish.

It's time for us to admit that we have allowed the process of discipleship and fulfilling the Great Commission to languish. In chapter 1, I pointed out the failure of the multiplication method as the sole strategy for obeying the Great Commission. Real life lacks the symmetry that charts and graphs so nicely display. I've never seen a real-life example of a person training two people for six months, then those two finding two and then reproducing that for the next six months, and so on. Life just doesn't work that way. Frankly, not enough can happen in six months for people to sustain reproduction of skill and character sufficient to transform.

Spiritual reproduction, on the other hand, creates spiritual generations that can be as short as a few minutes or as long as decades. I've known people who committed to follow Christ and later that day led their whole family to make the same commitment. While that would qualify as a spiritual generation regarding entry to the Christian faith, it wouldn't qualify under Jesus' more sweeping command to "[teach] them to obey everything I have commanded you" (Matthew 28:20).

Fortunately the church continues regardless of how poorly we attend to apprenticeship and training. Jesus promised to build his church, and he has kept his word. But God also asks for and needs our cooperation. He created the discipleship process with us involved, so we shouldn't be proud of mere survival. Instead we should live up to our calling to become little Christs who change the world where we live, work, and play.

Throughout church history, intentional and well-planned

training has mixed with the more casual influence of one person's life on others. The monastics, who held Christianity together through the Middle Ages, were intentional, disciplined, and formal. Millions of men and women, whose names we don't know, have held the faith together in the ordinary, unspectacular daily grind of life.

Perhaps the best situation would be to combine both reproduction and multiplication approaches into a discipleship that can dramatically change the world. Of course, as with all of discipleship, we surprisingly find what seems new to us in the pages of Scripture. This would certainly be true of the spiritual generations approach Paul and his followers modeled.

THE RESPONSIBILITY TO REPRODUCE:
A SACRED TRUST

We find the most compelling argument for passing on the sacred trust of the gospel woven into normal communication between a leader and his apprentice. Of course, I'm referring to the apostle Paul and Timothy. Paul wrote, "What you heard from me, keep as the pattern of sound teaching, with faith and love in Christ Jesus. Guard the good deposit that was entrusted to you — guard it with the help of the Holy Spirit who lives in us" (2 Timothy 1:13-14).

From our perspective some two thousand years later, we can easily dismiss Paul's words as simple encouragement to Timothy. But Paul wasn't just making a theoretical pronouncement. He was actually making a plea for faithfulness because he was losing support in the province of Asia and had been deserted by two friends, Phygelus and Hermogenes. So Timothy's faithfulness was necessary. It was a sacred trust.

In the first few centuries following Christ's death and resurrection, Christianity could have died. In an institutional and cultural sense, it was much more fragile than it is now. It became an integral part of culture about three hundred years later.

Today you can visit the ruins of Ephesus, the city in Turkey where Timothy lived and pastored when he received this letter from Paul. While the church is gone and Islam dominates the nation, Christianity survived because of the sacred deposit that was the gospel, not the church in Ephesus. So the gospel is the treasure that passes on from person to person. As the gospel spreads, God's kingdom will expand.

NEEDED: BOTH A PAUL AND A TIMOTHY

For the gospel to continue spreading, two kinds of people are necessary. First, a Paul. A Paul says, "I have this trust, and I need to pass it on to someone who has the character and competence to protect and promote it." You might be a parent wanting to pass the gospel on in your family. Not all children are equal in their faith journey; some reject the message, while others see it as a good thing but not as *the* thing. But by God's grace, you can find at least one person who can carry on the sacred trust after you're gone.

Second, a Timothy. The apostle Paul had more confidence in Timothy than Timothy had in himself. Timothy was under attack, and he was young. Around the church, people might have said, "That young man is no Paul!" Of course, they were right, but God also called Timothy, who stood faithful and willing to endure to the end. Paul exhorted him, "For God did not give us a spirit of timidity, but a spirit of power, of love and of self-discipline" (2 Timothy 1:7).

REPRODUCTION REQUIRES
INTENTIONAL REPEATED ACTION

Although Timothy's confidence was low, Paul affirmed him and exhorted him to action: "I have been reminded of your sincere faith, which first lived in your grandmother Lois and in your mother Eunice and, I am persuaded, now lives in you also. For this reason I remind you to fan into flame the gift of God, which is in you through the laying on of my hands" (2 Timothy 1:5-6).

Paul wanted Timothy to fan into flame the remaining embers of his recognized call to leadership. Paul called on him to "be strong in the grace that is in Christ Jesus" (2:1). He wanted Timothy to take effective action that would ensure the continuation and health of the gospel in his own life, in the life of the church at Ephesus, and in the larger kingdom. Then Paul issued the best-known statement on reproduction found in Scripture: "And the things you have heard me say in the presence of many witnesses entrust to reliable men who will also be qualified to teach others" (2:2).

Paul let Timothy know that the task isn't easy. To make it work requires the discipline of a soldier, the vision of an athlete, and the patience of a farmer (see 2 Timothy 2:3-7). Paul knew Timothy would encounter the temptations of laziness, boredom, and impulsiveness.

What is our culture's mantra? Victory without sacrifice, achievement without vision, and get it now and pay later. Yet Paul's simple exhortation rings out over the centuries: "Endure hardship with us like a good soldier of Christ Jesus" (verse 3).

THE QUALITIES OF REPRODUCTION AND MULTIPLICATION

In spite of his lack of self-confidence and need for encouragement, Timothy exemplified qualities that leaders look for in their own Timothys.

Proper Selection of Personnel

The foundational quality for giving someone responsibility is that person's faithfulness. A faithful person is one who shows up, who does what she says she will do, and who does it consistently. That's why Paul used the word *reliable* in 2 Timothy 2:2. Most successful people show up and show up on time. When you ask them to take responsibility for setting up a room or giving a speech, you don't have to wring your hands wondering if it will happen. But this doesn't come naturally for most people. They don't just fall out of trees already faithful. For most, reliability is a developed quality. Someone trained them, just as my grandfather trained me to be fifteen minutes early.

The Paul-Timothy relationship reveals one of the most common desires of many leaders: to surround themselves with reliable people they don't have to check up on. Of course, to work with people who don't need to be checked on is to invest a lot of time checking up on them. Even the most reliable people need to be accountable, but it's so sweet when they're so reliable that checking up becomes a formality. Leaders want people who are teachable, who don't make excuses, and who have a passion for the work. That's how you develop faithfulness.

Several Passes on the Sacred Deposit

Delegation remains the number-one challenge in management. Captains of industry find that passing on work to others is the most frustrating part of their job. But creating an environment of repro-duction is far more comprehensive than delegation.

Reproduction is about more than the completion of a task. It's about passing on a transformed life. Changed people help other people change; reliable people can teach others. They care. They can feel the passion beating in their breasts. They are infectious. They are an unstoppable tide.

Yes, delegating to these reliable individuals requires training, schedules, plans, and assignments. But a deep passion to change the world around them fuels them. That fuel will be necessary to keep the gospel moving from generation to generation.

If you're thinking about taking reproduction seriously, dig in and stir the passion within, and then offer what you have to faithful people around you. That's how to start.

Passing on to the Right People

The right people also can teach. That doesn't mean the gift of teach-ing; it means the interest and ability to explain to others and to show them the way of Jesus. Some people can't handle this because either they're spiritually weak or they don't have the interest. The *New International Version* uses *qualified* in 2 Timothy 2:2. Sometimes reliable people aren't qualified to teach. Others might be qualified in ability, but they're not reliable (and therefore not qualified). The right people have both faithfulness and ability.

Paul urged Timothy to be careful who he spent time with and who he invested in. Every leader faces this tough decision because needy people can gobble up his time. When a leader begins to focus on the reliable and qualified instead of on those with chronic prob-lems, disagreement sometimes arises about how she is spending her time. Many well-intentioned leaders get off-task by deciding that the bigger the problem, the more time it deserves.

Sadly the result is leaders who are generic in function and

ineffective in their calling. The Christian leader's calling is to guard the gospel, then to entrust it to disciples and to promote reproduction and multiplication of the gospel through faithful and qualified men and women.

Imitation, Not Impersonation

Impersonation of a greatly loved leader isn't the worse offense, with the possible exception of impersonating Elvis. Young people naturally want to wear athletic gear and clothes like those of their heroes. But Paul reveals the difference between impersonation and the biblical tradition of imitation in his correspondence to the Corinthian church.

The Corinthian church had a serious problem. At least four factions warred over control. The first was the Apollos party, people who loved the eloquent teacher. The Cephas party loved the ministry of the big fisherman, Peter. Another group claimed that no one but Christ was worthy to follow, which sounds noble but actually meant they didn't want to be accountable to anyone. Finally, some wanted to follow Paul, the church's founder and their spiritual father.

Paul wasn't a diplomat. As an apostle, he didn't restrain himself from speaking out when he needed to. In dealing with the battle for control in the church at Corinth, he delivered what the great baseball pitcher Dizzy Dean would call "a hard high one."

I am not writing this to shame you, but to warn you, as my dear children. Even though you have ten thousand guardians in Christ, you do not have many fathers, for in Christ Jesus I became your father through the gospel. Therefore I urge you to imitate me. (1 Corinthians 4:14-16)

Paul's bold solution called for a return to the basics. He made it simple: "Imitate me." Stop fighting and start living in the tradition of the gospel that I taught you. This bold statement is full of courage, because Paul put his life, all that he had modeled, and the words he had spoken, on the line for examination.

Next Paul made a remarkable statement: "For this reason I am sending to you Timothy, my son whom I love" (verse 17). Paul and Timothy couldn't have been more different in temperament and style. Paul was a hard-nosed driver renowned for his ability to focus. He had a quick mind and boldly fulfilled his calling regardless of the price he had to pay. When Timothy first met him, Paul had been left for dead outside of Lystra, Timothy's hometown. Instead of fleeing for a better situation, Paul dusted himself off and went back into Lystra. Now, that's tough. That takes someone with determination and courage.

Timothy, on the other hand, was shy and retiring, possessed a nervous tummy, and was easy to intimidate. Paul said, "Imitate me," and then sent a person nothing like himself.

What Can Be Passed On

Apparently what Paul passed to Timothy wasn't personality or wardrobe. The reason he sent Timothy involved at least three qualities:

He was faithful in the Lord. There's that word again: *faithful.* You don't send a shaky novice into a volatile situation. You send your best, someone you can trust, someone who is proven, someone who made it through the battles and came through the pain and trouble.

He reminded Paul of his way of life in Christ Jesus. First and foremost, Christ calls us to reproduce character in others. Paul sent Timothy because Timothy had taken on his qualities, teachings, and character—Christlikeness and godliness. Imitation had nothing to do with outward traits. Rather Paul had learned and then passed on Christlike character to Timothy, Titus, Priscilla, Aquila, Luke, and others.

He had the same message and strategy. Paul knew that the danger of various factions wrestling for control of the church in Corinth meant that different versions of the gospel would be championed.

He also spoke against this to the Galatian churches: "Evidently some people are throwing you into confusion and are trying to pervert the gospel of Christ. But even if we or an angel from heaven should preach a gospel other than the one we preached to you, let him be eternally condemned!" (Galatians 1:7-8).

Timothy came to the Corinthians with a message that agreed with what Paul taught everywhere he went. We still have those teachings in Paul's writings and sermons. The key to reproduction is having the same message and the same strategy. This allows the message to spread.

So, what does it mean to be a Paul and have a Timothy? The apostle Paul invested in people like Timothy and had them teach others. We can clearly see that character, message, and strategy result in effective reproduction. That's why so many different kinds of people can carry the message. We don't need to culturally clone disciples. We can let them be who they are, but emphasize character, message, and strategy.

Suggested Resources

Dedication and Leadership by Douglas Hyde (University of Notre Dame Press, 1995). An older book, but the very best on what it takes to train and reproduce.

Disciples Are Made Not Born by Walter Henrichsen (Victor, 2002). I don't agree with this book's title or thesis, but its mechanics of training are wonderful.

CHAPTER 12

THE FUTURE OF DISCIPLESHIP: LIVING THE JESUS WAY

I have a stack of books before me—books I very much enjoy. They're filled with philosophy, theology, and captivating narrative. They're written by leaders of what is called the emergent church, a movement that many think represents the future.

The emergent church is made up largely of younger leaders who hunger to bring freshness and a new power to the way we communicate the gospel. They use language filled with new ways of saying things, such as, "Stop counting conversions and start counting conversations." "Don't ask, where are we going; ask, what are we becoming?" "Don't measure it, instead experience it."

One of my favorite writers, Brian McLaren, has become the de facto leader of this movement. In his book *Generous Orthodoxy*, he calls himself a "post-protestant, liberal-conservative, Fundamentalist-Calvinist, a Methodist, a Catholic, a Mystical-Poetic, an Evangelical," and so on.

The term *generous orthodoxy* seems to be an oxymoron. McLaren cites the words of Hans Frei, who coined it: "Generosity without orthodoxy is nothing, but orthodoxy without generosity is worse than nothing." McLaren labels the "modern, exclusivist, absolutist, colonial version of Christianity" worse than nothing.[1]

A Challenge and a Worry

I have great admiration when devout men and women search for the Jesus life. They stand ready to challenge much of the cultural understanding of evangelicalism. They do this for two reasons: First, because many of them are young and that's what the young naturally do; second, because they hunger to get past the dead orthodoxy so common in the Bible-believing community.

Wait—let me restate that. They hunger to get past the dead orthodoxy so common in Bible-*knowing* churches that aren't believing and aren't communities. These churches have adopted faith as agreement, and they employ the doctrinal test for salvation, rather than Jesus' behavioral one. Notice I said "test for salvation," not "means of salvation," which I firmly believe to be faith alone in Christ alone. But faith's only character is action.

I'm with the emergent movement leaders in their challenge in many ways. Much of their literature creates a lot of questions, and I support them in asking the questions. They're wrestling with the mixing of conservative politics with evangelical theology. They're questioning the ungenerous orthodox doctrines of election, Jesus being the only way to God, the treatment of homosexuals, and the eternal nature of hell. My worry is that the questions abound, but the answers don't. My fear is that these writings in unknowing hands could be damaging to evangelical faith.

Like me, a lot of people don't like the answers we do have, but we're compelled to hold to them because of our commitment to the authority of Scripture. Someday those of us a bit older hope that the answers we have will bring us a more generous orthodoxy, but an orthodoxy that remains faithful to Scripture. As Dallas Willard aptly said, "Reacting against the modern church is not a gospel."[2]

McLaren asks us to consider this question:

> Is it possible that there is a way of seeing and being that is beyond modern exclusivism/absolutism and beyond plural-istic relativism? Could there be an approach that avoids both stagnant, modern fundamentalism and narcissistic boomeritis? Is it possible that modern, exclusivist, absolut-ist Christians are right — pluralistic relativism is dangerous? But is it possible that the way ahead is not to stop short of a pluralistic phase, but rather to go through it and pass beyond it, emerging into something beyond and better?[3]

My answer is, I hope so, and Godspeed.

However, I'm afraid that this sounds a lot like a Buddhist tour guide I once had in Beijing. As we sat together in the back of the car, he told me that all the cars around us were illusions and that we should search for a higher truth — a truth that went beyond the mind's empirical needs. So I asked him, "If one of those cars hit you, would that be an illusion?"

I'm afraid that going beyond Scripture and two thousand years of wisdom from those who have preceded us is a true illusion. Meanwhile I think other critical issues will shape our future. The more dangerous issues are subtle and deeply woven into our minds and ways of life. The following is my understanding of the conflict.

I believe that our culture, and the consumerism that dominates our culture, have taken the "good" out of the good news. The result is a filter on the future, regardless of what comes at us.

THE RIGHT THING IN THE WRONG WAY[4]

There's an old story about St. Patrick baptizing a Druid priest.[5] Both men stood in the water, and St. Patrick inadvertently placed his staff on the priest's foot. When the baptism was complete, Patrick said, "You can go now."

The priest answered, "I can't."

"Why not?" a puzzled Patrick responded.

"Your staff is on my foot."

"Oh, I'm so sorry," Patrick said. "Why didn't you tell me?"

The priest answered, "I thought that was part of it."

St. Patrick had done the right thing, baptizing the priest. But he'd done it in the wrong way, with his staff on the priest's foot. Like the Druid priest, we've learned to endure unpleasant experiences: Leaders who don't care that much about God or us. Churches that bore and drain the joy out of our souls. Silly power struggles that sicken the spirit. We think that's just the way it is.

Yes, being a Christian and living with other Christians will always be difficult. Sin is within us, and therefore in the church. But in the midst of the battle, we must know that we're doing things that bring transformation.

TWO PHILOSOPHIES

Two philosophies are at war. The first is the Jesus way. It is a way of sacrifice, submission, humility, and patience. In this worldview, God is at the center and his disciples live for others because Jesus was a man for others. In the Jesus way, life isn't about us; it's about God. The Jesus way shows us that the means is just as important as the end.

The other philosophy, which dominates, is the consumer way. This is a world of consumption, assertiveness, speed, and fame. In the consumer world, it's all about me. The consumer culture creates the consumer church, and that gives us consumer Christians. The consumer Christian culture focuses on receiving benefits and getting into heaven. The story is about us rather than God. We cultivate artificial needs, create an environment of instant gratification, package the teaching of Scripture into neat formulas, and conduct worship centered on personal needs and taste.

The distinction might be put as succinctly as this: In the Jesus way, Jesus becomes more. In the consumer way, humans become more.

These philosophies are mortal enemies, but many good Christian people live on without knowing they've been seduced by the culture. No one reminds them that "no one can serve two masters; for either he will hate the one and love the other, or else he will be loyal to the one and despise the other. You cannot serve God and mammon" (Matthew 6:24, NKJV).

This isn't just about material wealth; that trivializes the subject and misses the point. Instead it's about what Eugene Peterson said well: "The American Culture is stubbornly resistant to the way of Jesus."[6] The point is that the priorities and practices of the consumer religious culture aren't sufficient to form the person of Christ in his followers. Far too many ministries and churches are stuck in a rut of non-transformational religious activity. As a result, we've created consumers who are nice, moral people but who make little difference to the people in their life.

Mammon represents the entire superstructure of pride. We might think of Ayn Rand's superman, who objectifies everything and everyone.[7] In consumer Christianity, mammon plays out in the person who reads the Bible, goes to church, and uses his skills to take his church or business to the next level. It's part of an entire world system that elevates humans to a god-like status. It's about leaders manipulating, bullying, pushing, and pulling people to serve their own agendas and needs. And it's about depersonalizing God into a doctrine and our neighbors into a project.

THE JESUS WAY OR THE CONSUMER WAY?

There are four ways to show the conflict between the Jesus way of life and the consumer way of life.

1. Competence Before Prayer

Jesus modeled prayer as a priority. His actions demonstrated that his relationship with his Father was the basis for ministry. He prayed all night before important decisions. He slipped away to spend time with his Father (see Mark 1:35; John 5:19-30; Mark 1:16). He sought to relish his relationship with his Father and, in turn, could answer the only question that really counts: "What is the will of God?"

Dietrich Bonhoeffer left Germany in 1939 for New York City to teach at Union Theological Seminary. His friends and mentors thought it would be wise to spare him the Nazi persecution of the church. They reasoned that Bonhoeffer could return to teach and rebuild Germany after the war. But Bonhoeffer sought God's wisdom. He believed there was only one important question: "What is the will of God?" He boarded the last ship back to Germany before World War II began, and in 1945, he was executed for his part in a conspiracy to kill Hitler. Bonhoeffer's actions reflect a willingness to sacrifice that is the antithesis of consumer Christianity.

The consumer way is to act now, make an impact, get things done. The greatest temptation of the consumer way is to lead with competence. The danger of this is twofold. First, we falsely believe that after a period of time in the Christian way, we know enough and have cleaned up our life enough that we can get by without practicing disciplines such as prayer, solitude, mediation—the kinds of actions that build our dependence on God and culminate in the creation of character. Second, we start believing we can get the job done without contemplation.

I spent much of my life relying on my competence to lead people, create, speak, write, and sell ideas. In the end, it proved to be a cul de sac: I had to turn around and look for another way. That other way is a life of prayer, silence, solitude, and meditation, which multiplies and enhances competence.

So, there it is. The church has been doing the right thing—working to build the cause of Christ—in the wrong way—depending on competence rather than a prayerful life of dependence on God.

2. Individualism Instead of Congregation

Ever since the Renaissance, a revival in art and literature, and the Enlightenment, a philosophical movement based on rationalism and skepticism, people have moved God out of the center and replaced him with themselves. This focus on the individual taught that individual rights, individual thoughts, and individual needs are paramount. This was a serious shift from the previous worldview, which valued community and, in religious terms, the congregation.

The congregation provides the home base where we form our Christian life. In the congregation, we develop our identity. Again, the congregation isn't about us—it's about God. God's plan involves creating a new community wherever his disciples learn to love him by loving one another.

Disciples worship in the context of the community. The biblical metaphor for worship is sacrifice. We come to the altar to sacrifice, to serve, to set aside our own agendas. Like Jesus, we choose to live the life of submission to others, to consider their needs equal to ours—or even above our own (see Philippians 2:3-14). We gather to contribute to each other's lives.

Individualism turns congregation into a consumer enterprise. The advertising industry stirs up needs in us that we don't even know we have, and Christian leaders often join right in with gusto. We've recast the gospel into consumer items, entertainment, adventure, problem solving, and formulas to help us get an edge. We've learned to draw a crowd by offering them whatever the culture teaches them they need. We've become world-class consumers and providers of religious goods and services.

The problem, however, is that the discipleship offered in a consumer package targeted at individual needs isn't sufficient to form people into the image of Christ. Studying without reflection, measuring maturity by knowledge, and finishing curriculum for its own sake—these don't have any traction. It's not the way Jesus brings people into conformity to his will.

The consumer Christian culture makes us become more, while Jesus becomes less. As a result, we don't live sacrificially and we aren't available to others. This is the antithesis of the sacrificial, deny-yourself servant that Jesus was and calls us to be.

So, there it is. Doing the right thing—gathering people into congregation—but in the wrong way—cultivating consumer Christians.

3. Impatience Rather Than Endurance

Impatience might be the most accepted sin in America. We're an impetuous people. Everything seems to be available now, so we've been trained to expect it instantly. I marvel at how the Internet meets my insatiable appetite for knowledge, products, and services in just seconds. As the culture moves faster, the faster we go and the less we "become."

The people leaders serve want relief and answers today—or tomorrow at the latest. The culture forms them to want leaders who please them, not leaders who challenge and change them.

Have you seen the film *Super Size Me*? This entertaining documentary chronicles a young man who gained thirty pounds and developed medical problems from eating three meals a day for thirty days at McDonald's. Spiritual fast food will destroy us too. When we read the Bible with the goal of fulfilling our potential, of getting a handle on principles, of gaining an edge on others, or of increasing our capacity at work, we're consuming scriptural fast food.

Why do we know so much but live so badly? Don't read the Bible to enhance your self-image. Read it to receive, to respond, to submit, to listen to God's voice so you can serve and humbly obey. Read under the authority of God's Word, not to get ahead. Karl Barth said, "I have read many books, but the Bible reads me." As Jesus said, "The one who hears my words and does not put them into practice is like a man who built a house on the ground without a foundation. The moment the torrent struck that house, it collapsed and its destruction was complete" (Luke 6:49).

We can't hurry the formation of character into the person of Christ. It's slow and messy work. People fail, fear, delay, make mistakes, and resist. It can't be hurried; yet it's urgent, it can't be delayed.

In America, slow and urgent aren't compatible. They cancel each other out. But in God's kingdom, patience and urgency are yoked together. The consumer religious culture wants people to get things done and to look for shortcuts to becoming the person God builds over a long time.

The culture not only doesn't foster patience, it's contemptuous of that virtue. Patience is the first thing most people throw overboard in a storm. The storm today is the mania for success. We rush to build a great ministry, a great law practice, a wonderful business, because then we can feel affirmed, have the resources we desire, and do it in the time frame we have planned. However, this puts us in our own self-made pressure cooker: If we don't meet our expectations, we've failed. Then we must work harder and find someone to blame.

I think of Paul's words to the Galatians as the right alternative: "Let us not become weary in doing good, for at the proper time we will reap a harvest if we do not give up" (Galatians 6:9).

So, there it is. Doing the right thing—working to build a business or ministry for Christ—but in the wrong way—taking short-cuts, pushing, and manipulating others to meet our time frame and our desired results.

4. Celebrity Over Humility

Psychologist Robert Hogan wrote in the *Harvard Business Review* that humility rather than self-esteem is the key trait of successful leaders.[8] Wouldn't it be great if followers of Jesus believed him? The Christian world has a highly developed celebrity system indistinguishable from its secular equivalent. In fact, it isn't separate at all. Christian speakers and entertainers demand the same limos, dressing-room cuisine, and preferential treatment as their secular counterparts. Yet I'm not referring only to the elite, who comprise less than one percent of the population. Celebrities can display humility while people in the most humble circumstances can demand celebrity treatment.

I once hosted a local debate program on television. I had no problem getting congressmen, pastors, and advocates to appear. Something about that little red light on the camera has a seductive quality. In a culture that believes any publicity is good publicity, we shouldn't be surprised that part of the consumer religious culture includes a hunger for recognition. It begins with the small things, such as compliments that feed our need to know we've done well. But then we slip into addiction, needing affirmation, genuine or not. When others don't celebrate us, we feel empty because we've consumed their praise as our spiritual food.

The tendency of leaders and followers alike to celebrate themselves debilitates the Christian cause. Worship becomes about us—our tastes, likes, and dislikes. The drive within us is to see ourselves at the center of every song, every sermon, every event, every conversation. And every problem reminds us of our own problems.

Humility, on the other hand, removes self from center and puts God there. We become supporting players; the world and God's plan don't orbit around us. Jesus was a man for others. As his disciple, then, my life is about others; only then will I find myself. As Bonhoeffer said, "The church is only the church when it exists for others."

I'm Jesus' disciple when I celebrate him, not me. The gospel is about how to live. And the way we learn to live is by learning to die. Once you have life, Jesus says, "Now I'll teach you how to give it up."

So, there it is. Doing the right thing—trying to live for God—but in the wrong way—making it all about me.

CHOOSING THE JESUS WAY

The Jesus way is prayer, congregation, endurance, and humility. Seeking and living in a state of brokenness or humility enhances and multiplies competence. We must throw celebrity and impatience overboard and rearrange our lives around the priorities and practices of Jesus. We can expect an array of the popular and the fast to tempt us, but we must beware that it doesn't take us by the hand and pull us into the ditch!

If you make a commitment to this process, you will feel like a person driving the speed limit but being passed on both sides by those in a hurry to arrive at a disappointing or worthless destination. The best and the brightest will try to speed up spiritual growth and contort the gradual nature of normal growth. "How can we speed this up?" is the natural human response, but accelerated growth by any means only does damage.

Unfortunately these tactics bring out the "freak" in the church. The freak is armed with all the right religious phrases and clichés, but thoroughly disciples into the culture instead of into Christ.

So let's follow the simple ideas in our filter of prayer, congregation, endurance, and humility. The shape of discipleship in the future will determine the strength and ability of the church to be the church and to live for others instead of for itself.

SUGGESTED RESOURCES

A Generous Orthodoxy by Brian McLaren (Zondervan, 2004). Covers the waterfront of issues facing the church.

A New Kind of Christian by Brian McLaren (Jossey-Bass, 2001). Wrestles with the church and kingdom issues.

The Last Word and the Word After That by Brian McLaren (Jossey-Bass, 2005). A very hot treatment on the question of hell.

Blue Like Jazz by Donald Miller (Thomas Nelson, 2003). What are young people thinking? A wonderfully engaging discussion of the issues.

The Post-Christian Mind by Harry Blamires (Regent College Publishing, 2004). A master writes about the real differences in the way people think.

Reimagining Spiritual Formation: A Week in the Life of an Experimental Church by Doug Pagitt (Zondervan, 2004). An emergent church gives it a go. This book puts some feet on what the entire movement is advocating.

FIVE MODELS OF
EFFECTIVE DISCIPLESHIP

Researcher George Barna chose five churches that, in his judgment, were doing an effective job of making disciples. Each church followed a different model of discipleship. The following are short excerpts from his findings.[1]

THE COMPETENCIES MODEL:
PANTEGO BIBLE CHURCH, DALLAS

This model is a highly integrated approach to discipleship that stands out in its emphasis on personal assessment and integration. The model is based on the Great Commandment and the Great Commission and broken into thirty specific competencies: ten core beliefs, ten core practices, and ten core virtues. The process considers these thirty dimensions in light of the disciple's relationship with God and with other people.

This model requires the substantive integration of everything the church does. The worship services provide inspiration to become disciples, and the sermons are built around the thirty core competencies. The competencies model doesn't use events. This model also minimizes other church programs and specialized ministries in favor of accomplishing all ministry through these existing avenues. Each person in the church goes through assessment and then engages in practices that can improve their spiritual strength.

THE MISSIONAL MODEL: FELLOWSHIP BIBLE CHURCH OF LITTLE ROCK, ARKANSAS

This kind of approach matches the church's purpose with its programs. The mission of the church is to help people become spiritually mature as manifested in six core qualities or competencies:

1. Being passionately committed to Jesus Christ
2. Evaluating everything in their lives according to biblical standards
3. Being deeply committed to having a healthy family
4. Being morally pure
5. Being evangelistically bold
6. Being socially responsible and influential

The church sponsors small groups that make it possible for the members to create a Personal Development Plan. The church calendar is developed a year in advance to enable people to create a stable plan of activity. Once the personal plan is developed, the individual shares it with the others in his or her small group. The group encourages and prays for one another throughout the year in their efforts to grow in their areas of emphasis.

THE NEIGHBORHOOD MODEL:
PERIMETER CHURCH, ATLANTA

People new to the church attend an inquirer's class to gain a general overview of the church. Once they decide they want to get serious about involvement, they join a neighborhood congregation, which is a group of fifteen to twenty people from the same geographic location. That group meets twice each month. One meeting focuses on worship, teaching, and fellowship, with members encouraged to invite guests. Members can invite guests to either meeting. The group is led by a lay pastor who has received extensive preparation via a pastoral training process complete with qualifying tests, class-room teaching, textbooks, written tests, and oral examinations. The neighborhood congregation is the church's primary delivery point for spiritual nurture and care. It is also the main launching pad for outreach opportunities. Multiple neighborhood congregations are linked together for outreach activities, such as concerts at the church.

Members of the geographic units are encouraged to get involved in a more intensive discipling environment by joining a disciple-ship team. Each discipler leads five to nine individuals of the same gender through the developmental process. Each participant creates a personal life plan. The plan defines the person's mission, vision, values, goals, and schedule for pursuing desired growth outcomes. The plan also identifies how the individual will strive to mature in five specific areas:

1. Bible knowledge
2. Practical ministry skills
3. Outreach
4. Prayer
5. Accountability

The program runs on three-year cycles, divided into six six-week modules per year.

THE WORLDVIEW MODEL: FELLOWSHIP BIBLE CHURCH NORTH, PLANO, TEXAS

The primary thrust of the Worldview Model is imparting biblical wisdom that leads to personal transformation. This model is designed to increase people's participation in the church, to upgrade their level of service to other people, and to improve their ability to understand issues and make decisions from a biblical perspective. The primary objective of this process is to encourage people to think and behave biblically — in other words, to adopt a truly biblical worldview.

The model relies on a two-year process that gives groups of people a thorough grounding in the foundational truths of Christianity. The discipleship curriculum known as the Discovery Series encompasses four topical books requiring an average of sixty to ninety minutes per week in personal reading, study, and reflection. The training asks people to:

- Identify the issue at hand
- Study the Bible in relation to that issue
- Gather wisdom from other sources
- Make a personal response to the accumulated information
- Discuss that response with the other members of the group
- Develop personal strategies for living out the truth discovered

THE LECTURE-LAB MODEL: NORTH COAST CHURCH, VISTA, CALIFORNIA

This is the "loosest" or most casual of the five spiritual development approaches. In this case, the sermon becomes more than a warm and fuzzy-but-forgettable message. Because the sermon material forms the substantive foundation of a second go-round for small group participants, the biblical principles imparted are hammered home at least twice.

Clearly, the major downside of the model—but one that could be overcome without much difficulty—is the absence of any objective, broad-based evaluation system. The church does make some effort to determine the spiritual health of believers through head-counts, ease of recruiting participants for ministry opportunities, and anecdotal evidence.

A "BEST OF" MODEL

The following is Barna's summary of these five models. These may be the most helpful for application into life and ministry.

- The senior pastor is an irrepressible advocate of discipleship.
- Church membership is granted only when a person covenants to participate in a focused, demanding discipleship process.
- All ministry programs are intimately tied to discipleship outcomes.
- The number of programs is minimized in order to focus the church's ministry on and through the discipleship process.
- All teaching in the church, from Sunday morning classes

for elementary school children through the worship service and other adult teaching venues, is substantively coordinated.

- The church's mission statement serves as a practical tool for identifying necessary ministry outcomes that are tied to an annually updated series of goals that directly relate to the mission statement and to the spiritual state of the congregation.

RESEARCH FOR EVALUATING CONGREGATIONS

George Barna's *Growing True Disciples* provides some excellent hard data based on his research of congregations across America.

WHY CONGREGATIONS DO POORLY

Barna lists the following as some of the reasons evangelicals are doing poorly in developing their people:

1. Few churches or Christians have a clear, measurable definition of "Spiritual Success."
2. We've defined "Discipleship" as head knowledge, rather than complete transformation.
3. We've chosen to teach people in random rather than systematic ways.
4. There's virtually no accountability for what we say, think, do, or believe.
5. When it comes to discipleship, we promote programs rather than people.
6. The primary method that churches rely on for spiritual development (small groups) typically fails to provide

comprehensive spiritual nurture.

7. Church leaders aren't zealous about the spiritual development of people.

8. We invest our resources in adults rather than in children.

9. We divert our best leaders to ministries other than discipleship.[1]

WHAT MAKES CHURCHES EFFECTIVE AT DISCIPLE-MAKING

Barna's research showed that "a church engaged in effective discipleship is a church that will grow steadily and solidly."[2] In addition, the research demonstrated how churches can correct the nine flaws above. Every church doing well did a few of the following nine things well.

1. The leaders had passion for making disciples.

2. Depth: Personal growth and spiritual reproduction were one and the same.

3. Maturity: The end product was for a person to reach his or her highest earthly potential in Christ.

4. Practice: The repeated acting of the will created habits and therefore, character.

5. Process: Discipleship is not a destination but a journey. The process is lifelong and one must be patient.

6. Interactive: Discipleship is done in community, not in isolation.

7. Multifaceted: The process incorporates a variety of thrusts toward building us up in Christ.

8. Lifelong: Every day of life for all of life. Don't think program, trust the process.

9. Christ-like: The marker is Jesus, being formed into his image; all else is a waste of effort.[3]

While the research reveals nine things that leaders or churches are doing right or wrong, rarely (almost never in fact) are any leaders or churches doing all the listed things. They usually have five or six out of nine of the characteristics—good or bad—so please keep that in mind as you handle the data.

NOTES

Introduction

1. Dietrich Bonhoeffer, *The Cost of Discipleship* (New York: Macmillan, 1937), 64.
2. Bonhoeffer, 64-65.
3. Dallas Willard, notes taken at his speech at the Spiritual Formation Forum, Los Angeles, May 2004.

Chapter 1: Biblical Foundations of Discipleship

1. Armand M. Nicholi Jr., *The Question of God: C. S. Lewis and Sigmund Freud Debate God, Love, Sex, and the Meaning of Life* (New York: Free Press, 2003), 46.
2. When the Pharisees asked Jesus about the greatest commandment (see Matthew 22:34-40), it was a trick question. The closest Jesus came to repeating those words again was in the Upper Room when he commanded the disciples to "love one another. . . . By this all men will know that you are my disciples, if you love one another" (John 13:34-35). This means that loving one another is a mark of a follower of Jesus. However, his commission commanded his follower to be that kind of person *and* to teach others to live that way. The subtext of the Great Commission can be found in the other gospels and Acts: "Go into all the world and preach the good news to all creation" (Mark 16:15); "Repentance and forgiveness of sins will be preached in his name to all nations" (Luke

24:47); "Peace be with you! As the Father has sent me, I am sending you" (John 20:21); "But you will receive power when the Holy Spirit comes on you; and you will be my witnesses in Jerusalem, in all Judea and Samaria, and to the ends of the earth" (Acts 1:8). These four passages support the most clear or formal statement of the Great Commission found in Matthew. Those in Mark, Luke, and John constitute fragments of the larger picture, while the Acts statement specifically focuses on the necessity of the Holy Spirit to fulfill the commission.

3. William Law, "Christian Perfection 2," in *The Works of the Rev. William Law*, vol. 3, 263.

4. Gordon Mursell, ed., *Story of Christian Spirituality* (Minneapolis: Fortress Press, 2001), 284.

5. "Global North" refers to the northern hemisphere and "Global South" to the southern hemisphere.

6. *Koinonia*, a Greek word translated *fellowship* in Acts 2:42 and described in 4:44, involves sharing life together based on commonality in Christ.

7. Ephesians 5:18-21 teaches that a Spirit-filled culture is a culture of submission.

8. Michael Wilkins, *Following the Master* (Grand Rapids, MI: Zondervan, 1992), 38.

9. Wilkins, 40.

10. See Bill Hull, *The Disciple-Making Pastor* (Grand Rapids: Baker, paperback ed., 1999), 54-60. Also see Wilkins, 24-47, for a thorough history of the word *disciple*.

11. Of course, a tough issue for the church is how to get Christians to intentionally befriend and develop relationships with unbelievers in their sphere of influence.

12. The actual figure is 10,737,418.24 dollars.

13. These four points are adapted from Michael Wilkins, "Eliminating Elitism from Our Traditions through Biblical

Reunification of Spiritual Formation and Discipleship," *Spiritual Formation: An Evangelical Perspective* (forthcoming).

14. Lesslie Newbigin, *The Gospel in a Pluralist Society* (Grand Rapids, MI: Eerdmans), 184.

15. Newbigin, 256.

16. See Luke 9:23-25; Philippians 2:1-8. A tendency exists to separate the gospel that Jesus taught from the one Paul developed. Jesus spoke of behavior as the test of a person's faith. This creates a problem for some, because most of us feel more comfortable with airtight theology. I find that many evangelicals are theologically informed but biblically illiterate; they adopt theological positions without reading the plain teachings of Scripture for themselves.

17. Bill Hull, *Choose the Life: Exploring a Faith That Embraces Discipleship* (Grand Rapids, MI: Baker, 2004).

18. Dietrich Bonhoeffer, *The Cost of Discipleship* (New York: Macmillan, 1937), 64.

19. Hull, *The Disciple-Making Pastor*, 60-73.

20. Hull, *Choose the Life*, 35-39.

Chapter 2: Origins of Discipleship

1. "Woman gets beer from her kitchen faucet," *USA Today*, March 13, 2006.

2. Michael Wilkins, *The Concept of Disciple in Matthew's Gospel: As Reflected in the Use of the Term "Mathetes"*, Novum Testamentum Supplements, vol. 59 (Leiden, The Netherlands: E. J. Brill, 1988), 12, 15-41. Wilkins sets the gold standard for linguistic work on *mathetes* and academic work on the theology of *disciple*.

3. Paul used this verbal form of *mathetes*, meaning "to learn," thirteen times in his epistles.

4. The Sophist school saw learning primarily as academic, with

no emphasis on the personal relationship between master and disciple. Plato, Socrates, and a number of other Greek philosophers disagreed to the extent that they didn't want to be associated with the Sophists.

5. Wilkins, 70.

6. Wilkins, 41-42.

7. Wilkins, 45.

8. Wilkins, 52.

9. Aaron helped by speaking for Moses (Exodus 7:8) and served him in other ways. Jethro made organizational suggestions that helped relieve daily pressure on Moses (Exodus 18).

10. Scholars disagree somewhat whether "my disciples" refers directly to God's disciples or Isaiah's. The best evidence seems to indicate that it refers to both. The distinctive of religious disciples is the dual discipleship of being followers of God as well as to one of his leaders. So a disciple could follow Yahweh and Yahweh's prophet, Isaiah. God often employs humans to help other humans in their spiritual journeys.

11. R. Coggins, A. Phillips, and M. Knibb, eds., "Origins of Prophecy in Israel" *Israel's Prophetic Tradition: Essays in Honor of Peter R. Ackroyd* (Cambridge: Cambridge University Press, 1982), 19.

12. Michael Wilkins, *Following the Master* (Grand Rapids, MI: Zondervan, 1992), 63.

13. Josephus, *The Jewish Wars* 1.:33.2.

14. See John 1:19-28. John the Baptist lived in Bethany, on the other side of the Jordan River, a day's walk from Jerusalem. Matthew 11:2 records that John's disciples were in Jerusalem to see Jesus.

15. Josephus, *Wars* 2.56.71-75, Antiq. 17.271-72, 278-85.

16. See John 6:15. A group of Zealots wanted to make Jesus king after the feeding of the five thousand. Instead Jesus withdrew.

17. Wilkins, *Following the Master,* 93.
18. See 2 Timothy 2:2. The command to teach others who will teach others provides convincing proof that Jesus, Peter, and then Paul were all on the same page regarding how to spread the gospel.
19. Wilkins, *The Concept of Disciple,* 123.
20. Four of the five observations are adapted from Bill Hull, *Choose the Life* (Baker: 2004), "Discipleship to Rabbi Yeshua," *Rabbi Yeshua,* June 2001. Accessed at http://www.rabbiye shua.com/rabbiyeshua/2001/discipleshiptoyeshua.html.
21. Doug Greenwald, *Making Disciples Jesus' Way* (Rockville, MD: Bible-in-Context Ministries, 2005), 14.
22. Greenwald, 15.
23. Thanks to Pastor Thomas Lancaster of Kehilat Sar Shalom for his helpful insights and guidance in this section.
24. *Manthano* means "to learn" or "to find out, understand, and hear." Wilbur Gingrich, *Shorter Lexicon of the Greek New Testament* (Chicago: University of Chicago Press, 1965), 131.
25. See Mark 3:14-16. Jesus called the Twelve to be with him and so that they would go out to preach. They graduated in the Upper Room, when Jesus said, "I no longer call you servants, because a servant does not know his master's business. Instead, I have called you friends, for everything that I learned from my Father I have made known to you" (John 15:15). This demonstrated a move to the responsibility of finding and making other disciples who followed Christ.
26. Jesus consistently delivered this message; see Matthew 28:18-20; John 15:15-16; Acts 1:8.

Chapter 3: The Story of Discipleship
1. Richard A. Burridge, "Jesus and the Origins of Christian Spirituality," in *The Story of Christian Spirituality: Two*

Thousand Years from East to West, ed. Gordon Mursell
(Minneapolis: Fortress Press, 2001), 36.

2. Generally scholars accept that a letter from Athanasius in 367 finalized the canon of the New Testament.

3. Martyrdom later became cultic because martyrs achieved great status. As you might imagine, this was never a popular cult. History demonstrates that most people give in rather than become martyrs. After a period of persecution, one of the church's problems was how to deal with those who gave in when facing torture and death.

4. See 3.1 in Lightfoot Translation of Ignatius letter to the Ephesians, 1891 translation, accessed at www.Ignatius.com.

5. See Lightfoot, 2.2. What Ignatius called the presbytery, we might today refer to as elders.

6. Jerome, On Illustrious Men, 17 Early Christians Web page

7. Christendom, defined as the mixing of church and state, offered common culture and thought. The king served as head of the church in his domain. Evangelism became foreign policy and included an invading army. Christendom led to widespread intolerance, the Crusades, and power mongering; the church eventually rotted from the inside out.

8. In Acts 24:16, RSV, *ascetical* (Greek: *asko*) is translated as "take pains" in reference to Paul's means to a clear conscience. I believe Paul referred to going before God to confess his sins rather than to an extreme life of self-denial.

9. Gordon Mursell, ed., *The Story of Christian Spirituality: Two Thousand Years from East to West* (Minneapolis: Fortress Press, 2001), 57.

10. Eberhard Bethge, *Dietrich Bonhoeffer: A Biography* (Minneapolis: Fortress Press, 2000), 309.

11. Mursell, 101.

12. Mursell, 104.

13. Harry Blamires, *The Christian Mind: How Should a Christian Think?* (London: SPCK, 1963), vii, 3.
14. Charles Malik, *The Two Tasks* (Downers Grove, IL: InterVarsity, 1980), 33.
15. See discussion on Ignatius in chapter 3.
16. Reginald Heber, *The Presbyterian Hymnal* (Louisville, KY: Westiminster/John Knox, 1990), as quoted in Eugene Peterson, *Christ Plays in Ten Thousand Places: A Conversation in Spiritual Theology* (Grand Rapids, MI: Eerdmans, 2005), 201.
17. Niccolo Malermi's Italian translation of the Bible, 1490.
18. Ross King, *Michelangelo and the Pope's Ceiling* (New York: Penguin, 2003), 203.
19. King, 203.
20. Peterson, 202.
21. Relics—the remains or possessions of saints such as pieces of cloth or dust from a saint's tomb—were religious souvenirs people bought and sold at very high prices. It would be similar to people today buying Billy Graham's old tie or shirt and thinking it would somehow keep them spiritual or forgive their sins.
22. Mursell, 168.
23. Roman Catholics and some other traditions believe transubstantiation occurs during the Eucharist, meaning that the bread and wine become the actual body and blood of Christ.
24. King, 215.
25. John Calvin, *The Institutes of the Christian Religion* 3.1.3.
26. Mursell, 248.
27. Mursell, 180.
28. Philip Jacob Spener, *Pia Desideria* (Minneapolis: Fortress Press, 1964), 87-115.
29. John Jackman, "Count Nicholas Ludwig von Zinzendorf," *Zinzendorf: The Count without Borders,* http://www.zinzendorf.com/countz.htm.

30. Mursell, 182.

31. *Wesley's Works I*, 306, cited in Gloster Udy, *Key to Change* (Sydney: 1962), 8.

32. Sydney Stevenson, *Wesley Family*, 196, cited in Udy, 10.

33. George H. Jones, ed., *The Methodist Primer* (Nashville, TN: Methodist Evangelistic Materials), 11.

34. Udy, 11.

35. Nolan B. Harmon, *Understanding the Methodist Church* (Nashville, TN: Parthenon Press, 1955), 11.

36. Udy, 13.

37. Malcolm Muggeridge, *A Third Testament: A Modern Pilgrim Explores the Spiritual Wanderings of Augustine, Blake, Pascal, Tolstoy, Bonhoeffer, Kierkegaard, and Dostoevsky* (Mary Knoll, NY: Orbis, 2004), 167.

38. Dietrich Bonhoeffer, *The Cost of Discipleship* (New York: Macmillan, 1949), 67.

39. Bonhoeffer, 64.

40. Bonhoeffer, 57-58.

41. Bonhoeffer, 48.

42. Translation of "Wer bin Ich?" from *Widerstand und Ergebung*, 381-382, as quoted in Dietrich Bonhoeffer, *A Testament to Freedom,* eds. Geffrey B. Kelly and F. Burton Nelson (San Francisco: Harper & Row, 1990), 514.

Chapter 4: The Distinguishing Marks of a Disciple

1. Rueben Job and Norman Shawchuck, *A Guide to Prayer for Ministers and Other Servants* (Nashville: Upper Room Books, 1983), 60.

2. George Barna, *The State of the Church 2002* (Ventura, CA: Issachar Press), 83.

3. Alexander McClaren, *PreachingToday*, www.preachingtoday .com. A poojah, most commonly spelled *pooja* or *puja*, is a

NOTES

ritual prayer or sacrifice to Hindu deities. In the extreme pooja
to which McClaren refers, a participant is suspended by hooks
passed through the muscle over the collarbones from a long
rope wrapped around a mast. He is then whirled around so as
to fly out centrifugally, causing intense pain.

4. Similar material appears in a different form in Bill Hull,
Choose the Life: Exploring a Faith That Embraces Discipleship
(Grand Rapids, MI: Baker, 2004), 46-59.

5. *Webster's New World Dictionary*, s.v. "attitude."

6. Malcolm Muggeridge, *Something Beautiful for God* (San
Francisco: HarperSanFrancisco, 1986).

7. C. S. Lewis, *Mere Christianity*, as quoted in Rueben P. Job and
Norman Shawchuck, *A Guide to Prayer for Ministers and Other
Servants* (Nashville: Upper Room, 1983), 125-126.

8. The most common Greek word translated as *minister* or *serve*
is *diakonos*. The person who serves is called a *doulos*, or slave.

9. Ulysses S. Grant, *Personal Memoirs of U. S. Grant* (New York:
Penguin, 1999; first published 1885), 29.

**Chapter 5: The Disciple-Making Environment:
What Makes Things Grow**

1. Benedict of Nursia, AD 480-543. See "God in the Ordinary:
Benedict and the Benedictines" in chapter 3. While we'd think
of climbing as the opposite of humility, humility in God's
kingdom involves an ascension of character. Benedict's twelve
steps are (1) reverence, (2) doing God's will, (3) obedience to
others, (4) enduring affliction, (5) confession, (6) content-
ment, (7) self-reproach, (8) obeying the common rule, (9)
silence, (10) seriousness, (11) simple speech, (12) humble
in appearance. From Richard Foster, *Devotional Classics:
Selected Readings for Individuals and Groups* (San Francisco:
HarperSanFrancisco, 1990), 178-181.

321

2. Readings of the Greek imperative *tapeinothete* in 1 Peter 5:6 "humble yourselves" as found in William F. Arndt and F. Wilbur Gingrich, *Greek English Lexicon of the New Testament and Other Early Christian Literature* (Chicago: University of Chicago Press, 1957), 812.

3. The phrases used here are the intellectual property of Leadership Catalyst, whose founders Bill Thrall and Bruce McNicol have helped many with their insights into relationships.

4. Bill Thrall and Bruce McNicol, *Forming the High Trust Culture* (Phoenix: Leadership Catalyst, 2002), 3-1.

5. Thrall and McNicol, 3-1.

6. Thrall and McNicol, 3-3.

Chapter 6: The Stages of Discipleship

1. The above points were paraphrased from Robert Coleman, *The Master Plan of Evangelism* (Old Tappan, NJ: Revell, 1963).

2. Rick Warren, *The Purpose-Driven Life: What on Earth Am I Here For?* (Grand Rapids, MI.: Zondervan, 2002), 144.

3. A. B. Bruce, *The Training of the Twelve: Exhibiting the Twelve Disciples of Jesus Under Discipline for the Apostleship* (New Canaan, CT: Keats Publishing, 1979; first published 1871), 11.

4. These phases are presented in detail and with practical application in *Jesus Christ, Disciplemaker; The Disciple-Making Pastor;* and *The Disciple-Making Church.* This disciple-making trilogy first discusses Jesus as the model, then follows the disciples as they created the early church, and finally teaches contemporary pastor disciple-making principles.

5. Eugene Peterson, *Christianity Today,* March 2005.

6. See Bill Hull, *Jesus Christ, Disciplemaker* (20th anniv. ed., Grand Rapids, MI: Baker 2004), which gives the rationale for a clear distinction between "come and see" and "come and follow me."

7. Luke 4–8 provides examples of the doing before the teaching.

8. Abraham Joshua Heschel, "God in Search of Man," in *A Guide to Prayer for Ministers and Other Servants,* comp. Rueben P. Job and Norman Shawchuck (Nashville: Upper Room, 1983), 133.

9. Elton Trueblood, "The Company of the Committed," in James R. Newby, *The Best of Elton Trueblood* (Nashville: Impact, 1979), 26.

10. Excerpts from Newby, *The Best of Elton Trueblood,* 26.

Chapter 7: Christian Spiritual Transformation

1. For deeper-meaning buffs, the fact that this illustration is a triangle means nothing.

2. Rule, from Latin, *regula,* meaning a pattern of life. Used most often to describe the covenant on which a religious order would live.

3. For a more complete examination of this pattern of life, see chapter 5, "The Disciple-Making Environment."

4. For more on how Jesus trained the first disciples through their experiences, see chapter 6, "The Stages of Discipleship."

5. For more on our mission as disciples, see chapter 4, "The Distinguishing Marks of a Disciple," specifically the section "The Call to Discipleship."

6. See Richard Foster's *Celebration of Discipline,* Dallas Willard's *The Spirit of the Disciplines,* or Donald Whitney's *Spiritual Disciplines for the Christian Life.*

7. See Foster's *Celebration of Discipline.* Foster defines and explains each major spiritual discipline. I'm not attempting to duplicate the fine work Foster has already provided.

8. Dallas Willard, *The Spirit of the Disciplines* (San Francisco: Harper & Row, 1988), 10.

9. John Ortberg, *The Life You've Always Wanted* (Grand Rapids, MI: Zondervan, 1997), 55.

10. This is the reason Dallas Willard titled his 1988 classic *The*

Spirit of the Disciplines.

11. Ortberg, 49.

12. Holiness, from the root word *hagios*, can be translated "saint, holy, set apart." It really means "different." God is different—his attributes make him unique. Another way of saying "Holy, Holy, Holy" is "different, different, different." This definition rescues holiness from a legalistic image of dark and plain clothes or a boring life without joy.

13. *Gumnazo* is found in Hebrews 5:14; 12:11 and 2 Peter 2:14.

14. A fuller treatment of the resistance to spiritual disciplines and their connection to the monastic movement can be found in Willard, 130-154.

15. In chapters 8, 9, and 10, we'll explore the roles of one-to-one relationships, small groups, and congregational communities in being and making disciples.

16. See 2 Corinthians 5:17-21. Transformation qualifies us to be ambassadors, to take the message to others.

17. C. S. Lewis, *The Screwtape Letters* (New York: Macmillan, 1962), 113.

18. We've talked about spiritual disciplines and spiritual transformation, but we can't separate our bodies from this process. Paul made this clear: "Offer the parts of your body to him as instruments of righteousness. For sin shall not be your master, because you are not under law, but under grace" (Romans 6:13-14).

Chapter 8: Personal Approaches to Disciple-Making

1. Please note that for all three personal areas of discipleship, I've quoted extensively from others who have formed some of the best resources on these topics: J. Robert Clinton and Paul Stanley on coaching, James M. Houston on mentoring, and Bruce Demarest on spiritual direction.

2. James R. Newby, *The Best of Elton Trueblood* (Nashville:

Impact, 1979), 140.

3. Paul Stanley and J. Robert Clinton, *Connecting: The Mentoring Relationships You Need to Succeed in Life* (Colorado Springs: NavPress, 1992), 76.

4. Stanley and Clinton, 82.

5. Stanley and Clinton, 197-198.

6. James M. Houston, *The Mentored Life: From Individualism to Personhood* (Colorado Springs: NavPress, 2002), 12.

7. Houston, 34-35.

8. What Western culture calls self-sufficiency, the Bible calls sin. This image of self is blind to the need for divine grace.

9. Houston, 119.

10. Houston, 134.

11. Houston, 152.

12. Bruce Demarest, *Satisfy Your Soul: Restoring the Heart of Christian Spirituality* (Colorado Springs: NavPress, 1999), 202-203.

13. Houston, 162.

14. Demarest, 215.

15. Demarest, 193.

16. Demarest, 196.

17. Demarest, 197.

18. Demarest, 204-205.

19. C. S. Lewis, "Introduction to St. Athanasius," *The Incarnation of the Word of God* (New York: Macmillan, 1946), 6, as quoted in Demarest, 257.

Chapter 9: The Role of Small Groups in Discipleship

1. These descriptions are paraphrased from Bob Gilliam, TNET International Training Notebook, PS-9.

2. Bob Gilliam, *Lecture Infrastructure II* (lecture, The Vision 2000 Training Network, Evangelical Free Church of America, 1-3).

3. For examples of how to manage a small-group system, see Bill Hull, *The Disciple-Making Church* (Grand Rapids, MI: Baker, 1990), appendix by Randall Knutson.

4. Some of the material in this "Management of Commitments" section was previously published in some form in Bill Hull, *Building High Commitment in a Low-Commitment World* (Grand Rapids, MI: Revell, 1995), 165-195.

Chapter 10: Congregations, Pastors, and Discipleship

1. Eugene Peterson referring to Von Hugel in an interview with Mark Galli, "Spirituality for All the Wrong Reasons," *Christianity Today*, March 2005.

2. George Barna, *Growing True Disciples: New Strategies for Producing Genuine Followers of Christ* (Colorado Springs: WaterBrook, 2001), 91.

3. Parts of the following are taken from Bill Hull, *Choose the Life: Exploring a Faith That Embraces Discipleship* (Grand Rapids, MI: Baker, 2004), 189-221.

4. Elton Trueblood, *The Company of the Committed* (San Francisco: Harper & Row, 1961), 112.

5. Trueblood, 113.

6. Dallas Willard, *Renovation of the Heart: Putting on the Character of Christ* (Colorado Springs: NavPress, 2002), 250.

7. Christopher Lasch, *The True and Only Heaven: Progress and Its Critics* (New York: Norton, 1991), 13.

8. Henri Nouwen, *In the Name of Jesus: Reflections on Christian Leadership* (New York: Crossroads, 1996), 62-63.

9. My thanks to Judith Hougen for her fine work *Transformed into Fire: An Invitation to Life in the True Self* (Grand Rapids, MI: Kregel, 2002), 137.

10. In verses 1-5, the apostle Paul said he did not use persuasive words or great wisdom, but the simple power of God.

11. Nouwen, 29-30.
12. Nouwen, 90.
13. I introduced this in a nine-week series titled *Choose the Life,* followed by another series on each of the spiritual disciplines.

Chapter 12: The Future of Discipleship: Living the Jesus Way
1. Brian A. McLaren, *Generous Orthodoxy* (Grand Rapids, MI: Zondervan, 2004), 14, 287.
2. Dallas Willard, "The Apprentices," *Leadership Journal,* Summer 2005, 25.
3. McLaren, 288.
4. Here I borrow the title of Eugene Peterson, "The Right Thing in the Wrong Way" (lecture, Spiritual Formation Forum Conference, Los Angeles, CA, May 2004).
5. *Druid* means someone who is wise. The word is also a moniker for an order of priests, soothsayers, judges, and poets in ancient Britain and Ireland.
6. Peterson, "The Right Thing in the Wrong Way."
7. Ayn Rand taught a philosophy called Objectivism, which says that humans are best served when they don't succumb to emotions; the greatest of people operate on a purely rational basis. Her best-selling novel *Fountainhead,* first published in 1943, is a passionate defense of individualism and presents an exalted view of man's creative potential.
8. Roy F. Baumeister, "The Low Down on High Self-Esteem," *Los Angeles Times,* January 25, 2005.

Appendix A: Five Models of Effective Discipleship
1. Adapted from *Growing True Disciples.* Copyright © 2001 by George Barna. Used by permission of WaterBrook Press, Colorado Springs, CO. All rights reserved.

Appendix B: Research for Evaluating Congregations
1. Adapted from *Growing True Disciples.* Copyright © 2001 by George Barna. Used by permission of WaterBrook Press, Colorado Springs, CO. All rights reserved.
2. Barna, 107.
3. Barna, 108-110, overview.

INDEX

groups, 305. See also community; small groups
growth, 33, 191
of church, 27, 37, 232, 266
personal, 310
spiritual. See spiritual growth
working for, 25
guidance, 52, 183. See also
coaches and coaching;
mentors and mentoring
spiritual direction and directors, 221–24, 262

habits. See discipline
healing, 259
Hebrew culture, 55–59
hermit ministry, 82
Hermogenes, 281
Herodotus. See also teachers
heroism, 145
Herrnhut, 101
Hervey, James, 104
Heschel, Abraham Joshua, 181
Hezekiah, 58
history of discipleship, 73–111
pre-Christian, 52–59
in time of Christ, 59–62
Hogan, Robert, 298
holiness, 103, 197, 324 (n12)
Holy Club, 103–4
Holy Spirit, 182–84, 190
empowerment by, 194–95
fruits of, 114
healing by, 259
inspiration by, 197
submission to, 193
Houston, James, 214, 220, 221
humility, 25, 30, 44, 321 (n1)

in disciple-making environment, 158
of Jesus, 149–50
Jesus' practices, 144
of leaders, 298
in life pattern, 83, 131–32,
142, 190
relationships and, 102, 193
reward for, 70
submission as, 67

idolatry, 218–19, 220
Ignatius of Antioch, 75, 76–78,
80, 81, 89
imitation
of other disciples, 115
of teacher, 64, 80, 261,
286–87
imitation of Christ, 16, 47, 68,
84, 103, 287
Paul on, 114–16
practicing, 188
transformation for, 130–52
impartation, 166–67
impatience, 296–98, 299
impersonation, 286
individualism, 41, 76, 119, 219,
295–96
indulgences, 96
influence, 24, 28, 152, 267
from action, 132, 172
of character, 132–33, 156,
159, 270
from love, 133
need for, 158
transformation of, 149–52
integrity, 156, 244, 247
intellect, 86, 87

AUTHOR

BILL HULL's passion is to call all people to follow Jesus. He pastored for twenty years and has written several ground-breaking books on making disciples. Bill committed his life to Christ as a student at Oral Roberts University and was mentored by a Navigator in those formative days that set his course as a disciple-maker. After several years with Athletes in Action, he earned a Master of Divinity degree from Talbot School of Theology. He and his wife, Jane, live in Long Beach, California. You can reach Bill at Bill@billhull.com or at www.choosethelife.com. To watch or listen to Bill Hull or access his materials, go to www.Bible.org.

OTHER BOOKS BY BILL HULL

Jesus Christ, Disciplemaker (20th anniv. ed., Baker, 2004)

The Disciple-Making Pastor (Baker, 1987)

The Disciple-Making Church (Baker, 1990)

Choose the Life: Exploring a Faith That Embraces Discipleship
(Baker, 2004)

Building High Commitment in a Low-Commitment World
(Revell, 1995)

Revival That Reforms: Making It Last (Revell, 1998)

Seven Steps to Transform Your Church (Revell, 1997)

Anxious for Nothing (Revell, 1988)

Right Thinking (NavPress, 1985)

THE NUMBER ONE SELLING DISCIPLESHIP CURRICULUM, TRANSFORMED FOR A NEW GENERATION.

DFD 1

Your Life in Christ   1-60006-004-8

This concise, easy-to-follow Bible study reveals what it means to accept God's love for you, keep Christ at the center of your life, and live in the power of the Spirit.

DFD 2

The Spirit-Filled Follower of Jesus   1-60006-005-6

Learn what it means to be filled by the Spirit so that obedience, Bible study, prayer, fellowship, and witnessing become natural, meaningful aspects of your life.

DFD 3

Walking with Christ   1-60006-006-4

Learn five vital aspects to living as a strong and mature disciple of Christ through this easy-to-understand Bible study.

DFD 4

The Character of a Follower of Jesus   1-60006-007-2

This insightful, easy-to-grasp Bible study helps you understand and put into action the internal qualities and values that should drive your life as a disciple of Christ.

DFD 5

Foundations for Faith   1-60006-008-0

This compelling Bible study will help you get a disciple's perspective on God, His Word, the Holy Spirit, spiritual warfare, and Christ's return.

DFD 6

Growing in Discipleship   1-60006-009-9

This study will provide insight and encouragement to help you grow as a true disciple of Christ by learning to share the blessings you've received from God.

DFD 7

Our Hope in Christ   1-60006-010-2

In this study of 1 Thessalonians, discover how to undertake a comprehensive analysis of a book of the Bible and gain effective Bible study principles that will last a lifetime.

DFD Leader's Guide   1-60006-011-0

The leader's guide provides all the insight and information needed to share the essential truths of discipleship with others, whether one-on-one or in small groups.

Visit your local Christian bookstore, call NavPress at 1-800-366-7788,
or log on to www.navpress.com to purchase.
To locate a Christian bookstore near you, call 1-800-991-7747.

NAVPRESS
BRINGING TRUTH TO LIFE
www.navpress.com